Photojournalism and Today's News

This book is dedicated to the love of my life Gloria who makes every day more beautiful and meaningful than I could ever have imagined possible, and to Susan Langton, Bob Langton and Susan DiBonaventure, my mother, brother and sister who are always in my heart. And, to my brother John who remains a part of my life always.

Photojournalism and Today's News

Creating Visual Reality

Loup Langton

A John Wiley & Sons, Ltd., Publication

This edition first published 2009
© 2009 Loup Langton

Blackwell Publishing was acquired by John Wiley & Sons in February 2007. Blackwell's publishing program has been merged with Wiley's global Scientific, Technical, and Medical business to form Wiley-Blackwell.

Registered Office
John Wiley & Sons Ltd, The Atrium, Southern Gate, Chichester, West Sussex, PO19 8SQ, United Kingdom

Editorial Offices
350 Main Street, Malden, MA 02148-5020, USA
9600 Garsington Road, Oxford, OX4 2DQ, UK
The Atrium, Southern Gate, Chichester, West Sussex, PO19 8SQ, UK

For details of our global editorial offices, for customer services, and for information about how to apply for permission to reuse the copyright material in this book please see our website at www.wiley.com/wiley-blackwell.

The right of Loup Langton to be identified as the author of this work has been asserted in accordance with the Copyright, Designs and Patents Act 1988.

All rights reserved. No part of this publication may be reproduced, stored in a retrieval system, or transmitted, in any form or by any means, electronic, mechanical, photocopying, recording or otherwise, except as permitted by the UK Copyright, Designs and Patents Act 1988, without the prior permission of the publisher.

Wiley also publishes its books in a variety of electronic formats. Some content that appears in print may not be available in electronic books.

Designations used by companies to distinguish their products are often claimed as trademarks. All brand names and product names used in this book are trade names, service marks, trademarks or registered trademarks of their respective owners. The publisher is not associated with any product or vendor mentioned in this book. This publication is designed to provide accurate and authoritative information in regard to the subject matter covered. It is sold on the understanding that the publisher is not engaged in rendering professional services. If professional advice or other expert assistance is required, the services of a competent professional should be sought.

Library of Congress Cataloging-in-Publication Data

Langton, Loup.
Photojournalism and today's news : creating visual reality / Loup Langton.
p. cm.
Includes bibliographical references and index.
ISBN 978-1-4051-7897-6 (hardcover : alk. paper) — ISBN 978-1-4051-7896-9 (pbk. : alk. paper)
1. Photojournalism. I. Title.
TR820.L374 2009
070.4'9—dc22

2008033375

A catalogue record for this book is available from the British Library.

Set in 11 on 13.5pt ITC Century by SNP Best-set Typesetter Ltd., Hong Kong
Printed in Singapore by Utopia Press Pte Ltd

01 2009

Contents

Contents

Illustrations

Photos

Figures

Acknowledgments

Vin Alabiso
Monica Almeida
Thorne Anderson
P.F. Bentley
Jocelyne Benzakin
Geoffrey Black
Mary Kay Blakely
Richard Boeth
Cecilia Bohan
Bill Borders
Carlos Bruch
Torry Bruno
Mark Bussell
Zbigniew Bzdak
Michele Cardin
John Carroll
Howard Chapnick
Sanjeev Chatterjee
Jan Colbert
Patty Colletti
J. B. Colson
Guy Cooper
Randy Cox
Colin Crawford
Richard R. Crocker
Denise Crosby
Robert A. Daugherty
Pat Davison
Len Downey
Michel duCille
Joe Elbert
Peter Essick
Frank Falwell
Rob Finch
Denis Finley
Gail Fisher
Travis Fox
David Frank
Philip Gefter
Jackie Gonzalez
Kim Grinfeder
Todd Heisler
Rex Huppke
Kenny Irby
Michael Kaufman
Tom Kennedy
Kent Kobersteen
Kim Komenich
Alexis Kostanesky
Bill Kuykendall
Vincent Laforet
Carolyn Lee

Laura Lein
Rick Loomis
Tony Majeri
Maria Mann
Marianne Mather
Kirk McKoy
Rick Nagel
Todd Panagopoulos
Bill Parker
Carlos Perez
Edward Pfister
Hillary Rasgin
Tim Rasmussen
David Rees
Janet Reeves
Luis Rios
William Rood
Kathy Ryan
Robert Schnitzlein
Flip Schulke
Luis Sinco
Mike Smith
Zoe Smith
Michele Stephenson
William Stott
Scott Strazzante
Meg Theo
Mauricio Villarreal
Priscilla Villarreal
Roger Villarreal
Ken Weiss
Hall Wells
Michael Whitley

Special thanks to:

Lelen Bourgoignie-Robert
Michael Carlebach
Pablo Corral
Mike Davis
Sam Grogg
Carol Lewis
David Lewis
James W. McLamore Awards
Margot Morse
Andrea Paquin
Maggie Steber
Tom Steinfatt
Elizabeth Swayze
Mervyn Thomas
Mercedes deUriarte

Foreword

Mike Davis and Maggie Steber

From Mike Davis

What lies ahead for you, the reader of this book, is a journey. It is a path that takes you through the major conundrums that people who tell stories with pictures face. If you are new to this business of making pictures, every word will be a revelation; if you are seasoned, your experience will be equally, but differently, revealing. In these pages you hear an educator, journalist, and cherished colleague gather and present some of the strongest voices in the business in a way that sees beyond the obvious. Loup Langton, here on these pages, perceives a path that is as revelatory as light falling on a newly discovered cave.

Nearly before the ink had dried on my first published picture, I began to hear claims of the demise of photojournalism. That was more than 30 years ago. Almost 20 years ago I wrote an article discrediting such a claim for the Santa Fe Workshops. Granted, challenges are legion. But that's not a new phenomenon. From the day the camera was invented, photography has struggled to reach its potential. Or more precisely, those who endeavor in this profession are bound by history and a likely future to face challenge.

It occurs to me that the only way to conquer this inevitable challenge is to exceed one's seeing, to go beyond the images that you have made, to be more than you are today, to know more, to try more to perceive, and therefore, say more. And the only way to do that is to be more of a person tomorrow than you are today. It's as simple and as complex as that.

Few books of words come along to help us in that endeavor. Here is one.

Mike Davis
November 16, 2007

While picture editor for the White House Photo Office, Mike Davis edited more than a million images to tell the story of a presidency. As a picture editor at *National Geographic* magazine Davis worked with a range of the world's great photographers on far-reaching stories. He served as the visual director for the award-winning Copley Northern Illinois' Sun Publications and as a picture editor for 11 books, he helped mold massive bodies of photographs into cohesive forms. Davis was twice named National Newspaper Picture Editor of the Year. He has also judged Pictures of the Year International three times, as well as the Robert F. Kennedy awards, the W. Eugene Smith grant and many state competitions.

From Maggie Steber

By now, this sounds like the sad lament of an unsympathetic character in Shakespearian drama: the socio-cultural function of American newspapers changed drastically with the advent of radio, television, and the Internet, and the end is in sight. Almost everyone in the business agrees that newspapers are in trouble, but the how and why are debatable which begs the question: are newspapers sitting on death row? Might they get a reprieve of sorts if they reform? Is the news of their demise greatly exaggerated?

Today's newspapers are plagued with financial woes, laboring under the harsh yoke of delivering high profits to demanding investors. Newsprint costs soar at a time when concern about the environment and the continued use of trees as a paper source grows. The corporate owners of newspaper chains institute staff cutbacks and reductions in benefits to employees as a method of keeping profit margins high.

At the same time, newspapers continue with the impossible task of being all things to all people. And, there is a rush to the Internet without fully knowing if people will actually turn to it to get their news in the same way that newspapers delivered it – organized.

The competitive climate, disappointing coverage of diverse communities, antiquated newsroom hierarchies and failure to attract young readers signal a need for newspapers to consider new models of approach and presentation. Without change newspapers could find themselves dead in the water.

We visual journalists believe it is time to change how photography and presentation is considered and used in newspapers and on websites. Many of us believe that photography can help save American journals but only with some serious conversation about photography, design, and graphics and the compelling ways in which they can be used to deliver information. In what has become a visual culture, readers respond vividly to the use of dynamic photography throughout the papers. Websites, too, can host a new approach to visual journalism.

Loup Langton has been doing some deep and remarkable research into how newspapers use photography in the United States, how the culture in the newsroom reflects the visual choices, and who makes them. It is terribly important work because it has far-reaching implications that go beyond photography. The research reflects how the newsroom culture decides what is news.

Loup brings with this research a remarkable array of experience, as a university professor, a former photographer and former director of photography for Copley Chicago Newspapers as well as for Ecuador's *El Universo*. He has moved through newsrooms across the nation to observe and analyze news-gathering routines and photographic impact in newspapers. He speaks the language of the newsroom and the language of scholarly study. He takes us on a tour and acts as our guide, giving us a roadmap to figure out where newspapers and readers are headed. You won't find many people with his wealth of experience doing such fascinating reporting on such a critical aspect of American society and culture.

Maggie Steber
November 19, 2007

Maggie Steber has worked for more than 30 years as a freelance magazine photographer. Her regular clients include *National Geographic* magazine, The *New York Times Magazine*, *Life*, *Smithsonian*, and a number of prestigious international magazines.

She received the Alicia Patterson Grant to write and photograph in Haiti during years of turmoil there and the Ernst Haas Grant for Photography. Other honors include the Leica Medal of Excellence and the Overseas Press Club Award for Coverage from Abroad. In 2003, the University of Missouri presented her with their Medal of Honor for Distinguished Service to Journalism.

From 1999 to 2003, Steber served as Assistant Managing Editor for Photography and Features at *The Miami Herald*.

Introduction

Every generation experiences a number of news photographs that are etched into the mind's eye. These photographs recall the emotion of a tragedy, the exhilaration of sporting triumph or the drama of war. Some serve as historical documents for future generations. And, many are tucked away in scrapbooks along with other mementos. Yet, these photographs all have something in common. They were culled from millions of other real and potential images.

Why and how do editors select some photographs for publication and omit others? How are assignments created and by whom? How do photographers work in the field? How do editors select the words that will accompany the images and how does that affect the way in which news photographs are understood by news-consumers?

As sociologist Herbert Gans observes, journalists decide through selection what is news and through exclusion what is not news (Gans, 1980). Factors such as bottom-line considerations, US foreign policy, story variety and guidelines like "newsworthiness" and "objectivity" act as touchstones during this decision-making process.

Media coverage of Haiti during the past two decades provides a good example of how news is filtered. In November 1991 Reuters' staff photographer Pat Hamilton telephoned Robert Schnitzlein's Washington DC office. Schnitzlein was the Reuters picture editor-America and Hamilton's supervisor. Hamilton was calling from Haiti to ask if he could extend his stay on assignment since the

Organization of American States' representatives were arriving in Port-au-Prince the following day. These representatives were going to attempt to mediate a settlement between the deposed Haitian president, Jean Bertrand Aristide, and the military leaders who had ousted him. Schnitzlein's response to Hamilton was that if he had enough money to pay his own expenses, he could stay, if not, he had to leave. Reuters would not be giving him any additional advances. "A lot of judgments on what you do have to be made based on how much it costs. . . . And the [Haiti] story is getting absolutely no ink at all" (Schnitzlein, 1991).

Major news organizations do periodically send journalists to Haiti (usually during times of crisis), but even that doesn't guarantee that a story or photograph will make it into the publication.

> What we never take into account is the personality of the reporter and whether there is a real interest at the newspaper once the report gets there. For example, Joe Treaster [*New York Times* journalist who reported from Haiti from 1984 to 1989] hated Haiti. It didn't make any sense to him. He wasn't a racist in any way, but he didn't understand why people couldn't just get their acts together.
>
> There were a number of reporters from the *New York Times* reporting on Haiti after Joe Treaster. The one that immediately followed him . . . never went anywhere without the *Miami Herald* reporter and the *L.A. Times* reporter. They went around like the "Three Musketeers," and they would all write the same thing. They all hated Aristide. And, they would only talk to the same people, the elite. Those were their contacts. They never went into the slums, and if they did, it was to talk to someone who had a school there or something like that. They never really wrote about what it was like to live and breathe and exist in Haiti on any particular day.
>
> It wasn't until Larry Rohter started reporting on Haiti. He was much better. He seemed to have a gentler, kinder spirit, which is what Haiti needs. And, not everybody can do that.
>
> So finally you get someone who does a good job and then the foreign editor isn't really interested in the story, so he's not going to promote it. It's going to be buried in the paper. There are all of

> these decisions being made by people who are less than perfect, who either have agendas against somebody or against some place.
>
> For a photographer that can have a huge impact because let's say that you're with Joe Treaster, and he writes an article that gets buried in the paper. Now, there may not even be room for your photo. (Steber, 2004)

Less than three years after Schnitzlein refused to extend Hamilton's stay, stories about the turmoil in Haiti as well as impending US/UN intervention abounded in the US news media. Despite little change in Haiti's leadership, political policies and/or economic problems, it became part of what Gans calls, "the symbolic arena" (Gans, 1980). Why did Haiti become "news?" *Newsweek*'s International Photo Editor Hillary Rasgin (1992) suggests that at *Newsweek* the selection of international stories is strongly connected to US foreign policy, and indeed US foreign policy toward Haiti changed dramatically between 1991 and 1994.

Similarly, perceived interest among valued readership can dictate coverage. Shortly after Tim Rasmussen was hired as director of photography at the *South Florida Sun Sentinel* a number of Haitians landed in Miami and were arrested. As part of a follow-up to the story, the *Sun Sentinel* sent photographer Mike Stocker and foreign correspondent Tim Collie to Haiti.

> From that point on we did stories in Haiti four or five times a year because of the Haitian community here. We did a series of stories on young street kids being executed by the police in Haiti. That was one of our first victories because we ran a photograph, a kind of evidence photograph, of a mother holding a picture of her two twelve-year-old sons who were shot in the head.
>
> Out of that came a meeting between Mike Stocker, Tim Collie and myself to think about what we could do with Haiti, and we came up with, "the environmental collapse of the country." We had all been doing little different pieces on the environment and figured out that these all fit into a bigger story so we actually did a huge year-long project looking into the environmental collapse. (Rasmussen, 2006)

Rasmussen believes that the *Sun Sentinel* is now more reticent to support such projects. He says that editors are concerned about the economic commitment and the results of readers' surveys.

> Readers consistently say one thing in these surveys, now granted, there are only 36 different readers included in the surveys, and I've been to four of them [surveys] and 35 of the readers are white, and they keep saying the same thing, they don't want to read about Haiti. (Rasmussen, 2006)

Rasmussen concludes, "We still go to Haiti. We just don't go as much as we did."

In addition to deciding what is news and what is not news, journalists continue to make other selection/exclusion decisions throughout the news production process. For example, after editors decide to assign a particular story, reporters then determine which sources to approach, which questions to ask, etc. During the editing and packaging stages certain words or images are selected while others are excluded, and certain arrangements of elements on a page are accepted while others are rejected.

All of these decisions affect the way in which news consumers perceive the world. French researcher Roland Barthes (1972) believes that the symbols (the specific story, photograph, etc.) that appear in the news media are both purposefully selected and understood to be representations by journalists but perceived as something more by news consumers. Barthes contends that journalists begin with a concept and look for a way in which it can be symbolized. Audiences, however, do not perceive the story or photograph as a symbol, but as reality.

Continuing with the media's coverage of Haiti, former assistant managing editor for the *Miami Herald* and multiple award-winning photographer Maggie Steber offers an example of what Barthes has called, "mythologies." She recalls a discussion she had with another photographer who had taken a photograph of a Haitian man eating human flesh. Steber says,

> There was a big riot. I can't remember what it was about, but there were people killed, and this photographer saw this Haitian man take a knife and cut a piece of flesh out of a body and eat it. So, he had this picture that ran in *Time* magazine of this guy biting down on this flesh with fire from the barricades in the background, very dramatic.
>
> When I saw that picture published, I was livid. I talked to the photographer about it, and he said, "First of all, the man did that," and I said, "But he's looking right at you, and he did it for the camera, and had you ever seen a Haitian do that before?" That is a very old African tradition to do that, but I've never seen it in Haiti. Its' not really representative of what people do. It was something that happened in front of him, and he took the picture. I'm not saying that he shouldn't have taken the picture. You should always take the picture, but I think it's lamentable that that was the picture that got published. People see that and think that all Haitians are cannibals and wild and unruly.
>
> The truth is that it was a unique situation at least as far as I've ever seen, and I've been doing stories there since 1980. (Steber, 2004)

The photographer created a dramatic and aesthetically interesting image that the publication chose to represent the situation in Haiti. As Steber suggests, however, news consumers might see that photograph as more than a symbol. Since most people who viewed the photograph have never visited Haiti, they may believe that "all [or at least many] Haitians are cannibals and wild and unruly."

Photography is particularly subtle in the way that it is digested. It is unlike other forms of representation in that its interpretive nature is less obvious (Grundberg, 1990a, 1990b; Richin, 1989). Individuals believe what they see (Sontag, 1973).

Michael Kaufman, founder and co-editor of Impact Visuals, a New York based photo agency, says,

> There is a subjective process in editing with the camera, a whole host of things can come into play, your choice of subject, choice of lens, composition, your sense of light. . . . The argument that "I can send someone into a different culture and a picture is a picture

> is a picture" is really crazy. I think all too often photographers go into a culture that they're not familiar with, and they look for photographs that fit their preconceptions, and they can always find such a photograph, but that may actually be the cultural exception. (Kaufman, 1991)

The ability to interpret subjectively through the use of technical and aesthetic skills empowers the photographer to infuse his or her photographs with meaning and value. This empowerment, however, is limited since photographers must consistently choose symbols that are appropriate to the assignment (as most often defined by the word editors) in order to maintain their jobs and/or advance their careers in a highly competitive profession.

National Geographic magazine's former director of photography Kent Kobersteen says, "So much of photographic reporting is intuitive; you develop a working methodology based on who you work for – the publication" (Kobersteen, 1991). And, former J. B. Pictures owner/editor Jocelyn Benzakin says, "Most photographers just do whatever they're getting paid for, and they deliver their work on time – it's just a formula" (Benzakin, 1991).

Formulas for producing the "right" kinds of photographs come from a variety of sources. Unlike news photographers from earlier generations, many current photographers attend journalism schools where they are introduced to such news gathering strategies as "newsworthiness" and "objectivity." These strategies, as well as others, are reinforced and further developed in the newsrooms and photographic communities in which photographers work.

Newsworthiness, of course, is whatever the top editors say is worthy of coverage. By assigning the term newsworthy, however, an editor is able to objectify his or her reasons for selecting one concept over another for publication.

The concept of "objectivity" is particularly stressed in photography since many editors believe that the physical evidence is presented directly to the viewer through the photograph. Kaufman, however, says:

> Objectivity is basically a myth that some major media people delude themselves with. What you're seeing in a picture is real, but it's an edit. Maybe the coverage that we saw of the [first] Gulf War with all of its pictures of the high-tech weapons had very little to do with the war or why our troops were sent over there. It became sort of a sales pitch for weapons systems although it turns out that many of the things that were photographed at the time were not real in terms of how they actually performed. They were real planes; they really were flying, but you saw only part of it. That was only one edit on what really happened. (Kaufman, 1991)

Photographers also refer to contests and news photography magazines to aid them in developing successful formulas for photography.

Ultimately, however, photojournalists become successful by consistently providing photographic symbols that portray a reality similar to the reality of top editors. Benzakin offers this example:

> Maggie [Steber] did this story on Miami, and the editor thought there were too many blacks in her photographs, so they sent somebody else to shoot more whites because his [the editor's] perspective was that there were more whites.
>
> The editors [who assign the stories] have an idea and, if the photographer gives them something other than their idea, then it's like, "oh that's not what we wanted; that's not really there. You didn't get it." Meanwhile, the editor has never been outside the building, but his perspective prevails. (Benzakin, 1991)

The news media, as profit seeking institutions, create and maintain audiences as their primary commodity – audiences are sold to advertisers. Clearly, an affluent audience is a more valuable commodity than a poor audience.

The demographic qualities that constitute the ideal consumer are much like the demographic characteristics of most top editors. In this way the system of news dissemination is rather insular. While many top editors are smart and insightful, inevitably they select concepts that are rooted in or framed by their own views of the world. Photographers (with the approval of editors) create/select visual symbols that communicate the concepts selected by top editors. And audience members receive the symbols within a context that is similar to the framework within which top editors make their decisions.

The news media contribute to the creation and reinforcement of reality as described in Barthes' formula for myth. News media decision makers perceive the world from a particular perspective. They select concepts or stories that are newsworthy and then look for ways in which those stories can be symbolized. News consumers bring their own experiential perspectives to the table as they digest the news. That news takes on its on sense of reality, particularly as presented photographically. Art historian and critic, John Szarkowski (1966, p. 86) says: "To quote out of context is the essence of the photographer's craft."

References

Barthes, R. (1972). *Mythologies* (A. Lavers, Trans.). New York: Hill and Wang.

Benzakin, J. (1991). *Interview by author* [cassette recording] (November), New York.

Gans, H. (1980). *Deciding what's news.* New York: Vintage.

Grundberg, A. (1990a). Ask it no questions: The camera can lie. *The New York Times*, August 12, Sec. 2, p. 1.

Grundberg, A. (1990b). *Crisis of the real: Writings on photography, 1974–1989.* New York: Aperture.

Kaufman, M. (1991). *Interview by author* [cassette recording] (November), New York.

Kobersteen, K. (1991). *Interview by author* [cassette recording] (November), Washington, DC.

New York Times Company (1992). *1991 Annual Report.* New York: Author.

Rasgin, H. (1992). *Interview by author* [cassette recording] (March), New York.

Rasmussen, T. (2006). *Telephone interview by author* [digital recording] (May), Miami.

Ritchin, F. (1989). *In our own image: The coming revolution in photography.* New York: Aperture.

Schnitzlein, R. (1991). *Interview by author* [cassette recording] November, Washington, DC.

Sontag, S. (1973). *On photography*. New York: Farrar, Straus & Giroux.

Steber, M. (2004). *Interview by author* [cassette recording] (August), Miami.

Szarkowski, J. (1966). *The photographer's eye*. New York: Doubleday.

1

Brief History of Photojournalism in the United States

The photograph was the ultimate response to a social and cultural appetite for a more accurate and real-looking representation of reality, a need that had its origins in the Renaissance. (Rosenblum, 1984, p. 15)

Although advances in photographic technologies enabled the creation of photography (and later, photographic reportage), the social, cultural, and political environment of the nineteenth century allowed photography to develop and expand rapidly. A burgeoning middle class supported photography as a new art form (Rosenblum, 1984) and embraced the idea that the photograph could "objectively" document life (Carlebach, 1992). The earliest photographs, however, suffered from the necessity of long exposures and were for the most part limited to subjects of landscape, architecture, and portraiture. "Nonetheless, reportage was understood to be one of the most significant potentials – and goals – of photography at the very beginning of its history. From the 1840s on, American photographers tested the available technologies against this goal and established important precedents for what has become one of the most significant applications of the medium" (Stapp, 1988, p. 2).

Photography was made a practical reality in 1839 by two fundamentally different and competing processes, the Daguerreotype, invented by Louis Jacques Mandé Daguerre in France and the Calotype, created by William Henry Fox Talbot in England. Although the negative/positive process of the Calotype allowed virtually unlimited reproduction of the original, the majority of the public initially embraced the Daguerreotype (a positive process) primarily because it produced better-quality images.

The Daguerreotype, a monochromatic picture produced on a silver-plated sheet of copper appeared more precise and attractive than the early Calotypes made from paper negatives. Despite the long exposure times (from 5 to 60 minutes in 1839) that required the subject's head to be placed in a clamp, Daguerreotype portrait studios flourished across the US. Publications like *Frank Leslie's* and *Harper's Weekly* used Daguerreotype portraits translated into wood engravings for the press. Nevertheless Daguerreotype images could not be easily duplicated thereby limiting their usefulness.[1]

Although the negative/positive process initially suffered from technical flaws, the soft image caused by the diffusion of light passing through the paper negative being the most glaring, the ability to easily duplicate the original image was decisive in the process' eventual acceptance over the Daguerreotype (Newhall, 1982).

The quality of photographic images improved rapidly during the 1840s and 1850s. Opticians developed non-distortion lenses, and glass negatives coated with egg whites or albumen replaced paper negatives. The albumen negatives produced better images than the paper negatives but still required long exposure times. A moist (or "wet") glass plate negative coated with a substance called collodian subsequently dramatically curtailed the exposure times. This helped to create sharper images and allowed a wider array of subjects. It also meant, however, that the photographer had to work from a portable darkroom in order to sensitize each plate before using it and to develop it immediately afterward.[2]

The invention of the albumen print in the 1850s occurred at approximately the same time as the development of the wet plate negative. And, like the wet plate negative, it significantly boosted the overall quality of the image by creating sharper definition and strong contrasts. In addition, the albumen print image lasted a much longer time than its predecessors.

Despite the improvements to the negative and printing processes, photographs as illustrations for publication still needed to be translated into engravings or included as original prints or lanternslides. It wasn't until the last decade of the nineteenth century that photographic images could be directly incorporated into the text through the halftone process.

Other technological barriers remained throughout most of the 1800s. Exposure times were still too long to freeze motion,[3] and photographers continued to transport their darkrooms to the scenes of their photographs. Nevertheless, photographers from industrialized nations, particularly, England, France, and the United States traveled internationally to document life, architecture and nature. Of particular interest to photographers and their audiences were the "Holy Land," Egypt, the American West, and Japan. "Though under the impression that these documentations were 'objective' – that is, truthful records of what exists – those behind the cameras were guided in their selection and treatment of material both by a sense of being emissaries of a 'higher civilization,' as John Thomson called it, and by the desire for commercial success" (Rosenblum, 1984, p. 168).[4]

Regardless of the inability to photograph movement sharply since exposures were seconds long, the Crimean War (1850s) and the American Civil War (1860s) were photographed extensively using Collodion glass-plate negatives. In both England and America a combination of media desire for dramatic images, the public's appetite for information and governmental acceptance, even support of photographic documentation[5] made both wars accessible to photographers such as Roger Fenton and Mathew Brady.[6]

Nevertheless, technology dictated both the subject matter and style of war photography during the mid-nineteenth century. Images of battle action were not possible since photographers had to transport their darkrooms and equipment in wagons, and the large-format cameras took time to set up. In addition, recording movement was sacrificed for clarity of image. Instead, photographers focused on portraits of officers (see Photo 1) and ordinary soldiers, camp life and supplies but also upon the

Photo 1. Six officers of the 17th New York Battery, Gettysburg, June 1863 Library of Congress, Washington, DC.

wounded and the dead – the aftermath of battle. These photographs, although subdued by today's standards of graphic images, "had a profound effect on viewers used to artistic depictions of wartime heroics. . . . The absence of uplifting tone in camera documentations was especially shocking because the images were unhesitatingly accepted as real and truthful" (Rosenblum, 1984, p. 182).

President Abraham Lincoln's assassination immediately following the American Civil War and the subsequent capture of the conspirators engaged the nation's attention and created another kind of opportunity for photographic reportage, the photographic sequence. Photographer Alexander Gardner, who published the *Photographic Sketch Book of the War* containing photographs that he took during the Civil War, also photographed the hanging of the four convicted conspirators of the Lincoln assassination. Gardner made seven images of the hangings that together created perhaps the first sequential documentation of an event although as Marianne Fulton observes, "Only three of the seven photographs Gardner took during the hangings were reproduced in the popular press (*Harper's Weekly* used wood-engraved copies to illustrate its story on the executions), and the narrative element of the original sequence and the cumulative visual impact of the original images were thereby lost" (Fulton, 1988, p. 28).

Although photographers immediately following the Civil War period produced little in the way of news-event photographs, (Stapp, 1988) the American public provided a vast market for documentary photography (Foresta, 1996).[7] Using large-format cameras and wet-plate negatives, photographers documented architecture, industrialization, historical landmarks, and perhaps more than anything else, the American West. The West, dominated by a sense of space, adventure, and beauty, piqued the imagination of those living in the East and provided photographers with fertile content. Photographic prints were sold to individuals, "and to the periodical press, which continued to use photographs as a source material for wood and steel engravings" (Carlebach, 1992, p. 102).

During the second half of the nineteenth century, photographers began to develop ideas about photographically covering the news. It was, however, the technological advances that were most instrumental in the development of the modern conception of photojournalism.

> [Photojournalism] became possible only when photographic technology (both films and camera equipment), communication systems (the means for getting photographic images from where they were taken to where they would be used), and reproduction technologies (the means of disseminating the images) had all evolved to the point of conjunction where the photography of action, in the field, was possible and easy; where photographic images could be reproduced quickly and accurately, in quantity

> and cheaply; and where the time lapse between the event and the publication of the images reporting it was minimal. (Stapp, 1988, p. 2)

Technological progress reached a tipping point during the final two decades of the nineteenth century. Dry plates replaced wet plates allowing photographers to use much shorter exposures due to the heightened sensitivity to light and, perhaps most importantly, the halftone plate[8] was developed as a means to reproduce photographs onto the printed page, eliminating the need for engravers and creating an even greater sense of objectivity.

Other technological advances of the 1880s and 1890s enabled photojournalism to develop rapidly. The Eastman Kodak camera, introduced near the end of the nineteenth century, influenced the way in which professionals worked. Professional photographers using the hand-held cameras were able to produce more spontaneous and intimate photographs because they had greater mobility and drew less attention to themselves. And, the small and relatively easy-to-use cameras created a new market aimed at amateur photographers.[9] The invention of transparent celluloid roll film in 1889 made the hand-held cameras even more practicable.

Photojournalism, however, did not develop solely from the conjunction of various technologies. "Photojournalism existed – and still exists – in a context that includes economics, politics, technology, the attitudes of the public, the ideologies of critics, and, ultimately, teachers and purveyors of knowledge and information" (Jussim, 1988, p. 38).

At the turn of the century the owners and editors of news publications sensed the public's appetite for illustrated journalism and realized that photographs could provide an important edge in the growing competition for readership. As a result, management began to think about how photographs could be used more effectively.

> At first little imagination governed the way that pictures were incorporated into the text of articles, but soon after 1890

> periodicals began to pay more attention to page layouts. The pictures were not simply spotted throughout the story; images of different sizes and shapes began to be deliberately arranged, sometimes in overlapping patterns and even occasionally crossing onto the adjacent page. Also, feature stories and articles consisting of just photographs and captions made an appearance. (Rosenblum, 1984, p. 461)

News consumers also became more sophisticated as the demographics changed to a more educated and urban readership. The National Geographic Society published the first issue of *National Geographic Magazine* in 1888 aimed at an audience interested in nature and distant cultures often portrayed as "primitive" or exotic. *National Geographic* became (and has remained) a pioneering leader in the use of photography. Among other innovations, it was the first magazine in the United States "to build its own black-and-white and color photography labs [and began to feature color photographs in the early 1900s]; the first to publish flash photographs of wild animals at night; the first to publish underwater photographs of fish in natural color" (Carlebach, 1997, p. 181).

A new breed of photographer emerged to provide the illustrated publications with photographs from a variety of subjects. These news photographers were largely self-taught and street savvy. They were part of the new profession of journalism and yet separate (and thought inferior)[10] from the writers. The news photographers were (as today) either employed as staff photographers or worked as freelancers. The freelance photographers had little trouble selling their work as their photographs were in demand, and newly formed syndicates (analogous to today's wire services and photo agencies) marketed the photographs nationwide (Carlebach, 1997).

The public demand for photographs, however, was a double-edged sword as editors and owners of news publications sought to give the public what it wanted rather than exercising editorial judgment about what was important. Staff photographers accepted their assignments, and freelance photographers made photographs that they knew they could sell. In this regard, newspapers of the early 1900s were similar to many of today's news media that use surveys conducted among readers/audiences to help determine editorial content.

For more than a century, content decisions have been routinely made with advertisers in mind. Researcher, Estelle Jussim explains that during the final decades of the nineteenth century large department stores merged with and/or acquired smaller ones. They then used their increased wealth to purchase advertising space in newspapers. The size of the readership determined the price of the space, thus newspapers worked hard to give readers what they wanted.

> Inevitably, the relationship between advertising and circulation led to several unfortunate outcomes, some of which are still with us.[11] First, there ensued a wild race among the dailies to capture ever-greater readership by whatever means. Sensationalism being tried and true, it was to ever-increasing sensationalism that the publishers turned. (Jussim, 1988, p. 47)

As is true today, stories with mass appeal attracted large numbers of photographers, and their photographs (sometimes faked) received ample space in the sensational press. Catastrophes, crime, violence, and the unusual were the preferred subjects for publication (McChesney, 2004).

Yet, Carlebach points out that much of the sensational press had a liberal bent and because of that also pursued stories that contained subtexts, exposés of abuse and corruption perpetrated by the elite.

> On May 31, 1889, floodwater swept through Johnstown, Pennsylvania, a major steel-producing center not far from Pittsburgh. More than 2,200 people drowned, many of them the wives and children of immigrant steel workers. The story gripped the national press, and not merely because of the terrible toll in human lives. The flood occurred when the earthen dam that created a private trout-fishing preserve burst, sending an enormous wall of water, muck, and debris into the narrow streets of Johnstown, fourteen

> miles downstream. The lake was owned and used exclusively by the South Fork Fishing and Hunting Club, an elite group of Pittsburgh industrialists, bankers, and lawyers including Andrew Carnegie and Henry Clay Frick. Although forewarned of the dam's weakness, the club's directors did nothing, and heavy spring rains that year sealed Johnstown's fate. The popular press saw proof of meanness and criminal neglect among potentates who preside over America's burgeoning industrial empires. (Carlebach, 1997, p. 47)

Liberal newspaper owners such as Joseph Pulitzer also sponsored various public welfare endeavors. Social conscience, however, also made good business sense. "Pulitzer's marketing strategy was to juggle sensation with public crusades, themselves handily sensational. Pulitzer swiftly managed to achieve the highest newspaper circulation in the country" (Jussim, 1988, p. 47).

Still, the most successful marketing tool for visual reportage appears to be war. Author and critic, Susan Sontag, declares, "War was and still is the most irresistible – and – picturesque – news" (Sontag, 2003, p. 49). Moreover, technological developments after the American Civil War (particularly the advent of the hand-held camera and roll film) allowed photographers to document war visually as it happened and instilled in news consumers the belief that photographs offered proof of war's horrors.[12]

New York Journal publisher, William Randolph Hearst understood the power of the war image in the competition for readers. After being informed by artist Frederic Remington – who was on assignment in Cuba for the *Journal* – "Everything is quiet. . . . There will be no war. I wish to return," Hearst reportedly replied, "Please remain. You furnish the pictures. I'll furnish the war."

Collier's Weekly was likewise among the first publications to realize the ability of war photographs to generate readership. By sending English-born Jimmy Hare, perhaps the most famous photographer of the Spanish-American War and certainly one of the pioneers in war photography, to Cuba, *Collier's* "increase[d] both circulation and advertising, which in turn prompted other magazines to use photographs more generously" (Rosenblum, 1984, p. 463).

The military's laissez faire policy toward the press during wartime ended rapidly. Governments and military leaders realized the negative effect that reporting (particularly photographic) could have on civilian support. And, by the early twentieth century words and images were being filtered through military censors. In addition, the army created its own group of photographers who were given access to people, places and events that were off limits to civilian photographers.

> Assignments were doled out with great care; subjects deemed potentially problematic were simply not covered. By restricting access on the one hand, and providing its own carefully controlled coverage on the other, the army finally was able to manage and direct the visual representation of war. In order to accommodate the pictorial needs of both the press and the military, the army even established its own school in San Antonio for training still and motion-picture photographers. (Carlebach, 1997, p. 82)

The military attempted to justify its control of the press by claiming that civilian news reports could put soldiers' lives at risk. Other factors may have also contributed to the military course of action. Carlebach says that, "Military officials were unwilling to assume responsibility for the transportation, care, feeding, and protection of journalists, some of whom were probably critical of the armed forces anyway" (Carlebach, 1997, p. 84). He points out that despite the high losses among correspondents covering wars at the turn of the century, it was the military and not the correspondents or their publications that tried to curtail civilian reporting from the front.[13]

Despite governmental and military restrictions regarding photographers, publishers nevertheless tried to increase circulation during World War I through the promise of photographic documentation. The *New York Times*, for example, rushed into print with the following advertisement as early as November 5, 1914:

> START A COLLECTION OF WAR PICTURES. Start now to collect these magnificent illustrations of current history, the camera's story of churches in ruins, soldiers in trenches, sacked villages, fleeing refugees, armies on the march, faithfully portraying, week after week, the progress of the war. They will be treasured in years to come as no other souvenir of the conflict. (Jussim, 1988, p. 63)

Promises such as these created an atmosphere in which journalists (particularly photographers) were tempted, even compelled to cheat. Lacking access to the front lines, they created photographs that sometimes had a link to real events and sometimes didn't. Nevertheless, news consumers generally trusted photographs as being proof of an event and provided an enthusiastic audience for visual reporting.

Ironically, it was the military that gave history its best visual accounting of the war – even though these photographs, for the most part, were not available to news outlets during the war:

> Hundreds of ordinary soldiers were also snapping pictures at the fronts, illegally, but although hundreds of thousands of these often anonymous photographs exist in international archives, very few, if any, appeared in wartime publications. It was these images, however, culled from the archives and reproduced in books about the war many years later, that give us an intimate view of daily life in the trenches. (Jussim, 1988, p. 64)

Government leaders and military commanders managed information during World War I more tightly than in almost any other conflict. There were more than nine million deaths, yet civilian journalists fabricated stories and photographs because they were denied access to the front. This was a seminal event in the history of war photography. It set the stage for a continuing struggle between governments and the news media to determine restrictions against civilian journalists during a time of war.

Politics was another area in which news photography was testing the limits of access during the early twentieth century. The Democratic presidential candidate in 1904, Judge Alton

Brooks Parker, declared that he would not allow any candid photographs of himself. He was fearful (as many candidates are today) that he would be caught on film during an embarrassing moment. Unfortunately for Parker, his opponent was Theodore Roosevelt, who embraced the camera and realized its potential for shaping a positive image (Carlebach, 1997).

The extent of media access to political candidates remains contested. Contenders for office, like military generals, continue in their attempts to control the media to their own advantage.[14] News conferences and photo ops appear to dominate today's political coverage, but the struggle between journalists and politicians began more than a century ago.

Not all of the questions that emerged in covering the news at the end of the nineteenth century were related to the news subjects. Some issues were internal. Newsrooms were – and still are – male dominated. The competition between newspapers at the end of the nineteenth century, however, created opportunities for women wanting to work as journalists. Despite resistance from (male) editors who thought that proper women didn't belong in newsrooms or mingling with questionable subjects, women were hired as writers and photographers[15] and eventually received assignments that previously had been deemed too difficult for women.[16] This initiated a long history of struggle for women journalists.

Opportunities to work for mainstream publications came much later and have been more difficult for minority photographers. Stories about minority individuals, communities and events were traditionally written and photographed by white journalists. "There were numerous black photographers at the turn of the century . . . but their work was confined to the segregated districts in which the vast majority of them lived" and to the black press (Carlebach, 1997, p. 51). Gordon Parks was arguably the first African-American to have his work published by the "white press" but that wasn't until more than four decades after the turn of the century.[17]

While minorities and members of lower socio-economic status have traditionally been excluded from telling their own stories in mainstream media, these groups are frequently the subjects of photographers. In 1845 Octavius Hill and Robert Adamson photographed Scottish fishermen in a straight-forward style with the intention of collecting money to improve the working conditions of their subjects. The distribution of these photographs was limited since the invention of the halftone process was several decades away. Nevertheless, the work by Hill and Adamson initiated an evolution towards what would eventually become known as the documentary style – the subjects were photographed in a direct manner, yet the photographs were taken in such a way as to communicate a social, even moralistic, theme.

The documentary style continued to evolve as English photographers of the nineteenth century photographed London's destitute. The work of Henry Mayhew (*London Labor and London Poor*) and John Thomson (*Street Life in London*) was intended to not only draw attention to the poor living conditions of London's impoverished but also to act as agents for change.[18] Thomson's photographs, reproduced through Woodburytypes for *Street Life in London*, resulted in "the building of an embankment to prevent the Thames River from periodically flooding the homes of the London poor" (Rosenblum, 1984, p. 358).

At about the same time that Thomson was photographing London's impoverished, Native Americans were being photographed by photographers such as Jack Hillers, William Henry Jackson, and Timothy O'Sullivan. The straightforward approach in the portrayals of their subjects established a precedent for the photographic style of subsequent American documentary photographers.

It's somewhat difficult to make distinctions between the documentary style and early photojournalism. Both the social documentary and photojournalism came of age with the development of the halftone process which allowed the work to be broadly distributed, and both became popular with the masses during the period of competition among the "yellow" press. Liberal newspapers in particular used illustrated stories to draw attention to what they saw as unjust social conditions. The ultimate purpose of the work and the intention of the photographer, however, differentiated (and still do today) documentary style from photo reportage. The documentary photographer advocates social change.[19]

Jacob Riis' profession as a journalist for the *New York Herald* lasted 40 years and bridged the period of illustrating works using artists' renditions of photographs to the age of the halftone process – his most significant work, *How the Other Half Lives: Studies among the tenements of New York* (1890), included examples of engravings and halftone reproductions. He dedicated his career to documenting the lives of New York's impoverished. This group of mostly-recent European immigrants lived in desperate circumstances with little hope of assistance from the city or other organizations. Riis used words and photographs with the intention of bringing about social change, and his work is cited as an important factor in efforts to improve the living conditions of New York's most destitute.

Lewis Hine was the other great reform-minded photographer at the turn of the century. Born into a working-class family, Hine was drawn to the plight of laborers, particularly new members of the workforce coming from Eastern and Southern Europe. Hine photographed immigrants arriving at Ellis Island from 1904 to 1909, creating an impressive body of work that highlighted their uncertain futures.

Hine's other major body of work photographically documented the lives of child laborers and their terrible living and working environments (see Photo 2). These photographs were instrumental in prompting subsequent child-labor laws. Hine, like Riis, used the flashgun (made from magnesium powder – the flash bulb was invented in Germany in 1929) regularly to provide light for his photographs and is also remarkable for his dedication to aesthetics as a photographic tool.

> The confident atmosphere engendered by the Progressive Era sustained other projects in which camera images were used to document social conditions, but few photographers were as committed to lobbying for social change as Riis and Hine. Many worked for the expanding periodical press that by 1886 had increased its use

Photo 2. Manuel the young shrimp picker, 5 years old and a mountain of child labor oyster shells behind him. He worked last year. Understands not a word of English. Biloxi, Miss., February 20, 1911. Photograph by Lewis Hine. Library of Congress, Washington, DC.

> of photographs to the point where Frances Benjamin Johnston could describe herself as "making a business of photographic illustration and the writing of descriptive articles for magazines, illustrated weeklies and newspapers." (Rosenblum, 1984, p. 361)

But, by 1915 people in the United States were more concerned with the war in Europe than with tackling social issues at home. The photographic documentary diminished in importance until being revitalized by the political directives of the Farm Security Administration almost 20 years later.

Jussim concludes that the era between 1880 and 1920 was one of public naiveté about photography. She says that people were so impressed with the ability to reproduce images on a page that they were less concerned with what those images actually said, especially when paired with words. The images were accepted as providing proof to a condition or an event. "It was an era deluged by the products of the press and manipulated by warring publishers who displayed few ethical concerns. Photojournalist images would be perceived as visual fact, but were actually more often propaganda and pure sensationalism" (Jussim, 1988, p. 38).

The Farm Security Administration (FSA), originally called the Resettlement Administration, defined photography in 1930s America. There is little argument that the work of the FSA photographers was political, but it was also meant as an educational tool and as documentary reportage. In other words, the images were direct, honest and truthful portrayals that were also created from a particular perspective and with a particular mission to evoke sentiment (see Photo 3).[20] This seeming dichotomy of definitions began with the work of the nineteenth-century documentary photographers but matured through the work of the FSA photographers.[21] The Farm Security Administration body of work was a response by the Franklin Delano Roosevelt administration to document the disrupted lives of farm families and to extol the proactive governmental policies during the Great Depression (Stott, 1973).

Farm Security Administration photographs were used in government publications and supplied freely to the press, which made good use of them. Interestingly, the photographs also became art objects as they were exhibited through the Museum of Modern Art. Before the FSA project, documentary and art photography were considered separate and irreconcilable, but the FSA work combined documentation with aesthetics and emotive intent.[22] Whatever criticism was leveled at the Farm Security Administration's documentary work for being propagandistic, the images affected the lives of both the subjects and viewers of the photographs. In addition, the body of work became the prominent historical record of the era (Rosenblum, 1984).

Several technological developments of the 1920s generated a new approach to photography and spawned the next evolutionary stage of the illustrated magazine. The German-made Leica 35 mm camera became available in 1925 (the twin-lens Rolleiflex in 1930). The size of the camera along with the precision and speed of the lenses revolutionized photography, making it much more spontaneous and edgy. Images no longer needed to be perfectly

Photo 3. Migrant Mother, Florence Thompson, Nipomo, California, 1936. Photograph by Dorothea Lange. Library of Congress, Washington, DC.

sharp, and photographers were free to capture "moments" or slices of life.

The 35 mm roll-film camera not only changed the way in which photographers worked in the field but also altered their post-photographic workflow. Processing labs accounted for an ever-increasing amount of film developing and printing, and photo editors took on more of the responsibilities of film selection for publication (Rosenblum, 1984). This allowed photographers more time to actually photograph, and it allowed publications to more rigidly set deadlines.[23]

Another invention that changed the way in which photographers worked and extended the limitations of photography was the flashbulb. The first flashbulbs were produced in Germany in 1929 and brought to the United States a year later by General Electric. Flashbulbs replaced the dangerous and unreliable flash powder that had been used by Riis and Hine and made night and indoor photography a practical reality.[24]

These technological improvements facilitated the advance of the illustrated magazine during the 1920s and 1930s, particularly in Germany and later the United States. Illustrated magazines also thrived during this period because of "the continuing development of a truly mass audience, mainly in the urban middle class but augmented increasingly by a literate lower class" (Osman & Phillips, 1988, p. 76). And, the troubling state of affairs in Europe and Asia increasingly attracted world attention. "One writer was moved to say, 'All hell broke loose in the '30's and photography has never been the same since'" (Fulton, 1988, p. 107).

Hitler's ascendancy to power in Germany during the 1930s had consequences beyond creating an international audience for photographic reportage. Many of the photographers and photo editors who had put German illustrated magazines at the forefront of the photographic revolution left Germany for the more stable environment of the United States. They took with them the talent and ideas that would make the illustrated magazines such as *Life* and *Look* fixtures in American life.

These magazines not only printed photographs that were fundamentally different from the static, large-format images that had been previously published but also used them in ways that were totally new to readers.[25] Picture editors became an important element in the creative process. They increasingly became responsible for selecting which photographs would be used and how they would be used. Audiences, meanwhile, became more sophisticated in their appreciation and understanding of photographic reportage.

Newspapers and newspaper photographers of the 1930s and 1940s were not nearly as well regarded as their magazine counterparts. Tabloids, in particular, gave newspaper photography a bad reputation (this remains the popular perception today). Tabloid photographs were (and are) known for their lurid presentation and fascination with sex and violence. "[But] the real problem was with pictures that elbowed words right off the page, relegating them to a minor role as caption or brief explanation. Even worse, some tabloid publishers, eager to increase circulation and profits, encouraged the use of highly manipulated and 're-created' images" (Carlebach, 1997, p. 152).

Largely because they traditionally had little formal education and were known for their "pushy" ways as well as intrusive manner, newspaper photographers of this era received little respect from their colleagues on the word side or from the public. The creation of the National Press Photographers Association in 1946 as well as increased educational opportunities in photojournalism programs such as at the University of Missouri School of Journalism helped ameliorate these conditions, but some vestiges of newsroom hierarchy have remained into the twenty-first century. Despite the poor reputation for newspaper photography during this era, photographers were routinely given a variety of assignments such as immediate or "spot" news, planned or "general" news, sports, entertainment, and features. These diverse genres were later formalized into categories, and today almost every newsroom photographer must ably photograph a wide range of topics.[26]

The way in which photographs could be distributed was revolutionized in 1935 when the Associated Press (AP) made its first transmission of a photograph. The AP, established in 1848 by five

Northeastern US newspapers for the purpose of reporting the war with Mexico via the telegraph, made it possible for member newspapers to send and receive photographs by means of telephone wires. The introduction of this service enhanced the AP's value and helped to provide new sources of photographs to a readership clamoring for more information about the world around them.

Another source for news photographs were the agencies that developed in the 1920s and 1930s from the syndicate-concept of the nineteenth century. The photographic agencies of the twentieth century, however, did more than collect and distribute photographs from freelance photographers. "Agencies now concerned themselves with generating story ideas, making assignments, and collecting fees in addition to maintaining files of pictures from which editors might choose suitable illustrations" (Rosenblum, 1984, p. 465).

All of the advances made in photojournalism during the 1920s and 1930s were put to use as world war became inevitable. And, the circulations of picture magazines like *Life* and *Look* increased dramatically while readers followed World War II's destruction, heroism, and tragedy through the magazines' photographs. The 35 mm cameras allowed for a spontaneity and sense of immediacy that had not been present in war photography before this time.

Heightened expectations by editors and the public accompanied the advanced technology. Photographs were expected to arrive from the warfront to the publication in a timely manner. Military censorship[27] could delay the arrival of photographs for months unless the photographer was accredited by the military. And, in a kind of "Catch 22" arrangement, the only journalists who could receive accreditation were those associated with major news organizations.

Despite these and other obstacles to photographic reportage during the War, photographers, such as W. Eugene Smith, Robert Capa, and Joe Rosenthal, followed the troops into battle and recorded the daily lives and emotions of those under fire while putting themselves at risk. Their work has served as a blueprint for those war photographers who have covered subsequent wars.

Perhaps no other World War II photograph is more remembered than Joe Rosenthal's image of the US Marines raising the American flag on Mount Suribachi. While working as an AP photographer, Rosenthal was, in today's terminology, embedded with the Marines. "Old Glory goes up on Mt. Suribachi, Iwo Jima" illustrates the power of the photographic image to go beyond the literal and the two-dimensional to symbolize something much grander and universal. Although the image remained controversial for several decades because an original smaller flag was replaced by the larger one captured in the photograph, and there were suspicions that Rosenthal had requested the change in flags, "people believed in the spirit it conveyed and were cheered by its sense of victory over adversity. It had an immediate, overwhelming impact on the nation" (Fulton, 1988, p. 161).

Rosenthal, who died in 2006, insisted that the situation was not manipulated and that he recorded a real moment. *Life* magazine, which had initially declined to use the photograph for fear that it had been posed, published it three weeks later. The magazine reasoned that, whatever the circumstances under which it was taken, it had become to the nation, and to the marines, a symbol of their heroism. "Old Glory" was accorded iconic value because people believed in its truthfulness. Believing came first. In 1945, Rosenthal was awarded a Pulitzer Prize for the photograph (Fulton, 1988, p. 161).

The United States emerged as the preeminent world power at the end of World War II. Its power was based not only on its military and technological advances but also upon its economy and cultural exports. An American cultural empire began to expand worldwide through a variety of mediums such as radio, film, and printed publications. In the United States the picture magazines, like *Life* and *Look*, reigned over all others. Because the picture magazines demanded countless numbers of photographs, photographers, especially magazine photographers, gained in stature, became better compensated and were able to exercise more control over the stories and photographs that they pursued.[28] The honeymoon between magazine photographers and the publications was short-lived.

The attempts by magazine photographers during the late 1940s to have increased input concerning what stories to cover as well as photographic selection and captioning, sequencing and cropping of their photographs began a struggle between photographers and editors that continues today.[29] The strain between photographers and editors over these issues contributed to some photographers leaving the magazine world and finding other outlets for their work. W. Eugene Smith was perhaps the strongest proponent of photographers exercising control over their own photographs. Having made some of the most famous and elegant photographic essays for *Life* magazine, Smith repeatedly fought with editors and in 1954 resigned in anger (Rosenblum, 1984). He believed that the press's proclivity for "giving the public what it wants," was undermining the integrity and potential of photography. He subsequently pursued projects that he felt were worthy of serious photographic reportage.[30]

David Douglas Duncan was another photographer who worked for *Life* magazine, covering the war in Korea during the early 1950s. Although he followed the same path as the World War II photographers by assuming the perspective of the common soldier, his photographs pushed the aesthetic limits by filling the frames with the faces of his subjects. The compositional tension mirrored the emotional tension of the Marines. "Pushed to the edge of their endurance, the men display utter exhaustion and the gamut of emotions" (Fulton, 1988, p. 168).

Newspaper photography had become more professional as a result of the founding of the National Press Photographers' Association in 1946, but frequently fell prey to managed news events, hokey features and a prodigious use of wire-service photographs. The news consumers' seemingly unquenchable desire for all kinds of photographs may have lessened the overall impact and quality of the everyday newspaper work.

> Thus perhaps it was unavoidable, and even necessary, that the most influential figure in news photography in subsequent decades

> was a man who essentially spurned the medium, creating what might be called anti-photojournalism. Swiss-born Robert Frank said of his own work that he wanted to produce images that would make "all explanations unnecessary." In other words, abolish the necessity for text.
>
> At the same time that Frank was working to undermine the notion of the event, and even the individual, as a focus for news, photojournalism continued to expand its frontiers. In the blandness of the postwar [Korea], photographers turned their vision on the corporation and the suburb. (Russell, 1995, p. 127)

The proliferation of television posed dramatic challenges to photography in the 1960s. Advertisers moved marketing dollars from magazines such as *Life* and *Look* to television, and the mass audience went to television for day-to-day news about one of the major stories of the 1960s – the war in Vietnam. At the same time a group of committed photojournalists provided readers with hard-hitting and emotional images from the war that had "staying power." The images did not vanish on the screen but were viewed again and again by a public that increasingly turned against the war.

The photographers who covered the Vietnam War included men and women who came from varied backgrounds and encompassed the full range of previous experience as photographers. Women such as Catherine Leroy (the Overseas Press Club) won international awards for their work, and others like Dickey Chapelle were killed while on assignment. Associated Press photographer Eddie Adams had been a Marine during the Korean War while Philip Jones Griffiths had to beg Magnum to give him assignments so that he could maintain his credentials as a journalist and remain in Vietnam. Every photographer had his or her own story about why and how they were in Vietnam, but the small cadre of photographers that provided the overwhelming majority of images were deeply committed to their profession.[31] They visually and emotionally documented the brutal destruction and tragedy of war for combatants and civilians alike.

The lasting impact of these images – such as Huynh Cong (Nick) Ut's photograph of the Vietnamese girl after a napalm attack and Larry Burrows' photograph of a helicopter crew member's death – gives testament to the photographers and to the power of the medium. This did not go unnoticed by the government or the military.

> During the Vietnam era, war photography became, normatively, a criticism of war. This was bound to have consequences: mainstream media are not in the business of making people feel queasy about the struggles for which they are being mobilized, much less of disseminating propaganda against waging war.
>
> Since then, censorship – the most extensive kind, self-censorship, as well as censorship imposed by the military – has found a large and influential number of apologists. (Sontag, 2003, p. 65)

The other great story of the 1960s, the Civil Rights movement, had its origins in the 1940s, but was scarcely covered by the mainstream press (although it was reported in the black press) during the early years of protest. The issue was so politically and socially divisive that many hoped that it would just go away, but the movement for social justice pressed on and eventually could not be ignored.

Flip Schulke was one of the few photographers who began documenting the Civil Rights movement during the 1950s. Since the movement received little attention from the mainstream press, Schulke relied upon *Ebony*, a picture magazine directed toward an African-American audience, for his assignments. *Ebony* used Schulke, a white photographer, because black photographers were harassed and/or arrested when trying to photograph in the South (see Photo 4) (Fulton, 1988).

By the 1960s black photographers had been at least partially empowered through the insistence of Civil Rights leaders. Chapnick explains,

> In the United States, there is an ethnically and a racially based press, each of which has its own constituency. Moneeta Sleet, Jr., who graduated from a black Kentucky college, Kentucky State, and received a master's degree in journalism from New York University, opted for a career with black publications. . . . In 1969, he

Photo 4. A protester against integration in Birmingham, Alabama; 1963. Photograph by Flip Schulke. © Flip Schulke, All Rights Reserved.

> received the Pulitzer Prize for his photograph of Coretta King and her daughter, Bernice, at Martin Luther King's funeral in 1968. It was the first time that the Pulitzer Prize was given in feature photography . . .
>
> It was decided that there would be restricted coverage, and Sleet was designated as a "pool" photographer . . . Originally all the photographers were white, but because Andrew Young and Coretta King interceded and insisted that a black photographer be included in the pool, Sleet was able to be inside the church during the service. Mrs. King decided that either a black would be included, or there would be none at all. (Chapnick, 1994, pp. 104, 105)

The importance of women and minority photojournalists cannot be overstated. As W. Eugene Smith said, "There is nothing objective about journalism." A diverse group of (photo)journalists is necessary to address those perspectives that are often missing in the mainstream press. The independence and diversity of photographers during the Civil Rights movement and again during the Vietnam War provided the public with views that ran counter to those supported by institutions of authority and played a role in the social and political change of the 1960s. Furthermore, the photographic reportage from these events inspired the next generation of "concerned photographers" such as Eugene Richards, Eli Reed, and Mary Ellen Mark.

The final two decades of the twentieth century brought many technological changes to photojournalism. In the 1980s newspapers began to use color regularly.[32] This initially changed the way in which photographers had to work as the color film demanded that special care be taken with light. Photographers found themselves using flash more regularly than was necessary with the black-and-white films. As color negative film became more flexible and the Photoshop software was developed photographers were once again able to work more often with available light.

USA Today, founded in 1982, led the way in the newspaper industry's conversion to color photographs. Published by the Gannett Company, the nationally distributed newspaper used the front page to display a variety of stories accompanied by bold and colorful visual elements. Newspaper publishers across the country reacted by redesigning (some would argue "over-designing") their own newspapers and instituting color photography. At many newspapers photographers and editors were forced to consider packaging over content.

Digital cameras began to replace film cameras in many newsrooms in the early 1990s. As a result the routines for photographers changed in several ways. Photographic images are now stored electronically in cameras and in computers. Photographers are able to download their images from the camera to a laptop computer while working in the field and then transmit the edited and cropped images via satellite to almost anywhere else in the world. This technology has also resulted in a number of ethical transgressions and has altered the expectations of some editors.[33]

Despite the technological advances in photography, the goal of photographic reportage remains the same:

> Photojournalists . . . are more than spectators in an historical grandstand. Being there is important, being an eyewitness is significant, but the crux of the matter is bearing witness. To bear witness is to make known, to confirm, to give testimony to others. The distribution and publication of the pictures make visible the unseen, the unknown, and the forgotten. (Fulton, 1988, p. 107)

Photojournalists have historically exposed themselves to danger, endured substandard conditions and worked incredibly long hours to excel at their profession but also to give a voice to those who otherwise would not be heard (or seen). This is the real strength of photojournalism.

Notes

1 Despite the necessity of long exposures and the difficulty of making duplicate images, the Daguerreotype was (rarely) used as a means of visual documentation. "The photographers who took the images apparently had no intention or interest in distributing them beyond their immediate local audiences, who had themselves been witnesses to the actual events . . .

Perhaps the most significant and most historically important example of this phenomenon is the large group of daguerreotypes – about sixty plates are now known – taken in Mexico during the Mexican War by an as-yet-unidentified photographer who spent some time with the American troops" (Stapp, 1988, p. 8).

2 This often caused hardship as photographers working in extreme climates such as Egypt and the Middle East were forced to coat and process their film in enclosed tents where temperatures were well over 100 degrees with "the collodion fizzing – boiling up over the glass" (Rosenblum, 1984, p. 116).

3 Rosenblum points out that during the mid-nineteenth century "in order to present occurrences in which there was continuous, if not very rapid, action, it was necessary to restage the scene" (Rosenblum, 1984, p. 167). Present-day technology makes "restaging the

scene" to freeze the action unnecessary. Photographers have been known, however, to restage the scene for other reasons – composition, capturing a stronger moment, improving the light. Doing so has become an ethical taboo, as news publications need news consumers to believe that photographers are recording rather than creating the news.

4 Yeshayahu Nir examines the way in which cultural, national and religious predispositions affected the choice of subject and visual perspectives of nineteenth-century photographers documenting the "Holy Land." His research indicates that (Protestant) British photographers were generally interested in landscape while (Catholic) French photographers were generally interested in art and architecture (Nir, 1985).

5 The idea to "imbed" photographers with military units may be as old as war photography itself. Rosenblum says, "Civil War reportage owed its successes also to the readiness of the military to accept photography as a new visual tool, hiring photographers other than 'Brady's Men' to work with various units" (Rosenblum, 1984, p. 185).

6 Marianne Fulton declares, "In retrospect, that war [the Civil War] broke out at just that critical juncture in the history of American photography when advances in technology made reportage with the camera feasible, and a perceived demand for news-related images provided an economic incentive" (Fulton, 1988, p. 15).

7 Stapp says that there were no staff photographers or even freelance news photographers until late in the nineteenth century. He says, however, that the illustrated journals would publish "photographs of subjects that captured their readers' interest – usually the aftermaths of catastrophes. These photographs were often otherwise available on the market, usually as stereographs. It can be argued that stereographs provide the link between the pioneer journalistic photographers of the Civil War and the first professional photojournalists, who began to appear in the 1890s" (Stapp, 1988, p. 31).

Stereographs are instruments that hold two nearly identical images beside each other. The images are simultaneously viewed through an optical device that magnifies the images and makes them appear three-dimensional.

8 The halftone process relies on a screen that translates the photograph into small dots. "This involves coating a plate with a light-sensitive emulsion, exposing it to a negative through one of a variety of fine-or-course screens and processing the plates to make the

resultant 'dots' acid resistant. After etching the plate to remove the metal from around the 'dots,' its raised surfaces are inked with a roller . . . and the image is transferred under pressure to paper. . . . The development of the process halftone plate [patented in 1881] also inaugurated an era of photojournalism of a broader nature" (Rosenblum, 1984, p. 451).

An argument could be made that the halftone process accomplished for photography what Guttenberg's press had achieved for the printed word.

9 Carlebach says: "This market was catered to by George Eastman, an inventor and entrepreneur from Rochester, New York, with a keen sense of the profit potential in photography and a single-minded determination to dominate the field" (Carlebach, 1997, p. 16).

The popularization of the small digital and cell phone cameras of today might be akin to that of the hand-held cameras that were first sold at the end of the nineteenth century. In both cases it became easier for the general populace to visually document everyday life.

10 At the same time, the great number of photographs made available to news consumers by the halftone process may have also elevated the news photographer's professional standing among the public (Rhode & McCall, 1961).

11 Jussim says that another result of this relationship was (and is) that newspapers often failed to pursue stories that were potentially harmful to their advertisers since advertising provided a substantial portion of newspaper revenue.

12 Rosenblum says that photographer Jimmy Hare "regularly achieved the sense of real-life immediacy" covering the war in Cuba while using a handheld camera (Rosenblum, 1984, p. 463).

Two decades later Hare was sent to Europe by *Collier's* to cover the fighting in France, but by then military authorities had restricted civilian photographers to the point that Hare "complained that, 'to so much as make a snapshot without official permission in writing means arrest'" (Rosenblum, 1984, p. 463).

13 "According to one observer, during the British army's bloody operations against the Boers in South Africa in 1899, a remarkable 'thirty-three percent of the correspondents have been killed or wounded, or have died of disease incurred in the line of duty'" (Carlebach, 1997, p. 84).

14 Writing about the 1992 presidential campaign between Bill Clinton and George H. W. Bush, art and photography critic, Charles Hagen,

says, "In the mix of actions, ideas, and pageantry that makes up a Presidential race, two parallel campaigns vie for voters' attention. One is the explicit campaign of issues, while the other, equally important, deals with images and symbols" (Hagen, 1992).

15 "The number of women employed by major American newspapers averaged about five," wrote Anne O'Hagan in 1898, though on "some conservative sheets there are but two or three, reserved for such dainty uses as the reporting of women's club meetings and writing weekly fashion and complexion advices." It was different at the yellow papers. O'Hagan noted that on progressive newspapers as many as eight or ten women could be seen [covering a variety of stories]" (Carlebach, 1997, pp. 48–49). Even through the 1960s women reporters were mostly confined to covering "soft" news and "women's" pages.

16 One editor from 1901 says, "'I would rather see my daughters starve than that they should have ever heard or seen what women on my staff have been compelled to hear and see'" (Carlebach, 1997, p. 49). Remarkably similar attitudes may still be expressed – although rarely. Chapnick refers to a story told by photographer Judy Griesedieck. Griesedieck, who confronted an editor over the types of assignments she was receiving, was told, "'If I sent you to a bad part of town, and something happened to you, I'd feel really terrible. It would be like sending my daughter, and I don't think I could live with it'" (Chapnick, 1994, p. 92).

17 Gordon Parks contributed to the Farm Security Administration (FSA) project during the early 1940s and later became a staff photographer for *Life* magazine from 1948 to 1961, photographing several highly acclaimed essays.

18 "Fully aware of the purpose to be served, the photographer selected appropriate vantage points and ways to frame the subject, at times transcending the limitation implied in the title – that of an outsider looking at slum life from across the deep chasm separating middle- from lower-class life. While he may not have entered very deeply into the space occupied by the 'other,' his was not a casual view" (Rosenblum, 1984, p. 361).

19 "With their focus mainly on people and social conditions, images in the documentary style combine lucid pictorial organization with an often passionate commitment to humanistic values – to ideals of dignity, the right to decent conditions of living and work, to truthfulness" (Rosenblum, 1984, p. 359).

20 Although the intent of the photographer is a factor in the way in which photographs are read or interpreted, it's not the only factor. Each viewer brings his or her own background and perspective into the equation as will be discussed in Chapter 3 under the "construction of reality."

21 The Farm Security Administration documentary project provided an opportunity for some of the twentieth-century's most talented women (Dorothea Lange and Margaret Bourke-White) and minority (Gordon Parks) photographers to produce a large body of work that received national attention.

22 Carlebach says, "Consensus on the need to produce images of things as they are breaks down when considering the other major function of the documentary photographer: interpretation. Here, the objectivity of the lens gives way to opinion, and the raw visual data collected on film is molded into argument and narrative" (Carlebach, 1997). And, Howard Chapnick says, "The Farm Security Administration photographers walked in the footsteps of Riis and Hine during the dark days of the Great Depression, using documentary photography not just to record the urban and rural upheaval caused by adverse economic conditions, but also as an advocacy propaganda tool for forcing social change" (Chapnick, 1994, p. 16).

23 This phenomenon is sometimes being repeated with, in my opinion, disastrous results due to the replacement of film cameras by digital cameras. In 2000 as director of photography for Copley Chicago Newspapers I attended a meeting for the senior editors of the Copley chain in Illinois. During this meeting, the managing editor of a newspaper in southern Illinois announced that the average number of daily assignments per photographer was being raised from three or four to six or seven. He explained that the digital camera allowed the photographer to transmit her images to editors rather than having to physically return to the newspaper to process the film. Although there is probably some justification for increased expectations, the mindset of calculating expectations into a predetermined number of additional assignments does not account for a photographer's most precious resource – time – time to establish relationships with subjects, time to capture the strongest moments, time to create the most aesthetically pleasing images and time to get thorough and accurate caption information.

24 The Autochrome color process was invented at the beginning of the twentieth century and was commercially introduced by the

Lumiere brothers in France by 1907. Color wasn't used regularly in photographic reportage, however, until several decades later. *National Geographic* magazine first published several photographs using the Autochrome process in April 1916.

25 "For its concept, *Life*, a publication of Henry Luce, drew upon many sources. In addition to the example of the European picture weeklies, it took into account the popularity of cinema newsreels, in particular 'The March of Time' with which the Luce publishing enterprise was associated. The successes of Luce's other publications . . . also were factors in the decision to launch a serious picture weekly that proposed to humanize through photography the complex political and social issues of the time for a mass audience" (Rosenblum, 1984, p. 476). *Life* magazine, as well as the other illustrated magazines of the mid-twentieth century, worked with the premise that readers wanted to be informed and entertained. Each issue contained a variety of elements such as serious news, social commentary, entertainment, sports and "slices of life."

26 The categories for almost every major photojournalism contest today mirror the types of assignments that were given to newspaper photographers in the 1930s.

27 "With the declaration of war on December 8 [1941], censorship became a mandatory part of the routine editing process" (Fulton, 1988, p. 143).

28 "The majority of news photographers remained the employees of countless newspapers and major press organizations, but the 1947 founding of the photographers' cooperative, Magnum, established the revolutionary principle that picture takers should own the rights to their work" (Russell, 1995, p. 125).

29 Photographers sometimes believe that their subjects or their photographs or both are not given sufficient respect or consideration by an editor. Some photographers think that they know better than the editors which photographs should be published and in what order. And, at times the photographer worries that someone, who has not witnessed the event, person, etc. firsthand, making the editorial decisions will compromise the basic integrity of the story.

30 *Minamata*, a book detailing the effects of industrial mercury poisoning on a fishing community in Japan, is perhaps W. Eugene Smith's most famous work. Smith says of *Minamata*, "This is not an objective book. The first word I would remove from the folklore

of journalism is the word 'objective.' That would be a giant step toward truth in the free press. And, perhaps, 'free' should be the second word removed. Freed of these two distortions, the journalist and photographer could get to his real responsibilities. . . . My first responsibility is to my readers" (Smith & Smith, 1975, prologue).

31 The ability to document the disastrous effects of war so closely and so broadly was partially due to the fact that press credentials were so easily obtained. AP photographer Eddie Adams said, " 'Anybody could get accredited. I don't care who you were. You could just type your own little letter saying so-and-so is a so-and-so – it didn't have to be on a letterhead. It was a joke. You typed it up and then you were accredited' " (Moeller, 1989, p. 360).

32 During the 1950s several magazines began using color photographs (although rarely for news stories since the film speeds were still slow), and a handful of newspapers ran color on the front and/or back pages of the A sections. This practice encouraged (as it did in the 1980s) photographers to set up photographs and to rely heavily on artificial lighting.

33 The significance of these changes for good and ill is addressed in Chapters 4 ("Newsroom Culture and Routine"), 6 ("Ethics") and 8, ("The Iraq War").

References

Carlebach, M. L. (1992). *The origins of photojournalism in America.* Washington, DC: Smithsonian Institution Press.

Carlebach, M. L. (1997). *American photojournalism comes of age.* Washington, DC: Smithsonian Institution Press.

Chapnick, H. (1994). *Truth needs no ally.* Columbia, MO: University of Missouri Press.

Foresta, M. A. (1996). *American photographs: The first century.* Washington, DC: Smithsonian Institution.

Fulton, M. (1988). *Eyes of time: Photojournalism in America.* New York: Little, Brown and Company.

Hagen, C. (1992). Photographs and political families. *The New York Times*, October 25, p. H 28.

Jussim, E. (1988). The tyranny of the pictorial: American photojournalism from 1880 to 1920. In M. Fulton (Ed.), *Eyes of time: Photojournalism in America* (pp. 36–73). New York: Little, Brown and Company.

McChesney, R. W. (2004). *The problem of the media.* New York: Monthly Review Press.

Moeller, S. D. (1989). *Shooting war.* New York: Basic Books.

Newhall, B. (1982). *The history of photography: From 1839 to the present.* New York: Museum of Modern Art.

Nir, Y. (1985). *The Bible and the image.* Philadelphia: University of Pennsylvania.

Osman, C. & Phillips, S. S. (1988). European visions: Magazine photography in Europe between the wars. In M. Fulton (Ed.), *Eyes of time: Photojournalism in America* (pp. 75–103). New York: Little, Brown and Company.

Rhode, R. B. & McCall, F. H. (1961). *Press photography: Reporting with a camera.* New York: Macmillan.

Rosenblum, N. (1984). *A world history of photography.* New York: Abbeville.

Russell, G. (1995). New directions: 1950–1980. In R. Lacayo & G. Russell (Eds.), *Eyewitness: 150 years of photojournalism* (pp. 125–163). New York: Time Books.

Smith, W. E. & Smith, A. W. (1975). *Minamata.* New York: Holt, Rinehart & Winston.

Sontag, S. (2003). *Regarding the pain of others.* New York: Farrar, Straus & Giroux.

Stapp, W. (1988). Subjects of strange . . . and of fearful interest: Photojournalism from its beginnings in 1839. In M. Fulton (Ed.), *Eyes of time: Photojournalism in America* (pp. 1–35). New York: Little, Brown and Company.

Stott, W. (1973). *Documentary expression and Thirties America.* New York: Oxford University Press.

2

The Visual Newspaper

I believe that photographers are journalists in the fullest sense and they're not a service department to just illustrate the stories that other people think up. They're people who think for themselves and come up with stories and with reasonable ways of telling stories, whether their own or other people's stories, and I think that they're crucial to the success of a paper. We're living in a very competitive media environment, and you've got to have a paper that plays all the notes. (Carroll, 2004)

The role of photojournalism and the photojournalist is and has been a passionately debated topic for many years. At the best visual newspapers, photographs are recognized as an important part of the everyday story-telling process and a key ingredient in the competition for news consumers. Yet at many newspapers photographs are regarded as simply a means for illustrating word stories. Word journalists and even photojournalists often fail to recognize the strength of photography in reporting the news.

Word editors and writers traditionally set the course within newsrooms by selecting the stories and determining how those stories should be covered. Photographers and photo editors in most newsrooms are forced to follow the lead and play a game of "catch-up."[1] Visual Journalism Group Leader for the Poynter Institute, Kenny Irby says, "Throughout my career and travels, I have constantly heard frustrated photographers bemoan the fact that many of their writing colleagues and editors 'just don't get it. . . . They treat us like a service department. They don't understand our craft. They don't appreciate our need for time. And they don't run our best pictures'" (Irby, 2002).

Turf wars within newsrooms frequently affect the way in which stories are initiated and produced. Not long after I became director of photography for Copley Chicago Newspapers, I realized that the section editor was initiating virtually all of the stories in the features section. The photography department was not informed of the details until after the stories had been at least partially developed. I met with the section editor to discuss the possibility of involving photo editors and photographers earlier in the process. Our meeting didn't produce any changes, so the next week I announced at the senior editors' meeting that a photo editor would be attending the weekly meetings for features. I also mentioned that the photo editor would be bringing a list of story ideas initiated within the photography department.

When the senior editors' meeting ended, the features section editor visited my office, and a heated discussion ensued. Finally, I said to the editor, "Think of it this way, every week you're engineering a train that is your features section and you're leaving the station while the photo people are running down the tracks trying to catch up. I don't want to take over your train; I just want to be on it." From that point on photographers, with the editor's encouragement, initiated many of the best stories produced by the features section and worked together with the editor and section designers as a team. Together, they received numerous accolades, and the features' editor became a strong newsroom advocate for photography.

In this case the overall quality of the features section's photographs rose dramatically because photographers had increased input and more time to complete the assignments. More than technical execution and aesthetics, however, changed through the photography department's participation in the planning sessions. Stories initiated by the photographers were fundamentally different than those assigned by the editor.

Photographers spend a good amount of their time "in the streets" since they need to be present in order to photograph their stories. Their subjects tend to represent a diverse set of cultures, socio-economic levels, educational backgrounds, religious affiliations and racial and ethnic groups. And, their stories many times come from the grittier side of life. Editors, on the other hand, spend most of their time in the newsroom associating with colleagues who to a large extent come from backgrounds similar to their own and who have similar interests. They try to give readers stories that they perceive to be of popular interest, but that might not be the best strategy. Mike Davis, features picture editor for the *Portland Oregonian*, says:

> I would guess that if you looked at the number of papers that ran stories about the D'Vinci Code – the movie – last weekend, it would be astounding. We had three section fronts in three days – three totally different sections for one stinking movie that maybe 20 or 30 percent of the population will see.
>
> I think that if a newspaper or any other news publication tries to satisfy niche information delivery – a movie, a book, a new video game – there are so many better sources for that kind of information than a newspaper. If, on the other hand, what you're doing is trying to tell more universal, more wide-reaching stories – if the standard for what you're doing is that more than 20 percent of the readership will be interested in this – you will be a desired information experience in your community. (Davis, 2006)

Photographer Rob Finch's visual narrative, "To Be a Mom," provides a good example of a "more universal, more wide-reaching story" and one outside the norm for most feature sections. The *Aurora Beacon News*' (one of four daily newspapers that collectively were called, Copley Chicago Newspapers) news section assigned Finch to cover a community fund-raising event to aid the family of a young boy who suffered from "Black Fan Diamond Syndrome" a rare type of anemia. The assignment called for one photograph to be published with a story about the event. Finch, however, became emotionally drawn to the boy and his family and continued to work on the story for another one and a half years until the boy, Craig, died in his mother's arms (see Photo 5).

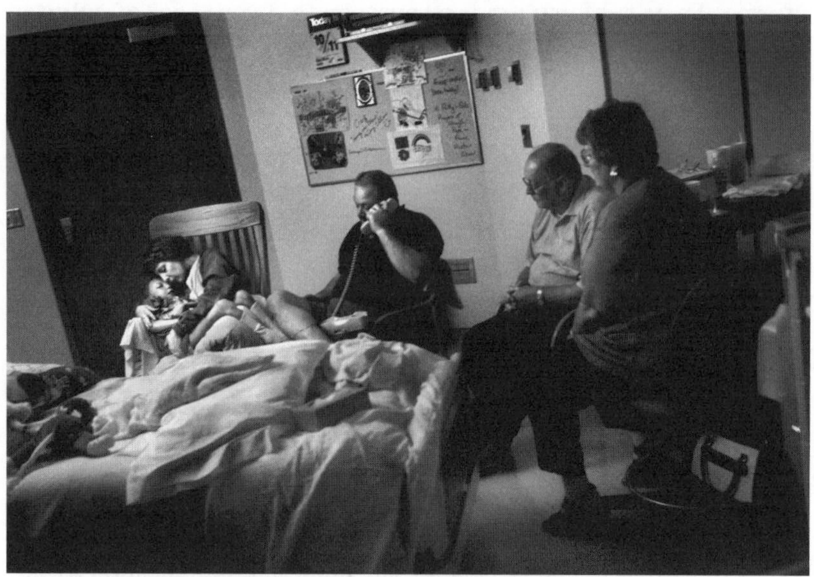

Photo 5. Patty Colletti holds her son Craig shortly after his death. Photograph by Rob Finch. As published in *Aurora Beacon News*. Copyright 1999 by Fox Valley Publications LLC. Reprinted with permission.

Finch, with the mother's blessing, pitched the idea for a photo-driven story to the features' editor. The editor suggested a two-part series and assigned several pages (including the section fronts for both days) to the photographs and text. She also agreed to publish the photographs in black and white at Finch's request (photographers often feel that black and white photographs imply a sense of respect for the subject).[2] "To Be a Mom" received an overwhelmingly positive response from the community and won several state and national awards.

Copley Chicago Newspapers and their sister papers, Sun Publications (a group of suburban Chicago weeklies also owned by Copley), however, were "really atypical of newspapers" (Strazzante, 2004). By and large newspapers remain word-driven. "The pictures that are locally produced to run in the paper – what's chosen and how they're played – that continues to be too much out of the hands of photo editors and photographers. The picture choices are too literal, and the photographs are too often slaves to words instead of being regarded as a way to tell a different facet of the story" (Steber, 2004). Some even argue that newspaper photojournalism is dead.

Poynter Institute's Anne Van Wagener says, "Visual journalists . . . have a hard time being taken seriously in some newsrooms. Changing the perception of visuals as information and not decoration continues to be a struggle." She continues, "That struggle comes in part from a lack of understanding about why visuals are used and how they fit into the publication's mission" (Van Wagener, 2004). Nevertheless, some newspapers understand the importance of visuals. Former *Los Angeles Times* editor of the paper, John Carroll says, "I've seen the eye-track research from Poynter [Institute]. I know that no one is going to read a story unless there is something visual to entice them whether it's a headline or a photograph or whatever. So, we're trying to make our paper like a symphony of all the crafts, and photography is one of those crafts, and it's crucial" (Carroll, 2004).

What then constitutes a visual newspaper? How does a newspaper attain a high level of visual reporting? And, how are news consumers affected when newspapers become more visually sophisticated?

Newspapers that are consistently strong visually have at least five factors in common. First, photographers are regarded as journalists in every sense of the word. They are given the respect to initiate, research, and tell stories visually. "I think that to succeed photography has to be accepted by the broader newspaper as a key piece in it. You can't just say, 'Go and do a good job,' but you've got to tell the rest of the newsroom staff that photography is important" (Carroll, 2004). When photographers become partners in the development of a story, the visual aspect of that story improves. Yet, despite John Carroll's enlightened approach to visual journalism, most newsrooms remain word dominated with little opportunity for photographers to initiate stories. Carroll's own *Los Angeles Times* newsroom experiences friction over the issue. *Times* photo editor, Hal Wells says, "There are some people here who resist sharing the power and the leadership of the newspaper with design and photo editors, but they're starting to see the light" (Wells, 2004).

The second factor in creating a visual newspaper derives from the first. Photographers take the responsibility to find out about their communities and originate stories from those communities. And, photographers find out how their newsrooms operate and how they can work most effectively to make their newspapers visually stronger.

Newspaper photo editors frequently decry the small number of story ideas initiated by staff photographers. *Los Angeles Times* photo editor, Gail Fisher, says,

> I don't understand it. I mean, as a photographer, when I was out in the field, I was constantly initiating things because I wanted to be working on stories as a photographer that I was interested in instead of having somebody hand me an assignment everyday. I'm not sure why – it might just be this culture [of receiving assignments without an opportunity to initiate them] that these people have been in for too many years – but, I'll tell you, there's not enough initiating, and I really want that to change. (Fisher, 2004)

The best photojournalists constantly look for stories. And editors at the best visual newspapers support those photographers. *Chicago Tribune* photographer Scott Strazzante talks about an earlier time in his career when he worked for the (Joliet, Illinois) *Herald News*:

> I wanted to do this story on a family being evicted from their trailer – actually, the entire trailer park was being evicted. The newspaper had covered it off and on as a news story and didn't really want to spend any more time on it. But I proposed a more in-depth story, limited to the one family, to Michael Hamtil [the photo editor]. They were part of our community, and I wanted to follow them through their transition. He [Hamtil] said, "Great, just let me know when you have to go out there, and I'll clear the schedule for you." I ended up spending more than a month – probably half of my [work] time – in that trailer park.
>
> By focusing on that family's situation, the photographs told the story of all the people that were there. The piece ended up running

> on the front of the paper and then a double truck inside. I don't even remember if we had a [word] story with it. I might have written a copy block or maybe a reporter went out and wrote something. It was definitely a situation where the paper allowed me to do something that they weren't immediately interested in, but they let me continue to shoot and watched how it developed. (Strazzante, 2004)

Strazzante is not only a talented photojournalist.[3] He also understands how newsrooms work and how to convince others that a story merits coverage. Many photographers do not sufficiently comprehend the newsroom culture or how to get things accomplished within that culture. Maggie Steber says:

> We [photographers and photo editors] have to become smarter about how we conduct our business. That's where I think the [visual] revolution has to occur because until we stop asking the question, "Why do they [writers and word editors] hate us," we will be the victims. We play victims as photographers. So, we really need to get beyond that, and we need to learn how to speak the language of the word people and to make intelligent discussions.
>
> Photographers are very aware of all of this, but they never get involved in it. I'm making a great generalization here, but my experience is that it's very rare that photographers fully understand the whole business side of the paper like the deadline issue. I never see photographers staying until the very end watching how the paper is put together.
>
> They should understand the restrictions they're working under, understand the political pressure in a newsroom, all of these things that do affect their work and their lives as creative people. But, they don't get involved. We have to change. (Steber, 2004)

Editors at visually strong newspapers understand that visuals don't have to repeat the information presented in the word story or mirror the preconceptions of the editor. This factor runs counter to the instincts of many word journalists, yet it's crucial to understand that the best visuals tell stories, they do not serve as illustrations for word stories.[4] "[A visual image] is no different than a carefully crafted story. . . . A visual image should be scrutinized for its visual content and its perceived message" (Van Wagener, 2004).

Freelance photographer Peter Essick talks about how editors' preconceptions can make photography difficult even at a publication as visually sophisticated as *National Geographic* magazine:

> In the Trobriand Island story I wanted to basically say, "Here is a group of people, and here's how they live," not show them off as some weird exotic group. There are some people at the *Geographic* who appreciated that, and it's going to run as that, but it would have gone a lot easier and quicker if I had done the old [photograph with] flash at sunset of funny looking people who look different from us. In fact, they [some editors at *National Geographic*] told me that it's harder for readers to understand a story like this than one that has some guy hanging from a rope in a cave. (Essick, 1991)

Newsroom journalists agree that pages require strong visual entry points, and writers know that the chances of their stories making the front page are often determined by the presence or absence of a photograph. Some stories almost force editors to allow the photographs to tell the story.

> There is a power in photography, sometimes good, sometimes bad. You look at, let's say Abu Ghraib and that was a huge story because of the photographs (see Photo 6). You could have written about it and people would have been stunned, but when they saw it, the outrage was phenomenal. Same thing is true about those contractors that were burned and hanged on the bridge [in Fallujah]. You could have written about that and people would have been appalled but to see those photographs it brought the horror of the scene home. (Crawford, 2004)

At the same time, visuals are treated differently than words. They are often judged by their ability to illustrate the word stories rather than tell a story in a different way or communicate compelling content. The Abu Ghraib photographs, taken by sources other than photojournalists, offer an excellent counterpoint to the word-driven story. Addressing the debate over whether and/or

Photo 6. Abu Ghraib prisoner Satar Jabar standing on a box with wires attached to his body. Originally published in *The New Yorker.*

how the Abu Ghraib photographs should have been published, *Time* magazine picture editor, Mary Anne Golon says, "'The inflammatory thing is not the images, it's what's in the images. Of course it's inflammatory, so is war.'" Golon concludes, "that the images' main source of power is that they serve as evidence for accusations of wrongdoing" (Tarbert, 2004).

Barbie Zelizer, professor at the Annenberg School of Communication at the University of Pennsylvania, says, "The [Abu Ghraib] images resonate culturally because they can conjure up dark collective memories. She noted that some of the photos bear a strong resemblance to historical images of lynchings. The images of dogs attacking prisoners, are 'absolutely directly taken from Nazi iconography . . . These photos certainly undermine our sense of how we like to think of ourselves during wartime'" (Tarbert, 2004). Visuals can powerfully communicate strong content.

Writers and word editors initiate most story ideas. More enlightened senior editors are receptive to a story changing directions and/or being expanded because of the photographic reporting. While serving as the director of photography for Ecuador's *El Universo*, I became involved in a discussion over the use of a photograph that the section editor wanted to bury inside the paper. Staff photographer, José Sánchez, had been assigned to accompany a writer who was reporting from a small indigenous town in a mountainous region that suffered several days of flooding. The story about the town's travails was slotted for page 4 and included space for a two or three-column photograph to be published in black and white.

While exploring the town's homes, stores and restaurants for subject material, Sánchez befriended two indigenous women who had walked several miles of perilous mountain trails to obtain food and medicine for their village. They told Sánchez that this was a common trek for themselves and for people from other communities in similar circumstances. He asked if he could join them and photograph their return to the village. They agreed, and he produced a compelling set of photographs documenting their dangerous journey (See Photo 7).

When Sánchez returned to the newspaper the next day, I went through the photographs with him and asked him more about the story. He told me that the women's journey over terrain made dangerous by landslides and steep cliffs was taken over and over by women from remote villages during the rainy season. I went to the section editor and asked that we delay publishing the story and instead do a more extensive piece detailing the dangers to these women. The editor flatly denied my request and asked for one photograph that would run two columns in black and white. I refused to give it to her and instead took the issue to the managing editor.

After some discussion between the three of us, the managing editor asked to see the photographs. He looked at the first one and said, "Okay, let's send the writer back to the town for more information. We'll hold the story." In the end, the story and photographs made a strong front-page package that told a meaningful

Photo 7. Two indigenous women pass over a treacherous bridge during flooding near Chanchan, Ecuador. Photograph by José Sánchez. Copyright, 1999, *El Universo*, Guayaquil, Ecuador. Reprinted with permission.

story about the everyday lives of a group largely underreported. In this case the managing editor realized that there was much more to the story than the one originally conceived. For him it was a non-issue that a photojournalist had been responsible for finding the further complexities in the story. He was more interested in producing a good newspaper.

The fourth factor that influences strong visual reporting is education. That includes training journalists to recognize and develop stories with visual potential, teaching even experienced photographers to use their craft to create better visual stories and working with editors to be more sophisticated in their visual thinking. Joe Elbert, former assistant managing editor for visuals at the *Washington Post*, says, "My role here is really as a picture editor, which I love, but it's also really teaching photography if you get down to it. That's my job, every day, editing film and teaching, seeing what people can do and challenging them to do it better" (Elbert, 2004). And, photo editor Gail Fisher adds, "Throughout the process (of working on a project) there is constant communication between myself and the photographer. I go through every frame, and I give them feedback weekly, maybe biweekly or even monthly depending on whether they're going to be traveling for three or four weeks" (Fisher, 2004).

Working with senior editors to broaden their approach to visual story-telling sometimes becomes a difficult process because editors must be willing to participate in order for change to take place. The process frequently ruffles feathers, but usually everyone benefits including the readers. Mike Davis describes a moment in this process during his time as picture editor for the *Albuquerque Tribune*:

> There was one project that we did in Albuquerque where Pat Davison was the photographer. I remember sitting in the editor's office with the managing editor, the city editor, the writer and the photographer and myself as well as the AME for graphics. This was a story about the point at which children's voices change, essentially a story about puberty.
>
> The editor was dead set that it should run as a multi-day series – kick off as the lead package on day one and then subsequently drop down on the page and go as a twenty-something inch story four or five days. I knew the visual potential of doing it that way would be minimal and that the chances of any reader staying with something like that would be pretty limited, so I was very strongly against doing it that way.
>
> I suggested an approach in which we would simply write 4 to 6 inches [of text] about each kid. We'd do ten or twelve kids and run them on the features section and run about three a day so that the readers could see the range. Boy, it was a dog and catfight, and I finally said, "Look if you want to run it like that, I don't want to have anything to do with it. You can take the ball and run with it." And, I started to walk out of the room, and everybody said, "Whoa, whoa, wait a minute." So, I came back in and talked about it more and drew out how it might work out on the page and talked more about why we should do it that way instead of the standard approach. That year it won a first place in Pictures of the Year.

> And, a lot of readership responded, but it was their [the editors] willingness to stop and reconsider. (Davis, 2006)

The success of that project was also, at least partially, due to Davis' willingness to educate the word editors as to why the less standard and more visual approach would work better.

The fifth factor in establishing a strong visual newspaper is the coordination and planning between the two visual areas of the newsroom, photography and design. Big news stories often bring out the best in newsroom cooperation. *Los Angeles Times* deputy design director Michael Whitley, in recalling his involvement in the Ronald Reagan funeral coverage, highlights several points that lead to excellent visual storytelling. He says that his work began before the photographs were ever taken when he wrote memos to the managing editor as well as the space accountant outlining his thoughts about the number of pages that would be required for the package. He believes that it's important for the design and photography departments to work together from the start to ensure that sufficient space is allotted for photographic images to have full effect. In regard to the Reagan funeral, Whitley says, "It was going to be something that people would remember more for the images than the words. . . . [A photograph] is a frozen moment that you can observe and study, and you can see every tiny detail" (Whitley, 2004).

Whitley received the space that he requested, an open double truck (two facing pages that are totally clear of advertising) for the day when Reagan's body was taken to lie in state, and another open double truck for the day of the funeral service. He explains, however, that there was a lot of back and forth discussion about it since it was going to put the paper over budget, and the *Times* was in the midst of a "belt-tightening" mode mandated by the Chicago based Tribune Company ownership. "Ultimately, it came down to (managing editor) Dean (Baquet) saying that we needed to do the right thing with the pictures, so we were given the space" (Whitley, 2004).

Whitley says that he assigned himself to design the pages because he gets personal satisfaction out of designing photo-driven pages. Part of that pleasure derives from the team approach to editing and design. On the day that Reagan's body was taken to lie in state, a small group from photography and design as well as the deputy managing editor gathered in a conference room to make the final selection of photographs. Photo editors had already winnowed the group of photographs that were laid out on the conference-room table from hundreds that had been received throughout the day. Their job had been to judge the overall quality of the individual images and to eliminate those not really publishable. The group of design, photo and word editors who gathered in the conference room had other criteria. "We discussed what images were going to really fit well together, which ones would tell the most complete story, and we discussed which images we thought were repetitive so that we would say, 'It's either this one, this one or this one, but we can't use all three.' It was very much a group editing process" (Whitley, 2004).

Since the Reagan package was a news event the editors worked under deadline pressure to select the final group of photographs. The longer that it took to edit the photographs, the less time Whitley had to design the pages. Whitley, however, says that taking the necessary time to select the "right" photographs is the proper approach. To most efficiently use the little time he had, Whitley began thinking during the editing process about how the various photographs on the table fit together proportionally. He says that while they were all the same size on the table, he was thinking about which ones might work as lead images and which ones might be able to be sized small. "I'm trying to decide which pictures need size and which pictures don't because we can't pick only pictures that need scale, we can't have all five or six-column pictures" (Whitley, 2004). Another issue that he thought about was face sizes within the images. He says that if the faces are essentially the same size in every photograph, the reader will become disinterested.

During the final edit the editors also discussed whether and how individual photographs needed cropping. Whitley says that although it might be evident to everyone that a particular image needs to be cropped, it is often difficult to agree on how much cropping is necessary particularly since the editors are working with small printouts during the edit. He says, however, "once you put it on the page some of the flaws at the edges of the picture become apparent, and you can really sharpen the focus by cropping the edges or through cropping you can get more impact in the crucial areas of the picture" (Whitley, 2004).

Because issues like cropping were not settled during the conference-room edit of the Reagan package, interested parties checked in regularly as Whitley laid out the pages. Whitley says that the whole process needs to be discussion oriented. "It's no good if I just go off and do what I think is right because it needs to be something that we all feel good about. For example, if we're really scaling [enlarging] a picture up, it needs to be because it's a picture that's worth it for the people that read the paper not just because it serves our egos" (Whitley, 2004).

In the case of the Reagan pages Whitley enlarged the lead picture (Reagan's horse-drawn casket) to twelve columns (see Photo 8). Although he had originally made it smaller, he kept enlarging it until it ran all the way across both pages. He believes that the increased size made people want to look at the photograph for a long time, taking in the small details and the context of the large crowd. He says that the smaller versions just didn't have the same impact or story-telling qualities.

Although Whitley feels good about the size of the lead photo, he also admits that using a photograph that large makes things more complicated. He says that once half of the space is taken by one photograph, the number of other photographs that can be used is more limited, and for that reason he has to think very carefully about which photographs work together the best to tell a multileveled story without repeating one another. Once the remaining photographs are chosen for the pages, he goes about determining the sizes of each and then starts "to fit the puzzle together."

Whitley's description of the production of the Reagan package offers an example of how the process works at a visual newspaper. The cooperation between photography and design, the commitment from senior editors, the planning, the allocation of space, the belief that photographs tell stories and the desire to do the right thing for readers are key ingredients in making the *Times* one of the best at telling stories visually.[5] Whitley concludes:

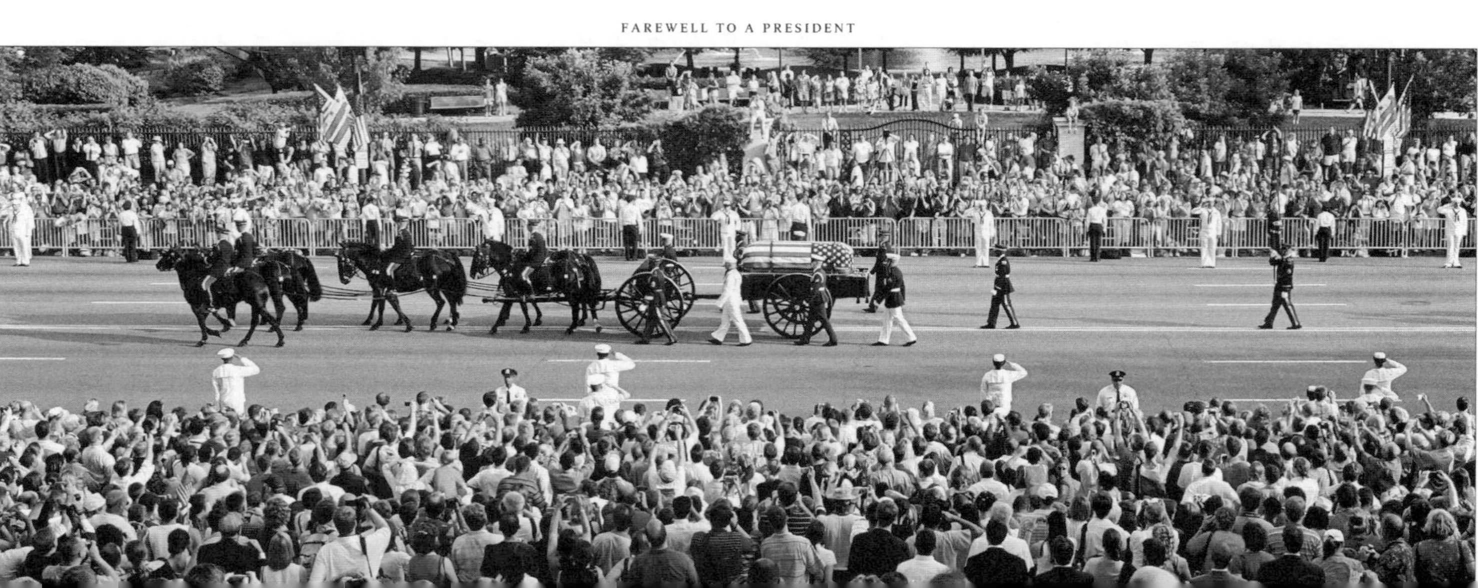

A DAY OF SOLEMN POMP, PAGEANTRY

Tyrone Turner *For The Times*

SOLEMN TRIBUTE: *Sgt. York is led behind the caisson. The horse bore an empty saddle and Reagan's own riding boots reversed in the stirrups to symbolize a warrior who will ride no more.*

Francine Orr *Los Angeles Times*

QUIET MOMENT: *With him in death as in life, former First Lady Nancy Reagan pauses to touch the flag-draped casket before leaving the Capitol Rotunda after the state funeral for the former president in Washington. The casket rested on a catafalque that originally was designed for Abraham Lincoln's funeral in 1865.*

Carolyn Cole *Los Angeles Times*

A RICH LIFE: *Mourners remember Reagan with mementos from his life: a license plate bearing the nickname earned during his film career and a ball cap sporting a ship named after him.*

Carolyn Cole *Los Angeles Times*

FOR THE CHIEF: *Cadets from the U.S. Military Academy at West Point, N.Y., march along Constitution Avenue during the funeral procession to the Capitol.*

Photo 8. *Los Angeles Times*, June 10, 2004. Copyright, 2004, *Los Angeles Times*. Reprinted with permission.

> Part of my job is looking out for what's in the best interests of our readers in terms of stories, graphics, and photography, and this [the Reagan funeral] is one of those times where you know that photography is going to be the most important piece. It's what people will most respond to, and if you mess it up, they'll hate you for it.
>
> We invest in the front page, but we invest in our inside pages too. And, our inside pages are where I think we really show what we can do, for example, these open Reagan pages. It's about telling a complete story. We push to have enough photojournalism included as an important part of the storytelling because people respond to it. They see it, and it's so different to have something told to you in words than to have something shown to you. (Whitley, 2004)

The *Los Angeles Times* only recently received acclaim for its photography, design and use of photographs. How then do newspapers become visual newspapers? Hiring a strong advocate for visuals is one way. Tim Rasmussen, former *South Florida Sun Sentinel* director of photography and now assistant managing editor of photography for the *Denver Post*, describes his experience upon being hired to lead the photo department at the *Freelance Star* in Fredericksburg, Virginia. "When I arrived, Suzanne Carr and Bill Blevens were the photographers, and there was nothing there photographically except Suzanne's talent and Bill Blevens' enthusiasm for actually doing something with the department" (Rasmussen, 2006). By the time Rasmussen left there were six full-time staff photographers, a photo editor, a photo assignment editor, two imaging technicians and a visuals editor, and the *Freelance Star* had won Pictures of the Year International's "Best Use of Photography" for a newspaper with under 100,000 circulation as well as numerous POYi photo editing awards. He says simply that the photography department kept delivering and the publisher in return kept giving them new positions.

Rasmussen says that although it was easier to effect change at the *Freelance Star* than at a larger newspaper, there were nevertheless constant battles over assignments, space and editing. Rasmussen admits, "I'm not sure they wanted to hire me at first, but I do think that Ed Jones [editor of the paper] wanted change, and he wanted the photographers and the photo department to be successful. I think that he had no idea what I would do or that I would institute things that they had never heard of like photo editing" (Rasmussen, 2006).

Among the difficulties Rasmussen faced were rules created by the publisher that prohibited photographs from being sized larger than four columns and stories from running more than two pages. Rasmussen says that the newspaper "broke that rule every day" through his pitching ideas, cajoling, arguing and cultivating allies like assistant managing editor Jim Mann. Rasmussen credits Mann with breaking the rules even though he knew he would get into trouble. And, he says the publisher helped build the photographic department even though they often advocated things that ran counter to his idea of what a newspaper should be.

Within five years after Rasmussen arrived at the *Freelance Star* the newspaper and its photo staff had developed a national reputation for photography and photographic usage. Rasmussen had been able to assemble a talented staff as well as add several innovative touches to the newspaper such as a string of photographic projects published quarterly in which all of the staff participated. He says that it was after one of these projects that he was summoned to a meeting with the editor and publisher. They told him that all photographs would in the future be turned over to the advertising department for possible use and that staff photographers would be required to produce advertising photographs in addition to their editorial work. That same night Rasmussen began looking for another job. In his subsequent interview with the *Sun Sentinel* Rasmussen says that he told the editor of the newspaper, Earl Macher, "If you want me to be your voice in the photo department, don't hire me because I will be their advocate from the day that I begin. He [Macher] said, 'I want exactly what you want'" (Rasmussen, 2006).

Joe Elbert, former director of photography for the *Washington Post*, receives much of the credit for turning the *Post* into a newspaper that attracts award-winning photographers and features strong photographic editing. At one time, his aggressive style and passion for photography and design helped the *Washington Post* and its photographers win numerous national awards.[6] He says that he (like Rasmussen) wanted to be clear about his strong personality and advocacy for visual storytelling from the beginning.

> The *Post* had 30 candidates in '87 for the job I now have. They kept whittling it down, whittling it down. Finally it got to five, and they brought each of us in [Elbert was at the time director of photography for the *Miami Herald*]. I've always had a bit of an attitude, and plus I had weird spiked hair, and looked like Don Johnson with my sleeves rolled up – not you're typical *Washington Post* interview kind of guy.
>
> I got into a disagreement with [editor of the *Post*] Len Downey while I was interviewing. I just wanted to see how far I could push because why be somebody you aren't? You get the job, and then what are you going to do? Ben [Bradley, the publisher] was watching the whole thing and enjoying it tremendously. They brought me back for a second interview because I guess I made a couple of AME's [assistant managing editors] that aren't here any longer really nervous, and Ben loved that. He wanted edge, he wanted attitude and that was not going to be a problem. One thing is certain; you always have edge and attitude in photo at the *Washington Post.*
>
> Let me give you a story that kind of sets the tone. The first time I'm here [to attend the daily news meeting] there was a giant conference table for all the editors to sit with Ben and Len. There was no chair for art and photo. I went in a bit early, and I took Ben's chair. He came in [later] and saw that I was sitting in his chair, and he had no space to sit except in the back row with everybody else. Everyone has a designated chair, but I had no chair so I took Ben's. When he came in, he had a smile on his face. Everybody else thinks, "What the Holy shit? What's going to happen?" Nothing happened. He took a seat in the back. I came to the meeting the next day, and there was a chair for photo and a chair for art that perfectly matched all of the other furniture. (Elbert, 2004)

Elbert had made a statement that the art and photography departments at the *Washington Post* would not be taken for granted.

Not all advocates for strong visuals come from the art, photography, or design departments. The confluence of the September

11, 2001 attacks on the World Trade Center and the hiring of a new editor of the paper thrust the *New York Times* into an elite group of visual newspapers.[7]

Although photography and design teams had begun to make important changes years before, prior to September 11 the *Times* not only had a reputation for being a "writers' paper," but also for being a non-visual paper. In a 1991 interview assistant managing editor Carolyn Lee said, "The important thing to know about this paper is that writers hold sway here; that's just an established fact. If a particular writer doesn't enjoy working with a photographer, then the writer gets his way, and the photographer trails along" (Lee, 1991). Yet, 10 years later Mike Smith, deputy editor for visuals says that writers who had never complimented photographers or photo editors "will stop us and say, 'Who took the picture on the front cover today?' or 'The pictures look good' " (Smith, 2004). What changed?

Editor of the paper, Howell Raines, began his fifth day of work with the *Times* on September 11, 2001. He had met with several photographers and picture editors before that day, and listened as they told him that the *Times* had a history of not using visuals well. Smith believes that Raines saw September 11 as an opportunity to do something different with photography, "something he could put his mark on." Smith adds, "[The hiring of Raines and 9/11] helped catapult us into sustained intelligent picture use. We had this huge story, the biggest story of our careers right in our backyard. And, on every level the staff responded brilliantly" (Smith, 2004).

> That day the first thing I tried to do was to make sure that all parties were on deck which doesn't sound like much but bridges and tunnels are being closed and security clamped down everywhere. . . . [Then] we tried to get everyone deployed and set up a system to deal with the freelance film. At that point we were still trying to figure out exactly what had happened. And, we were trying to figure out what kind of pictures we had to have, what might the front page look like.
>
> The first hours were so chaotic and everyone was at the scene and shooting and staying alive and keeping the communications

open. The TV's were on in the newsroom. We had meetings every couple of hours with the top editors of the paper. We would meet with the page designer to figure out how many stories we were going to have, how long they were going to be, how many pages we were going to need. . . . We were going to have a package on the attacks themselves, and we were going to have a package on the injured – at the time we thought there would be thousands of injuries, but as it turned out almost everyone died. We were trying to divide the coverage along those lines and make sure we had people in all those places and the clock just seemed to turn and before you knew it was 4:00 or 5:00 and nobody had stopped.

I don't think we had much of anything in terms of photos until early afternoon, but by the 4:30 newsroom meeting we had scores of pictures to show. Things were coming in so fast that you couldn't have one person look at everything; it would have just been too overwhelming. At least a couple of times during the day we got together a group of editors – the metro editor, foreign editor, the main news-desk picture editor – we looked at all the stuff [photos]. I've forgotten how many pictures we published that first day. I want to say it was close to 80 or 90 . . . a lot of pictures. It was just page after page.

Howell [Raines] came back to photo that day and looked at what we had. He was absolutely involved from the very beginning because he was concerned with the front page. I remember by mid afternoon or so having a discussion with [deputy photo editor] Margaret [O'Connor] and probably [chief photo assignment editor] Jim [Wilson] about what should be on the front. We knew we needed something of the towers, something dramatic, an explosion kind of picture of the planes crashing into the building, but we also needed something of people's reaction to it, the fact that people were hurt and then we had this amazing picture that we used very small of the second plane flying over. We also thought that we needed to have something from Washington because it wasn't an event that happened only in New York. So those were the four we ended up with – the picture of the plane colliding with the building and the building exploding, the picture of the woman on the street with the bloody injured, the picture of the plane flying on the skyline crashing into the building and the picture that came from Washington.

> That's kind of our page-one philosophy, we want page one to reflect what happened on that day in the world, the nation and in the metropolitan area and so the mix of stories usually falls along those lines – put the newsy stuff at the top and the less newsy stuff at the bottom. Of course on this day we knew there would be only one story, and so we applied that also to the pictures. Looking back I don't think I would do anything differently. We got it about right . . .
>
> By eight or nine that night we pretty much got the first edition done and we could start to think, "Oh my God what do we do now? What is tomorrow going to be like?" Then we realized that we were going to be working like that for a long time. (Smith, 2004)

The *Times* commitment to strong photography and good picture use continued even after the departure of executive editor, Howell Raines.[8] Current executive editor, Bill Keller, continues to support visuals (Frank, 2004) and former *Fortune* magazine picture editor, Michelle McNally, was hired and given the title of assistant managing editor. She is known throughout the industry as a tireless advocate for visuals, and the *Times* has allowed her to hire additional photographers even in the face of economic shortcomings.

Newspaper studies show that the eye goes first to the photograph, then to the headline and finally to the word story (Moses, 2000). Photographs, however, do more than just attract attention for word stories. When planned, executed, and played well, photographs are capable of telling rich, emotional, and informative stories on their own. Few newspapers take advantage of the particular story-telling qualities that photography and design together can offer; they are not "playing all the notes." Editors often don't understand that good visual reporting does not have to be at the expense of good word reporting. The two are intimately connected and yet mutually exclusive. Good visual reporting only happens when there is communication across all departments of the newsroom. At the same time, readers respond to visual storytelling differently than they react to words. The best newspapers allow words and pictures to tell stories on multiple levels in their own unique ways.

Notes

1 The reasons for this are not always the consequences of a hierarchical system or a result of competition. *Los Angeles Times* writer, Ken Weiss, explains, "There are some photographers I'd rather work with. Some are less obtrusive. Others insert themselves in the story, and it becomes a problem. When I have an experience like that I tend to avoid them. Some come between the subjects and me, and that's difficult. Some people get nervous around cameras, and they get even more nervous around video cameras. It really can change the dynamic" (Weiss, 2004).

For some writers, however, having a photographer who "inserts himself in the story" turns out to be beneficial. *Chicago Tribune* writer, Rex Huppke, discusses a project that he, two other writers and photographer, Terrance James, worked on together, "A lot of times Terrance doesn't even shoot anything because so much of what we have been doing is getting people to trust us and being comfortable with having us around. He'll come along, sometimes he will shoot stuff, depends on the level of comfort, other times he won't. A lot of the stories that we're doing are in African-American communities, and Terrance is black, and basically we're [the writers] three white guys, and we stand out. I've done a lot of interviews where the person I'm interviewing won't even look at me, but he maintains eye contact with Terrance and kind of talks almost through Terrance. Terrance just adds a great deal to the whole endeavor. He's not at all shy to ask questions, and he asks very good questions" (Huppke, 2004).

2 Photographer Richard Olsenius says, "There is a special 'otherness' to the black-and-white image. . . . Black and white distills the message; it helps you see through the camouflage of color to the essence of a thing, a person, or a place. It is timeless" (Olsenius, 2005, p. 6). And, photography educator and researcher Kenneth Kobré says, "Black-and-white images convey an air of dignity and seriousness. Shades of gray connote the traditional, respected, documentary style. Black-and-white journalistic photos stand out against competing, colorful advertisements" (Kobré, 2000, p. 241).

3 Scott Strazzante was named "Newspaper Photographer of the Year" in the 58th annual Pictures of the Year International contest for the year 2000. Pictures of the Year International is the oldest and one of

the three most prestigious international contests in photojournalism. Amsterdam's World Press Photo and the National Press Photographers Association's Best of Photojournalism are the two others.

4 The power and story-telling attributes of visuals are not limited to the print medium. "Television news managers understand that the visual images always overpower the spoken word. Powerful pictures can help explain stories better or they can distort the truth by blurring the important context of the report" (Radio-Television News Directors Association & Foundation, 2004).

5 The *Los Angeles Times* won the Pictures of the Year International award for "Best Use of Photography" (newspapers with above 100,00 circulation) in 2004 and 2005.

6 *Washington Post* photographer Carol Guzy, for example, became the first woman photojournalist to win the Pulitzer Prize and she was named Newspaper Photographer of the Year five times.

7 The *New York Times* won "Best Use of Photography" (newspapers with above 100,00 circulation) in the 56th annual Pictures of the Year contest, and the newspaper won its first Pulitzer Prize for photography for its coverage of the September 11, 2001 attacks.

8 The path to becoming a strong visual newspaper at the *Los Angeles Times* almost mirrors that of the *New York Times*. September 11, 2001 became the impetus for its ascension in photography and design. And two key players, executive editor, John Carroll, and director of photography, Colin Crawford had been at their jobs for only a short time before 9/11.

References

Carroll, J. (2004). *Interview by author* [cassette recording] (June), Los Angeles.

Crawford, C. (2004). *Interview by author* [cassette recording] (June), Los Angeles.

Davis, M. (2006). *Telephone interview by author* [digital recording] (May), Miami.

Elbert, J. (2004). *Interview by author* [cassette recording] (June), Washington, DC.

Essick, P. (1991). *Interview by author* [cassette recording] (August), New York.

Fisher, G. (2004). *Interview by author* [cassette recording] (June), Los Angeles.

Frank, D. (2004). *Interview by author* [cassette recording] (June), New York.

Huppke, R. (2004). *Interview by author* [cassette recording] (June), Chicago.

Irby, K. (2002). Why photojournalism matters. July 31, *poynteronline.org*

Kobré, K. (2000). *Photojournalism: The professional's approach.* Boston: Focal Press.

Lee, C. (1991). *Interview by author* [cassette recording] (November), New York.

Moses, M. (2000). The elements of powerful pages. March 20, *poynteronline.org*

Olsenius, R. (2005). *National Geographic field guide: Digital black & white.* Washington DC: National Geographic Society.

Radio-Television News Directors Association & Foundation (2004). Ethics: Graphic images. May 13, *rtnda.org*

Rasmussen, T. (2006). *Telephone interview by author* [digital recording] (May), Miami.

Smith, M. (2004). *Interview by author* [cassette recording] (June), New York.

Steber, M. (2004). *Interview by author* [cassette recording] (August), Miami.

Strazzante, S. (2004). *Interview by author* [cassette recording] (June), Chicago.

Tarbert, J. (2004). The power of images, May 17, *dartcenter.org*

Van Wagener, A. (2004). Visual credibility. January 16, *poynteronline.org*

Weiss, K. R. (2004). *Interview by author* [cassette recording] (June), Los Angeles.

Wells, H. (2004). *Interview by author* [cassette recording] (June), Los Angeles.

Whitley, M. (2004). *Interview by author* [cassette recording] (June), Los Angeles.

3

Construction of Reality

> *Lip service is frequently paid to the awesome power of the photograph, but there is little general discussion about the enormous strengths and pitfalls of visual journalism. The furor over pictures of captured Taliban "illegal combatants" (or were they "prisoners of war?") . . . underlines how essential it is for the context and meaning surrounding photographs to be made clear. (Jacobson, 2002, p. 4)*

For more than a century mainstream journalism in North America has pursued "the truth" through the concepts of "accuracy" and "objectivity" (Altschull, 1984; Gans, 1980; McChesney, 2004; Parenti, 1986; Schiller, 1979; Schudson, 2003; Sigal, 1973; Sigelman, 1973; Tuchman, 1972). But mainstream media have not cornered the market on "truth." Peter Essick who has photographed for numerous publications including *National Geographic* magazine and the *City Sun* (An African-American newspaper in Brooklyn) says:

> At the *City Sun* I've always felt that my editors see things as right and wrong, and they've tried to get me to think in the same way. I've always resisted that by basically saying that this doesn't make sense to me within my [Anglo] cultural framework. If you grow up in Detroit as a black kid and come to see the world through a certain set of eyes, then basically the way that the *City Sun* sees things seem like the truth. The *Sun* even has this motto that says, "Speaking Truth To Power." But, the more I've thought about it, the more I realize that I don't know what truth is. I look at it more

> as speaking the Black perspective, or a perspective that's often missing from public dialogue. (Essick, 1991)

Essick questions the absolutist concept of truth and instead suggests that historical and social/cultural values contribute to a particular society's "truth/knowledge." The very nature of human existence within a particular socially constructed reality presupposes ideas and concepts; it virtually creates the way in which the world is organized and perceived.

News media contribute to as well as reflect the reality of any given society. Researchers (Snow, 1983; Tuchman, 1978) suggest that news production and news comprehension are structured within frameworks that make news meaningful. These frameworks are said to be culturespecific – what might make sense for the *New York Times* and its readers may not do so for the United Arab Emirates' *Gulf News* and its readers. This does not assume a necessarily passive audience uncritically accepting everything the news media offer. Rather, the way in which the news media frame their "news products" not only contributes to a social construction of reality but is also affected by what the news consumers within that "reality" perceive as important. For this reason, news media often conduct reader/viewer surveys with the expectation of developing strategies for framing the news product to make it appealing to consumers.

At the same time, however, the "reality" of these consumers has been at least partially constructed by the way in which the news media have framed information. "Reporters operate within a net, which is a strategic organizational device to draw upon news sources as effectively as possible" (van Dijk, 1988, p. 8). In the United States this "net" utilizes such strategies as: the classification of news events; the assignment of newsworthiness; and an adherence to the concept of "objectivity." Furthermore, this net of strategies permits (forces?) journalists, including photojournalists, to "focus" on small portions of a much larger "picture," while editors and designers further narrow the focus by their editing of words, selection (exclusion?) of photographs and layout/design processes.

In addition, most US mainstream news publications employ a hierarchical system of decision-making. Top editors determine how their publications can best attract the "right" readers. In turn, editors are influenced by their own ideologies, social class and perhaps age, race, and even gender (Kaufman, 1991).

> The systems and the people within those systems have everything to do with the creation of reality in photographic images – much more so than the subjects themselves. For example, if an editor has an interest in a particular subject, then he will push that, and if he's a managing editor, he will be able to push it even harder. (Benzakin, 1991)

The perspectives or realities of women and minorities suffer in this hierarchical form of management since there is little diversity among top editors. "When you look at the upper echelons, those who are making the real decisions in journalism are male rather than female, and most of them are White rather than Black or Hispanic" (Chapnick [Black Star picture agency president, 1964–91], 1991). It could be added that most top editors enjoy upper-middle to high-income status, and many have been educated at elite schools and universities.

Ultimately, the frameworks used by the news media to "report" "reality" become "taken for granted" by both media professionals and media readers/viewers. The *structure* used to frame the news affects the *content* of the news and, by extension, contributes to a social construction of reality.

Semiotics, as the study of symbols (signifiers), their meanings and how they relate to the concepts (signifieds) they refer to, offers a fresh method for analyzing the way in which news photographs are produced and comprehended. In this view the relationship between the symbol and the concept is arbitrary and learned, therefore society specific.

For example, Jocelyne Benzakin, owner and founder of J. B. Pictures, a former news photo agency in New York, describes her criteria for editing:

> I edit with aesthetics in mind. But I also try to have a message especially in the sense of the story. For example, with [former

> leader of the Ku Klux Klan and former presidential candidate] David Duke, I'll try to find an expression or something that reveals his background or if there's a supporter in the background that has a swastika, I'll try to stick that in if it's small, just to give information so that we know who he is just by looking at the picture. (Benzakin, 1991)

In this example, a visual element, the swastika, acts as symbol within the photograph (also referred to as the "sign" in semiotics). The concept is presumably Nazism and beyond that perhaps, racism. The important point here is that the relationship between the symbol, swastika, and the concepts of Nazism and racism is an absolutely "arbitrary" one. The relationship is entirely dependent upon the learned association between the symbol and concept. And the association must be the same for both the photographer/editor and the viewer. The same photograph shown to a person living in some parts of Asia, for example, may not only be meaningless because he or she does not know who David Duke is, but might actually take on an entirely different meaning since the swastika is a holy symbol in Hinduism. It isn't the swastika that contains meaning, but rather its learned relationship to Nazism/racism – or as a holy symbol.

Berger (1982) delineates three important points that are implied in the David Duke example: first, both the photographer/photo editor and the audience know the learned relationship between the symbol (swastika) and the concept (Nazism); the photographer and the audience have a shared framework of reference. Second, both the producer and the audience know the conventions of the (photographic) medium and thus the relationship between the photograph (symbol + concept) and the subject (David Duke); someone looking at the photograph would presumably understand that photographs interpret the three dimensional as two dimensional and that the two key elements (swastika and David Duke) are positively related to one another by the way in which they are juxtaposed within the composition.[1]

Finally, and perhaps most importantly, "is the fact that, generally speaking, people are not consciously aware of the rules and codes and cannot articulate them, though they respond to them" (Berger, 1982, p. 22).

Berger and Luckmann (1966) contend that "knowledge" and "reality" are socially produced. But, more than that, their production is never a *fait acompli* but always an ongoing process. "Meaning" is not something that can be precisely pinned down. It is more like a "constant flickering." "Reading a text [including visual texts such as photographs] is more like tracing this process of constant flickering than it is like counting the beads on a necklace" (Eagleton, 1983, p. 128); language (including visual language) is a temporal mechanism, consequently, there is a complex relationship between symbols that are in the past, present, and future. "Each sign [word, photograph, etc.] in the chain of meaning is somehow scored over or traced through with all the others . . . to this extent no sign is ever 'pure' or 'fully' meaningful" (Eagleton, 1983, p. 128). Furthermore, because a sign is always reproducible, meaning is never identical with itself. Signs are always produced contextually; contexts are never the same, and thus meanings created by the same sign are never exactly alike.

A photograph published in the *New York Times*' "Living" section (see Photo 9) as discussed by assistant managing editor and former photo editor Carolyn Lee (a white woman) provides an example of the elusiveness of meaning in photographs:

> [We were doing a] section on Marylou Whitney at the Kentucky Derby, and when the art director was laying out the . . . page, he came to me and said, "You ought to look at this picture and offer it for page one." I looked at it and went crazy. There she [Whitney] was in her aging blond pageboy, sort of matronly dress with the black servant displaying frou-frou dresses over her arm, one of which would be worn to the Derby party, and behind her on the wall a portrait of her as a young girl, absolutely beautiful. It [the photograph] was so stunning and said so much about the lifestyle that still exists in the Blue Grass country. So, I offered it for page one, and they selected it for page one, and the "Living" editor, a white woman, came out and said, "I think this is just awful, people will think we're endorsing an ante-bellum way of life if we put this on page

Photo 9. Marylou Whitney and Gladys Hardin, left, display party gowns. Photograph by Jim Wilson. From the *New York Times*, ©1987 The New York Times, Inc. All rights reserved. Used by permission and protected by the Copyright Laws of the United States. The printing, copying, redistribution, or retransmission of the material without express written permission is prohibited.

one" – whereas, we saw it as an exposure of something still existing. . . .

The photographer [an African-American male] was out of town and couldn't be included in the discussion, so the photograph was moved inside. Ultimately, we pulled outside a picture of Whitney sitting on her patio with a black groom holding the halter of her horse, which I thought was not nearly so compelling an image and which still had the same message, just more subtle.

When the photographer returned, I told him a little about the debate without telling him who took which sides, and I asked him what prompted him to take that photograph. He told me about his

> day there as a guest of Marylou Whitney and while having lunch and watching all the black servants doing all of the work, he listened to her say, "I just don't know how I'm going to be ready for this party; there's so much work to be done, all this food to be prepared." Then, she took him to the kitchen, and there were six black women doing all the cooking, and he said there was no way to illustrate that until she had this black woman displaying these two dresses. (Lee, 1991)

An analysis of this photograph and the pre-publication debate highlights the difficulties in using hard and fast rules to interpret meanings within photographs. First, we can refer to the temporal nature of reality. As evidenced by the pre-publication discussion, it was thought by some that the audience would read this photograph as a repudiation of the lingering white supremacy in certain Southern societies; others felt that the audience would read it as an endorsement of the old Southern way of life, and for this reason it was subsequently not used on the front page. If the same photograph had been taken 50 years ago, it's doubtful that a similar discussion would have taken place. The photograph would or would not have appeared on the front page because of other considerations; the sensitivity for African-American concerns would probably not have been a part of the deliberative process.

The context of the *New York Times* itself also influences the reality ultimately constructed by the Whitney photograph. Had the same photograph appeared in a white supremacist publication, the meaning would be unarguably altered.

The participants in the discussion, both for and against running the photograph on the front page, engaged in a discussion in which the symbol is the holding of the dresses by the black woman and the concept is subservience. The message, therefore, is the continuance of a system of white domination and black subservience.

It is possible, however, to derive other meanings from this photograph. For example, the African-American photographer who took the photograph might have been attempting to communicate the continuation of a system of oppression in which those with power even take credit for the work of others or he may have been trying to convey the dependency of this Southern white woman upon African-Americans.

French researcher Roland Barthes (1972) advances the discussion of relationships between symbols and concepts one step further. He believes that these relationships, although arbitrary, are perceived to be natural. He calls the process of naturalization the "myth."[2]

Myth analysis of the *New York Times*' March 19, 1992 front page (see Photo 10) provides an example of how symbols and concepts are linked by the news media and perhaps understood by news consumers.

The *New York Times*, like most newspapers, places a heavy emphasis upon the contents of its front page. In 1992, news editor, Bill Borders was the person responsible for the day-to-day composition of the *Times*' front page. "I'm more concerned with the front page than anything else. . . . It's obviously our showcase" (Borders, 1992). In addition to Borders, the various section photo editors also played an important role, along with the section editors, of identifying which photographs were to be offered for the front page.

These suggestions were passed along to the picture editor and to the senior word editors through informal discussions and more formally through a list of stories and photographs that each section prepared called the "noon list."

After the senior editors had an opportunity to review the noon list, they met with the news editor at 12:45 to discuss the options for the next day's front page with special emphasis on photography. "Part of the idea of the 12:45 meeting is to anticipate what we need for the front page before we get to the end of the day" (Borders, 1992).

More information about stories and photographs was gathered at the three o'clock "turn around" meeting. During this meeting the daytime planners turned everything over to the nighttime production people.

The picture editor continued to devote time to the front page throughout the afternoon, accumulating photographs and

"All the News That's Fit to Print"

The New York Times

Late Edition

New York: Today, 3-6 inches of snow, then sleet, rain. High 35. Tonight, rain then flurries. Low 32. Tomorrow, clearing. High 42. Yesterday, high 45, low 31. Details are on page D22.

VOL.CXLI . . . No. 48,910 — Copyright © 1992 The New York Times — NEW YORK, THURSDAY, MARCH 19, 1992 — 50 CENTS

SOUTH AFRICAN WHITES RATIFY DE KLERK'S MOVE TO NEGOTIATE WITH BLACKS ON A NEW ORDER

Agence France-Presse

South African blacks celebrating the white electorate's approval of negotiating an end to white rule.

THE VOTE IS 2 TO 1

Big Turnout 'Closed the Book' on Apartheid, Joyful Leader Says

By CHRISTOPHER S. WREN
Special to The New York Times

CAPE TOWN, March 18 — South Africa's whites gave President F. W. de Klerk a stunning victory in Tuesday's referendum, approving his moves to negotiate an end to white-minority rule by a margin of more than 2 to 1, according to results announced today.

Of the 2.8 million whites who cast ballots, slightly more than 1.9 million — 68.7 percent — voted to give Mr. de Klerk the mandate he had sought. Only whites were allowed to take part.

Exhilarated by a success that exceeded what practically all political experts expected, the South African President declared that his referendum had now "closed the book" on the ideology of apartheid, the country's system of racial separation under white control.

Mr. de Klerk, who turned 56 today, told the nation that "today is the real birthday" of the new South Africa that he had promised when he was sworn in two and a half years ago.

Steps in Liberalization Process

Since then Mr. de Klerk has legalized anti-apartheid groups, freed political prisoners, obtained the repeal of the laws that underpinned apartheid, and initiated negotations with black groups on ending the system of minority rule.

The negotiations are expected to take on a new impetus as a result of the backing from whites that Mr. de Klerk can now assert.

"Today will be written up in our history as one of the most fundamental turning point days in the history of South Africa," the President said in a victory statement. "Today we have closed the book on apartheid — and that chapter is finally closed."

Mr. de Klerk spoke on the garden steps of the presidential office adjoining Parliament before he learned the full extent of his triumph. Almost 88 percent of registered white voters cast ballots, making the endorsement he received all the more authentic.

'A Powerful Message'

At a news conference later, he said: "The massive positive result sends out a powerful message to all South Africans that those who have the power in terms of the present imperfect constitution really mean it when they say, 'We want to share power.' "

The 1.9 million whites who supported him appeared to have been motivated by more than good will toward their black compatriots. They were also influenced by predictions of revived international economic sanctions, a freeze on sports contacts and renewed black rebellion if the Conservative Party, which led right-wing opposition to the referendum, was successful.

Some whites were also offended by the Conservatives' tactical alliance during the referendum campaign with the Afrikaner Resistance Movement, a neo-Nazi group that uses violence in defending white supremacy.

Mr. de Klerk, in attempting to negotiate the best deal he can get for whites in the transition process, has sought to avoid the path taken under white rule a decade and a half ago in secessionist Rhodesia under Ian D. Smith. Mr. Smith fought a long, costly war against

Continued on Page A14, Column 1

Reuters

President F. W. de Klerk, with his wife, Marika, announcing results.

Clinton Taking The Campaign To Tsongas Turf

Associated Press

Paul E. Tsongas addressing an audience yesterday in Hartford.

Connecticut Is Looming as Vital Battleground

By KIRK JOHNSON
Special to The New York Times

HARTFORD, March 18 — Gov. Bill Clinton of Arkansas, fresh from decisive victories Tuesday in Illinois and Michigan, laid the groundwork today for his campaign in Connecticut, the backyard of Paul E. Tsongas, which is reeling from the effects of the depressed economy.

Mr. Tsongas, badly battered by a second-place finish in Illinois and a third-place effort in Michigan, raised the stakes for himself today. The former Massachusetts Senator proclaimed at a news conference in Hartford that Connecticut was now a "must win" state for him.

Just weeks ago, Mr. Tsongas was heavily favored in the Democratic contest here, and such a statement would have seemed far-fetched. But the combination punch in the two Rust Belt states clearly enlivened the March 24 Connecticut primary.

While Mr. Clinton and most of his staff spent the day in Little Rock for some rest and reassessment, they pointedly noted that Mr. Tsongas was already back in New England — with all the advantages of operating on home turf.

Rally Hastily Arranged

Behind the scenes, however, Mr. Clinton's staff began a television advertising campaign this afternoon, going head to head with Mr. Tsongas's advertisements in the Hartford television market. And a rally was hastily organized for Thursday night in downtown Hartford, where Mr. Clinton plans to appear.

Edmund G. Brown Jr., who fought his way to a second-place finish behind Mr. Clinton in Michigan on Tuesday, arrived in Connecticut tonight for at least three scheduled campaign stops

Continued on Page A18, Column 3

PENTAGON CHARTS MILITARY OPTIONS FOR BOMBING IRAQ

BUSH SAID TO WEIGH MOVE

Officials Suggest President Is Likely to Use Force Unless Baghdad Yields on Arms

By PATRICK E. TYLER
with ERIC SCHMITT
Special to The New York Times

WASHINGTON, March 18 — The Pentagon has given President Bush a set of military options for a graduated bombing campaign to force Iraq to eliminate its remaining weapons of mass destruction in compliance with the United Nations cease-fire resolution that ended the Persian Gulf war.

Administration officials, who are reticent in discussing military planning so as not to appear to be prejudging United Nations Security Council decisions, emphasized that President Bush has not made any decisions on the timing or the targets of any attack. But there is a wide view among military leaders that Mr. Bush is predisposed to use force soon if President Saddam Hussein of Iraq does not meet the United Nations demands.

Administration officials said military planning was proceeding swiftly to give Mr. Bush the option of striking Iraqi targets by the end of next week. A decision to launch an attack hinges on whether Baghdad meets a March 26 deadline to present a detailed plan to the United Nations on destroying equipment and buildings associated with Iraqi ballistic missile production, the officials said.

Attack May Be Avoided

A confrontation may still be avoided if Iraq complies, the officials said. In that sense, the American preparations are part of a war of nerves: Baghdad is testing the willpower of the Security Council in the hope of bringing a 19-month-old trade embargo to an end, while Washington is seeking to hold together a coalition willing to use military power to force Mr. Hussein to comply with rigorous cease-fire obligations.

Some of the officials who discussed the plans and political problems associated with renewing the use of force against Iraq said the military option has been implicit in the conditions attached to the cease-fire since the war ended more than a year ago.

Those officials said the options drawn up for Mr. Bush were not intended simply to intimidate Iraq. There has been a concerted attempt to avoid giving any signal of impending military action that might stir opposition in the Security Council or in Congress, or open the issue to debate in the American Presidential campaign.

A list of targets drafted by the Pentagon has been reviewed by Mr. Bush. It parallels the list of sites to be de-

Continued on Page A15, Column 1

ISRAEL SHIFTS WAY OF PICKING PREMIER

Direct Vote Will Begin in '96 in Move to Enhance Office

By CLYDE HABERMAN
Special to The New York Times

JERUSALEM, March 18 — Parliament voted today to approve what some Israeli experts view as a historic change in the country's electoral system by passing a law providing for direct election of the Prime Minister.

The change would take effect in elections that are to be held in 1996, and will not be in place for national elections scheduled for June 23.

But supporters were delighted nonetheless because, in the final hours of the old Parliament, they managed to push through revisions that had seemed doomed under the weight of opposition from Prime Minister Yitzhak Shamir and most of his Likud Party.

A Mixed System

Uriel Lynn, a Likud member of Parliament who had sponsored the new law, called the revision "historic" and said, "We will now have a mix between presidential and parliamentary systems." No major democracy has such a system.

In Israel, voters choose their preferred political parties, and the Prime Minister generally has been the No. 1 person on a list prepared in advance by the party with the most votes. The rest of a party's parliamentary bloc is selected from that list in proportion to the share of the popular vote.

Stronger Leader Seen

But no party in the country's 44-year history has had enough votes to govern on its own. The result has been a helter-skelter system of coalition politics that critics complain leaves national leaders hostage to small fringe parties and to blatant political extortion.

Those favoring change argue that a directly elected Prime Minister, once liberated from the narrow political interests that now dominate, would be in a stronger position to negotiate with the Arabs and impose budgetary discipline that many here believe has been conspicuously lacking for too long. Considering the possible consequences for developments like the present Middle

Continued on Page A12, Column 5

F.A.A. Warns Port Authority On Transit Links to Airports

By JACQUES STEINBERG

The Federal Aviation Administration is threatening to block plans to build mass-transit links to the metropolitan region's three main airports unless the Port Authority of New York and New Jersey abandons efforts to strengthen jet-noise restrictions at the airports.

For months, the F.A.A. has been trying to discourage the Port Authority from taking a tougher stand on noise at the airports than the Federal agency demands, but it has made little headway. In linking the mass-transit plan to the noise-control dispute, the aviation agency is hoping to bolster its position.

At stake for the authority is a $2 billion plan to build a network of airport rail links to Kennedy, La Guardia and Newark Airports. Planners have long sought the links to relieve automobile congestion, a critical component of the airports' economic viability.

A Passenger Tax

The F.A.A.'s weapon against the Port Authority is its power to reject a $3 passenger tax that would be levied on airline tickets to finance the mass-transit plan. The authority said yesterday that it could not construct the mass-transit links without the money from the passenger tax, which is expected to generate $100 million a year.

At stake for the Federal agency is its attempt to protect the airlines from having to quickly scrap or refurbish older, noisier aircraft. The F.A.A. has its own noise rules for airports, which would use a slower method of phasing out such aircraft than the Port Authority is proposing.

After the dispute had been at a standoff for months, an F.A.A. official stepped up the fight with the Port Authority last week, writing the authority to say that its proposal for noise regulations could cause Federal officials to reject the $3 passenger charge.

Michael C. Moffett, the official who wrote the letter, said the Port Authority's rules, which have yet to be proposed to its board, "might well be found" in violation of Federal regulations. Under those regulations, Federal officials said yesterday, the F.A.A. can reject an airport's application for a tax on passengers if the airport is deemed not to be following Federal noise rules. The F.A.A. would contend that by imposing stricter rules, the Port Authority was not following the Federal rules.

"We once again urge the Port Au-

Continued on Page B4, Column 5

Biggest Maker of Breast Implants Is Said to Be Abandoning Market

By PHILIP J. HILTS
Special to The New York Times

WASHINGTON, March 18 — After months of criticism, the leading maker of silicone gel breast implants, the Dow Corning Corporation, has decided to bow out of the implant business, Government officials said today.

The company had no comment but scheduled a news conference for 9 A.M. Thursday in Washington.

The current climate makes it impossible for the company to let such a small part of its business drain resources, the company has reportedly told the Government officials. Even though the company has held the largest share of the national implant market, about 30 percent, implants account for less than 1 percent of Dow Corning's annual sales of $1.84 billion.

Dow Corning faces hundreds of lawsuits from women who contend that they suffered ill effects from the implants, and it has $250 million worth of insurance to cover its possible liabilities. Several verdicts have gone against Dow Corning, including one for $7 million in California last December.

A voluntary moratorium on the use of implants is in effect, but until recently, an estimated 100,000 to 150,000 women got breast implants each year.

Most Have No Complaints

Dow Corning is the third manufacturer of silicone gel implants to stop making them since problems with the implants were reported last April. Bristol-Myers Squibb stopped making polyurethane-coated gel implants last summer, and Bioplasty announced last week that it would stop making gel implants.

There are still two manufacturers on the market, both companies that make saline-filled as well as gel-filled implants, the Mentor Corporation and McGhan Medical Corporation, a subsidiary of Inamed Corporation. Saline-filled implants are thought to be safer because they contain sterile salt water instead of several ounces of silicone gel, experts say.

An estimated one million American women have had silicone gel breast implants, and even critics concede that most of them have had no complaints. But some doctors have argued that the implants can rupture, allowing the silicone to migrate to other parts of the body, possibly causing local tumors and immune disorders. In addition, studies show that it is more difficult to

Continued on Page B11, Column 3

On Further Review, Instant Replay Dies

National Football League owners voted yesterday to eliminate the instant-replay rule.

Under the rule, officials off the field reviewed questionable plays on TV monitors and had the power to uphold officials' calls or overturn them. Last season such replays were used on 570 plays, and 90 reversals were made.

The rule was debated and second-guessed annually, but it had survived for six years by winning over 21 of the 28 owners. It did not win the needed 75-percent margin this time, with only 17 yes votes.

Commissioner Paul Tagliabue said the issue was not closed; replay officials and new equipment will be used experimentally this season.

SportsThursday, page B13.

INSIDE

Japan Cuts Car Export Quota

In an election-year gesture to President Bush, Japan lowered its ceiling for automobile exports to the U.S., but only to a level slightly below what it exported last year. Page D1.

Transit Union Rejects Pact

New York City bus and subway workers rejected a new three-year contract, raising the possibility of slowdowns or other disruptions. Page B1.

They Done It

A new entry in Washington's power-novel steeplechase is a mystery by Marilyn Quayle and her sister. Washington at Work, page B9.

The State of the Projects

As a new leader takes command of New York City's public housing, often considered the best in the country, she faces increasing complaints of crime and disrepair. Page B1.

Banks Taking a Plaza Stake

In a deal with his creditors, Donald J. Trump has agreed to turn over 49 percent of the Plaza Hotel to a group of banks led by Citibank. Page D1.

Fashion from Silicon Valley

The latest in fashion? Wearable computer accessories like Palmpad, a computer that can be strapped to the wrist or lower arm. Page D1.

0 354743 12

THE NEW YORK TIMES is available for home or office delivery in most major U.S. cities. Please call this toll-free number: 1-800-631-2500 ADVT.

Photo 10. *New York Times*, March 19, 1992. © 1992 The New York Times, Inc. All rights reserved. Used by permission and protected by the Copyright Laws of the United States. The printing, copying, redistribution, or retransmission of the material without express written permission is prohibited.

eventually mounting them on a magnetic board to be presented at the 4:45 page-one meeting. Senior word editors, the graphics editor and the picture editor attended this meeting, chaired by the executive editor, Max Frankel. Stories and photographs were selected by committee during this meeting, but all front-page content was subject to the approval of the executive editor.

The news editor subsequently laid out the front page, and all stories and photographs not selected for the front page were made available to the individual news sections.

Traditionally, the *New York Times*' front page is heavily laden with national and international news at the expense of local, metropolitan news. Despite the predominance of national/international news, in 1992 the *Times*' front page stories were almost exclusively written by *Times*' writers or by writers as a "special to the *New York Times*." The same could not be said for front-page photographs.

The *Times* rarely sent staff photographers on overseas assignments. The *Times* was reluctant to do so for several reasons including the increased work load that would result for the remaining members of the *Times*' relatively small photo staff, the expenses involved (especially since the *Times* was already paying the wire services for photographs that might duplicate those of the *Times*' photographer) and the disdain that many *Times* writers had for working directly with photographers (Lee, 1991).

The March 19, 1992 lead story headlined, "South African Whites Ratify De Klerk's Move to Negotiate with Blacks on a New Order," was written by Christopher S. Wren as a "special to the *New York Times*." The two accompanying photographs were from the wires (one from Agence France Presse [AFP]; one from Reuters). The *Times* also hired a freelance photographer in Cape Town, but it was decided by all of the editors that the wire photographs were superior.

The South African referendum was a planned event, and editors at the *Times* knew in advance that it would be a front-page story. The decision to publish two front-page photographs (see Photo 10) from South Africa, however, came during the page-one meeting.

> We decided at the page-one meeting . . . that this story [ratification of de Klerk's anti-apartheid policy] was worth two front-page pictures. And it needed two pictures because this is a picture of the black beneficiaries of the vote. But this is certainly the man who engineered it, and so we thought it warranted both. (Borders, 1992)

Borders says that although there were several choices of photographs from South Africa, the celebration photograph was clearly the best. There were, however, three strong photographs of de Klerk from which to choose. The photograph of de Klerk that the *Times* published was selected by the executive editor, Max Frankel. "It wasn't really the one that I liked best, but my choice was hard to crop, and it just worked out that way" (Borders, 1992).

In explaining the criteria used in selecting one photograph over another, Borders not only identifies his perception of differences between word and visual communicators, but also reveals how cultural perspectives play a role in decision-making at the news media.

> [Picture editor] Bussell has artistic criteria [for preferring one photograph over another]. I don't have those artistic criteria, or at least Bussell would tell you that I don't – I think that I do. But this [the celebration photo] is clearly great. I mean it just says it all. It has jubilant black people and a sign that says, "vote for all" and that's what happened.
>
> Now, where Bussell would use aesthetics as his criterion, I would say that, first, it needs to be a great picture and, second, it needs to tell a story. And that's why we wanted de Klerk on the front page too. Because this is not just something that these people did. In fact, they didn't do it. It was done for them, and the person who did it was him [de Klerk]. This whole achievement in South Africa is so much his – so much a one man deal – that it would have seemed very strange not to have de Klerk's picture on the front. (Borders, 1992)

Borders never mentions the years of political protest at great risk by the majority race in South Africa.[3] He does not refer to Mandela,

Tutu, the ANC or international sanctions, but rather gives total credit to the white president.

Both March 19, 1992 front-page South African referendum photographs were published above the fold. The demonstration photograph was placed immediately above the photograph of de Klerk, and the demonstration photograph was sized slightly larger.

A four-column headline, “South African Whites Ratify De Klerk’s Move to Negotiate with Blacks on a New Order,” ran immediately above the three-column demonstration photograph as well as above the one-column story, sub headed “The Vote is 2 to 1: Big Turnout ‘Closed the Book’ on Apartheid, Joyful Leader Says.”

The concepts that were important to the *New York Times* as it reported the South African referendum results were plainly described by Borders: show the jubilation of the black beneficiaries; show the statesmanship of the white protagonist. Each photograph worked splendidly in symbolizing its appropriate concept (see Figure 1).

The demonstration photograph is immediately placed in context by the “Vote For All” sign and the exclusively non-white demonstrators. The smiling faces quickly give the viewer a sense of mood, and the large number of people in the frame suggests the size of the demonstration.

At the same time, this image of the “masses” offers a group identity rather than a more personal identity. And the elevation of the camera suggests group subservience to a higher authority.

These attributes are in marked contrast to those of the de Klerk photograph. There are other individuals standing behind de Klerk, but the photographer’s use of a longer lens and the resulting narrower depth of field renders them somewhat less sharp; de Klerk emerges from the group. Additionally, the camera angle is pointed slightly upward, giving de Klerk an air of authority, reinforced by his formal clothing and the bank of microphones in the foreground.

A limited range of camera angles in the de Klerk photograph can be explained by the government’s control of media access,

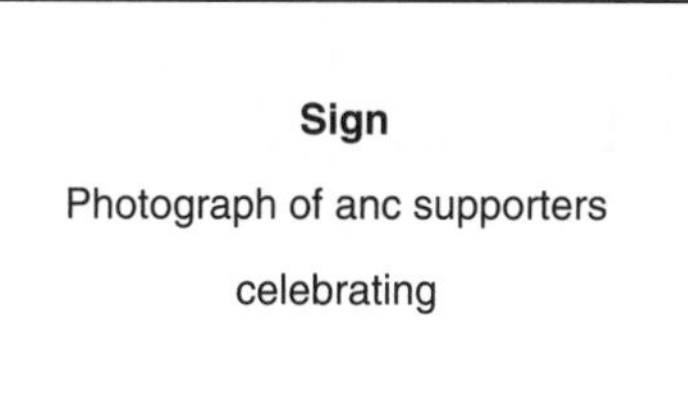

Signifier
Photograph

Signified
Passage of right to vote referendum in South Africa

Figure 1. Barthes' semiotic analysis in the first stage.

and large groups are more easily photographed from a higher camera angle. Likewise, de Klerk is obviously dressed formally for the occasion; the demonstrators are not. However, photographers working in the field make decisions about type of lens, depth of field, moment of exposure, framing, etc. And, photographers know the concepts that they are to visually communicate (Rosenblum, 1979) and the kinds of images that editors like Borders and Frankel are likely to select.

Concepts are further represented by the words that accompany the photographs. The most common way in which words are paired with photographs is through captions. "We [the *New York Times*] make the link between the photograph and the story through the caption – always" (Lee, 1991).

At the *New York Times* caption writers write the captions. This tends to improve the overall quality of captions from a technical perspective, but it also potentially changes the reality as the photographer experienced it. The caption that appeared with the demonstration photograph offers a good example.

The original caption sent via the wire reads, "African National Congress supporters celebrate 18 Mar the passing of the whites-only referendum. The mandate will require the South African government to share power with the black majority." The caption that the *New York Times* printed reads, "South African blacks celebrating the white electorate's approval of negotiating an end to white rule."

The meaning contained in the original caption has been altered in several ways. First, by failing to identify the demonstrators as African National Congress supporters, the *New York Times* has negated a history of political activism by the black majority and instead emphasized Borders' point: these are the beneficiaries of an act accomplished by someone else (de Klerk and the white electorate).

Second, the original caption says, "The mandate will *require* [my italics] the South African government to share power." This statement empowers the black majority; it does not suggest that the government has an option or will share power through goodwill. It states clearly that the (white) government will be required to share power.

The *Times*' caption reads, "South African blacks celebrating the white electorate's approval of negotiating an end to white rule." This caption robs the black majority of power. It suggests that the black demonstrators were left to celebrate a decision made by an enlightened white electorate; thus, blacks were helplessly dependent upon white approval.

Finally, the wire caption says, "The mandate will require the South African government to share power with the black majority." The *Times*' caption never acknowledges the majority status of blacks in South Africa; to do so would sully the concept put forth, a celebration of the great achievements by de Klerk and the white electorate. Reminded of black majority standing, a US audience might question why blacks were excluded from the democratic process for so long rather than applaud the nascent efforts by the white minority to share power.

Barthes contends that news consumers ultimately "naturalize" the symbols chosen by journalists to represent concepts.[4] A news photograph through interaction with the news consumer's cultural/historical, etc. background becomes reality.

For example, the symbols that Borders, with the approval of Frankel and input from other senior editors, chose for the front page represented a reality, perhaps a reality that was already similar to the reality experienced by many *Times*' readers. After all, the *Times* boasts: "a record number of affluent, influential and well-educated readers start each morning with the *New York Times*" (New York Times Company, 1992, p. 10).

To define a reader as affluent, influential, and well educated assumes, both explicitly and implicitly, certain characteristics about his social, cultural, historical, political, etc. experience. According to Barthes, it is the reader's experience that infuses the symbol, in this case the photographs and captions with meaning. A racial and political struggle has been transformed into an affirmation of white generosity towards other races as well as the triumph of democracy. At the same time, the maintenance of authority and stability is realized in the photograph of de Klerk. As Susan Sontag has noted in her book, *Regarding the pain of others*, "The photographer's intentions do not determine the meaning of the photograph, which will have its own career, blown by the whims and loyalties of the diverse communities that have use for it" (Sontag, 2003, p. 39).

News media help to define and reaffirm the values and beliefs of the cultures in which they exist. They, like other institutions such as schools, political systems, and religious bodies, contribute to a "social construction of reality." News photographs (most times[5]) depict something that actually did exist. But, the reality contained within the photographs is created within cultural frameworks and through cultural interpretation.

Notes

1 Sless (1981) relates an interesting case where the conventions of photography were not known; individuals from a forest culture were shown a photograph of large animals in the distance across an open plain. Unfamiliar with both the concept of uninterrupted landscape and the visual properties of a photograph, these people mistook the animals in the photograph for insects.

2 Myth according to Barthes is carried through discourse and, like semiotics, is concerned with the relationship between two elements, a signifier (the symbol) and a signified (the concept), which together produce a sign (for example, a photograph).

3 While the US media described the protesters in Eastern Europe and China as "pro-democracy" demonstrators, black South Africans demanding a system based on one-person one-vote were rarely, if ever, referred to as "pro-democracy" activists (Lee & Solomon, 1990, pp. 326, 327).

4 Barthes calls this the myth. Myth is "a peculiar system, in that it is constructed from a semiological chain which existed before it: it *is a second-order semiological system*" (Barthes, 1972, p. 114). In other words that which was a sign in the first round of analysis becomes a signifier in the second. The combination of this second-signifier plus a second-signified, then, establishes a second-sign or a myth-sign (see Figure 2). This, for Barthes, is the point at which messages in a subtle way become naturalized.

He explains it in the following way: the first-sign is also the myth-signifier, thus it has both meaning and form. It has meaning as the first-sign. "The meaning is *already* complete, it postulates a kind of knowledge, a past, a memory, a comparative order of facts, ideas,

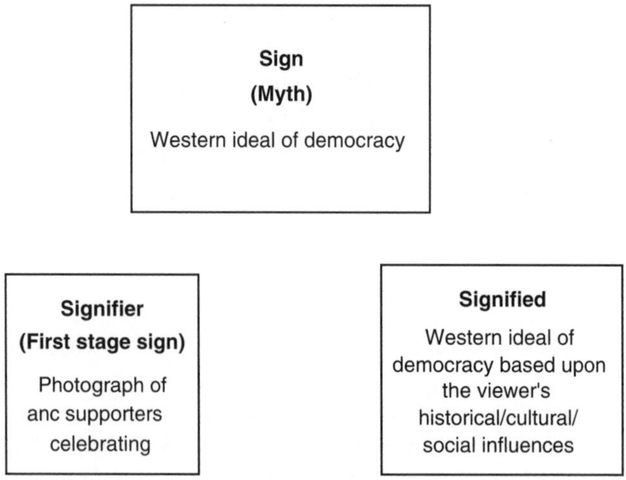

Figure 2. Barthes' semiotic analysis in the second or myth stage.

decisions" (Barthes, 1972, p. 117). For example, in the celebration photograph, the first-sign is a completed and rational whole; a photograph of ANC supporters celebrating the passage of the voting rights referendum. The members of the group are smiling and holding a sign that reads, "Vote for all", and the frame is filled with the demonstrators. In other words, there is a completed meaning to this photograph, one that is immediately recognizable, perhaps especially because it is a photograph; this actually did exist.

When this first-sign subsequently becomes a myth signifier, it changes from having meaning to having form. And, "[w]hen it becomes form, the meaning leaves its contingency behind; it empties itself, it becomes impoverished, history evaporates, only the letter remains" (Barthes, 1972, p. 117).

Returning to the celebration photograph, in its capacity as a first-sign, we realize a history and fullness. The "beneficiaries" are celebrating the South African referendum results. The photograph offers "proof" that the system works.

As a myth-signifier these meanings are put at a distance by form. But, explains Barthes, meaning is only impoverished, not suppressed. In fact, its new role as form is always rooted in its meaning. "It is this constant game of hide-and-seek between the meaning and the form which defines myth" (Barthes, 1972, p. 118).

The second part of the process is the myth-signified. This, says Barthes, "is at once historical and intentional; it is the motivation which causes the myth to be uttered" (Barthes, 1972, p. 118). In the celebration photograph the myth may be driven by the Western ideal of democracy evidenced through the referendum to give South African blacks the right to vote.

The myth-signified also infuses the process with a new and expansive history; it will include any variety of historical/cultural/social influences brought to it by any given reader/viewer. In the celebration photograph, for instance, a viewer may meld her own experiences as a voter; as a formally educated citizen through which she learned of the struggle for independence; as an informed citizen which caused her to look at the *New York Times*; as a news consumer reading about the lack of democracy in other countries; as a regular viewer of news photographs in which she learned to put words and pictures together to create a unified message, and of course any other "knowledge of reality" that she brings with her in viewing this photograph.

It is because of this great variety of "knowledge" that Barthes says, "[one] must firmly stress this open character of the concept [myth signified]; it is not at all an abstract, purified essence; it is a formless, unstable, nebulous condensation, whose unity and coherence are above all due to its function [myth-signifier]" (Barthes, 1972, p. 119). This is, of course, crucial; it gives the myth-signifier its power to structure or "form" the history contained in the myth-signified while at the same time the myth-signified injects new meaning to make up for the impoverishment of meaning within the myth-signifier.

Barthes further describes the myth-signifier/myth-signified relationship as quantitatively disproportionate; there may be many signifiers for every single signified. For example, the celebration photograph may act as a signifier, but the cover photograph of a news magazine may also act as a signifier to the same signified. Likewise, a television news story or a similar piece in the *Washington Post* may function as a myth-signifier of this same myth-signified. "This repetition of the concept [signified] through different forms is precious to the mythologist, it allows him to decipher the myth: it is the insistence of a kind of behavior which reveals its intention" (Barthes, 1972, p. 120).

As discussed earlier, the semiotic relationship is triadic; the third element, the sign, is the alliance of the first two. Barthes relates that this myth-sign or signification is the myth itself. In what way, then, do the myth-signifier and myth-signified become associated to form the myth? For an answer we must return to the hide-and-seek quality of meaning and form. "We now know that myth is a type of speech defined by its intention . . . much more than by its literal sense . . . and that in spite of this, its intention is somehow frozen, purified, eternalized . . . by this literal sense" (Barthes, 1972, p. 124). This inherent equivocation within myth between form and meaning creates two consequences for the myth-sign: first, the myth-signifier's meaning is impoverished only to be restored by the myth-signified, thus the meaning has changed. But, because the form of the myth-signifier is still present to structure the meaning of the myth-signified, the transition appears natural in the myth-sign.

As an example, we once again turn to the celebration photograph. The meaning provided by the myth-signified, that of the Western ideal of democracy based upon the viewer's historical/cultural/social influences, is associated with the form of the myth-signifier, namely the photograph of those celebrating the results of the referendum. The meaning has changed from the specific referendum to allow South Africans the right to vote to one of a reaffirmation of the Western ideal of democracy. At the same time that change goes unnoticed; it's perfectly natural; the Western ideal of democracy is evidenced in the photograph.

The second consequence of moving from the primary semiotic relationship to the myth stage is inherently related to the first. Barthes says that in the first part of semiology the relationship between the signifier and signified is always arbitrary, but that in the second or myth stage the relationship is never arbitrary; there is always a level of motivation within the myth-signified that urges on the myth-signifier and a degree of analogy between the myth-signifier and myth-signified. He offers the following extreme case to demonstrate the importance of motivation in myth: several objects are strewn throughout a room at random, and no order can be made out of their randomness. Barthes then puts forth that the disorder itself becomes the form, making "absurdity" the myth. This point is reminiscent of the Berger and Luckmann (1966) contention that humans have an innate need to create structure, to construct reality – a need to make sense of the world.

Ultimately, the significance of myth production is located within the way in which myths are received. This happens in three ways, according to Barthes (1972): the first is to concentrate on the myth-signifier as meaning-empty so that the meaning of the myth-signified fills the form "without ambiguity." For example, the celebration photograph *stands for* or *symbolizes* the success of democracy. This, says Barthes, is what journalists do; they begin with a concept, a signified, and look for a form in which it can be symbolized.

The second way of receiving a myth is to concentrate upon the myth-signifier as meaning-full. Viewed in this way, it can be seen that within the celebration photograph the myth-signifier meaning, a photograph of South Africans celebrating the results of the referendum has been impoverished and replaced by the myth-signified meaning of "the Western ideal of democracy." This is the way in which a mythologist receives myth.

The final, and perhaps most important, way in which myth is received is by concentrating on the myth-signifier as composed of both meaning and form. Thus, the photograph of South Africans celebrating actually *becomes* the Western ideal of democracy. This is how the reader/viewer receives myth. Barthes rhetorically asks the question of how this is possible, however, since [in this case] if the viewer does not see the connection between the photograph and the Western ideal of democracy, why publish it, and if the viewer does see the connection, there is no myth, just a "political proposition." Barthes addresses his own question with the answer that "it [myth] transforms history into nature" (Barthes, 1972, p. 129) so that myth, rather than being seen as a semiological relationship is seen as fact; the relationship between myth-signifier and myth-signified is natural. "Semiology has taught us that myth has the task of giving an historical intention a natural justification, and making contingency appear eternal. . . . What the world supplies to myth is an historical reality, defined . . . by the way in which men have produced or used it; and what myth gives in return is a *natural* image of this reality" (Barthes, 1972, p. 142).

There is, however, a "flickering" in the way relationships between signifier, signified and sign are perceived. A news consumer may view the celebration photograph (myth signifier) as both meaning and form (the Western ideal of democracy). During a more reflective time, however, this same news consumer who may be at least marginally aware of the way in which news is produced may view the photograph as a symbol of the Western ideal of democracy.

Likewise, the North American journalist is not only a member of the newsroom culture, but is also a member of North American culture. He may most times perceive the myth signifier as symbol [journalist's perspective] but at other times may perceive the myth signifier through its relationship with the myth signified as reality (myth sign).

5 Software programs such as Photoshop have made it more difficult to detect manipulation of photographs. The wars in Iraq and Lebanon have spawned several high-profile cases of digital manipulation in which photographs were merged, smoke from fires was distorted, etc. This topic is dealt with more thoroughly in Chapter 8 ("Iraq Wars").

References

Altschull, J. H. (1987). *Agents of power*. New York: Longman.

Barthes, R. (1972). *Mythologies* (A. Lavers, Trans.). New York: Hill and Wang.

Benzakin, J. (1991). *Interview by author* [cassette recording] November, New York.

Berger, A. A. (1982). *Media analysis techniques.* Beverly Hills: Sage.

Berger, P. L., & Luckmann, T. (1966). *The social construction of reality: A treatise in the sociology of knowledge.* New York: Doubleday.

Borders, B. (1992). *Interview by author* [cassette recording] March, New York.

Chapnick, H. (1991). *Interview by author* [cassette recording] November, New York.

Eagleton, T. (1983). *Literary theory: An introduction.* Minneapolis: University of Minnesota.

Essick, P. (1991). *Interview by author* [cassette recording] August, New York.

Gans, H. (1980). *Deciding what's news.* New York: Vintage.

Jacobson, C. (2002). Introduction. In C. Jacobson (Ed.), *Underexposed: "Pictures can lie and liars use pictures."* London: Vision On Publishing.

Kaufman, M. (1991). *Interview by author* [cassette recording]. November, New York.

Lee, C. (1991). *Interview by author* [cassette recording] November, New York.

Lee, M. A., & Solomon, N. (1990). *Unreliable sources: A guide to detecting bias in the news media.* New York: Lyle Stuart.

McChesney, R. W. (2004). *The problem of the media.* New York: Monthly Review Press.

Parenti, M. (1986). *Inventing reality: The politics of the mass media.* New York: St. Martin's.

Rosenblum, M. (1979). *Coups & earthquakes.* New York: Harper & Row.

Schiller, D. (1979). An historical approach to objectivity and professionalism in American news reporting. *Journal of Communication, 29*, 46–57.

Schudson, M. (2003). *The sociology of news.* New York: W. W. Norton.

Sigal, L. V. (1973). *Reporters and officials.* Lexington, MA: D. C. Heath.

Sigelman, L. (1973). Reporting the news: An organizational analysis. *American Journal of Sociology, 79*, 132–151.

Sless, D. (1981). *Learning and visual communication.* New York: John Wiley and Sons.

Snow, R. P. (1983). *Creating media culture.* Beverly Hills: Sage.

Sontag, S. (2003). *Regarding the pain of others.* New York: Picador.

Tuchman, G. (1972). Objectivity as strategic ritual: An examination of newsmen's notions of objectivity. *American Journal of Sociology, 77*, 660–679.

Tuchman, G. (1978). *Making news.* New York: Free Press.

van Dijk, T. A. (1988). *News as discourse.* Hillsdale, NJ: Lawrence Erlbaum Associates.

4

Newsroom Culture and Routines

If video captures immediate attention, the still frame is a lasting image. It defines a story and fixes it in the collective memory. . . . What people forget, however, is that a picture can mislead as easily as a set of words. When Asian refugees streamed out of Kuwait into Jordan, I went to the border each day to write what I saw. Photographers came along with instructions. Sometimes, a distant editor asked for tragic pictures. On other days, he wanted happy ones. (Rosenblum, 1993, p. 93)

The culture of a newsroom and the routines that journalists follow often define what is news and how news is covered. Newsroom culture exists within a hierarchical framework. The top editors prescribe the journalistic direction of their papers and make the final decisions, particularly with regard to potentially controversial images or stories, the front page and special coverage.[1]

Multiple award-winning photo editor, Mike Davis, says, "The most important thing for determining whether visuals will or will not be strong in a publication is who is sitting in the corner office" (Davis, 2006). The person "sitting in the corner office," however, also sets a tone for the publication's standards and policy and strongly influences decisions regarding "what is news."[2]

For example, *New York Times* executive editor Bill Keller decided that the *Times* would publish the photograph of bodies hanging from a bridge in Fallujah on the front page. *New York Times* deputy director of photography David Frank says:

> The way that it [the decision to publish the photograph of the bodies on the bridge on the front page] happened was that the [daily] noon meeting happened first. I had taken a stack of prints in with me, and when it was my turn to talk about the pictures that we had for the day, I just handed him [Keller] the whole stack. He and Jill [Albertson, the managing editor] were sitting next to each other, and they started going through them. They had already seen a lot of footage from television. A lot of people were like, "Oh my God," so he suggested that we gather after lunch. At 2 o'clock we got back together in his office, and all of these people came down.
>
> It seemed to us that [Keller] had already had a chance to think this through. He pretty much went right to one of the pictures on the bridge. There were a couple of different versions of this where you really saw the bodies much clearer. I think this [the photo that was published] was his compromise. (Frank, 2004)

Los Angeles Times editor of the paper, John Carroll opted to put a photograph of the bodies on the bridge inside the paper rather than on the front page. He says:

> I was deeply involved in that decision, and there were quite a few people here that felt that we should put that [the photograph of the bodies on the bridge] on page one. You know, when you're making those decisions, you're making a judgment in the middle of an event, and you don't really know how you'll feel when you look back on it after a year, five years or ten years.
>
> I didn't feel, as some argued, that that picture was a particularly enduring image. People in our discussion mentioned the famous pictures out of Vietnam, the picture of the young girl and napalm, and of course, the Eddy Adams' piece[3] – I was in Saigon at the time that was shot – and I paid attention to those things. I just didn't think this had the composition – it was disgusting, but it didn't capture much that was human.
>
> So, we played it inside. I don't know if that was the right decision or the wrong decision, but I haven't really had any regrets about it. And, I don't really know what other people think looking back on it, but that was my decision to put it inside. . . . The buck stops with me on a decision like that, and I decided. (Carroll, 2004)

Neither decision is necessarily right or wrong, but each reflects the thinking of the top person at the individual publications. Top editors and publishers are aided in their decisions by the traditions and culture of the newsrooms that employ them and also by their individual experiences as journalists and citizens.[4] In a 1992 interview, *Time* magazine's managing editor, Henry Muller,[5] said, "[My vision of *Time*] probably developed just from being around here a long time. If someone asked me 10 or 15 years ago to define *Time* magazine, I don't think I would have had the faintest idea, but I've been around this institution a long time, and I've learned within it, and in that process I've figured out what I think works and what I think doesn't work" (Muller, 1992).

At the same time he expressed the belief that the person who is ultimately responsible for the editorial content of the magazine leaves his/her personal stamp on the product. "Another way to look at it is that when a company or an owner chooses an editor for a magazine, they have to know that what they're getting is that person and whatever they like or dislike about that person is going to emerge in the magazine" (Muller, 1992). This can have significant consequences for the publication and its presentation of the news. "Ultimately, Henry Muller makes the final decisions. He decides, for example, if he wants a manic George [H. W.] Bush, a tough-looking George Bush or a befuddled George Bush because out on the campaign trail George Bush is all of these things. If you take enough pictures of anybody, you can make them look any way that you want" (Boeth, [*Time* associate picture editor], 1992).

Washington Post executive editor Len Downie says, "Our newsroom is decentralized in nature. We're much more participatory than at a news magazine." He also says of himself, however, "I am typically very hands on; I'm involved in everything that goes on the front page," and "there's definitely a *Washington Post* look and content that are identifiable with the newspaper" (Downie, 1992).

Often, the top editor doesn't need to be directly involved in a decision to exercise his influence. Former *Washington Post* assistant managing editor, Richard Crocker says that editors at the

Post are aware of Downie's personal taste in regard to certain types of photographs, and they make some of their own decisions accordingly. Crocker says that Downie does not want to see photographs of bodies on the front page – that informal rule has been broken a "couple of times" – nor does he want to see them prominently displayed on the inside of the paper. Knowing these beliefs, Crocker says that most times editors will just make the decision to keep photographs of bodies off the front page or out of the paper altogether (Crocker, 1992).

News magazines and newspapers are divided into sections each overseen by a section editor who exercises a strong influence upon the way in which photographs are used in his or her section. Since most section editors began their careers as writers,[6] words are generally favored over images. *New York Times* senior editor and former deputy director of photography Mike Smith says that the *Times* only recently became more visually sophisticated:

> This was not a paper that valued photographers. It valued the written word; it valued reporters; it valued writing . . . I think that whether folks would admit it or not, text editors just didn't value what pictures did. They were considered soft – necessary, yeah you have to have a few, but you don't have to make them big and you don't have to make them too dramatic, and we certainly don't want to spend much money on them. (Smith, 2004)

Although some newspapers value photography and photographic reportage more than others, all newspapers follow routines that are essentially the same. Story ideas are generated (usually by a writer or word editor). Photo orders or requests are initiated, and photographers are assigned to stories. They complete their assignments in the field (or photographs are selected from an alternative source such as the wire services). Photographs are edited, cropped, and tonal ranges are adjusted using digital software such as Photoshop. Captions are written, and pages are designed necessitating photographs to be sized and placed on the page. Each of these newsroom routines affects the visual presentation and the publication's interpretation of the news.

The ability to define "what is news" through the origination of story ideas is perhaps the newsroom's most influential practice. Gans describes the process of pitching story ideas as "a quasi-commercial transaction in which story suggesters [correspondents, etc.] are sellers, offering their ideas to story selectors [section editors and top editors] acting as buyers" (Gans, 1980, p. 90). As in any commercial transaction, the sellers attempt to make their wares as attractive as possible. This, says Gans, is one reason why news stories tend to concentrate on well-known personalities and intense circumstances. For example, *Chicago Tribune* reporter Rex Huppke explains a recurrent metro section story that has dramatic appeal:

> I'm doing a homicide project, looking into why Chicago has such a high murder rate. We were the murder capital last year so we're trying to get beneath the surface of that, looking at the root of the problem – what the police are doing now . . . Murders are down quite a bit this year so they're (the police) doing something right. But, we're sort of investigating that. We're doing stories about homicide continuously throughout the year – we've already done four or five [this year]. (Huppke, 2004)

Like the *Tribune*'s homicide story, most story ideas come from section editors and writers. This tends to limit the diversity of subjects and topics.[7] Unfortunately, many photo editors are content with accepting the photo requests, assigning the photographers and ensuring that they get the desired images in on time. "Today the photographer is sent off to illustrate the preconceptions, usually misconceptions, of the desk-bound editor – an editor biased not by any knowledge of the subject but by the pressure to conform to the standard view ordained by the powers that be. Any deviation from the 'party line' is rejected" (Jones Griffiths, 2002, p. 65). The lack of assigned stories proposed by visual journalists, however, is not entirely the writers or editors' fault. Many photographers and photo editors fail to take the initiative even at newspapers that appreciate visual story telling (Fisher, [*L. A. Times* photo editor], 2004).

Some photographers, however, take advantage of more visual-oriented newsrooms. Pulitzer Prize winning photographer Todd Heisler says of his experience at Copley's Sun Publications in suburban Chicago:

> [It] was a pretty rare situation; everybody was responsible for stories. We had weekly staff meetings, even the office manager was required to go, and each person was required to have two story ideas. That's where a lot of good story ideas came from; everybody was bringing a different perspective to the table. If you really wanted to do something that was personal as a photographer, you had to go out and find your own stories. (Heisler, 2006)

Kathy Ryan, picture editor for the *New York Times Sunday Magazine* says, "We're set up where we do a lot of group brainstorming to get the best possible ideas on what we're working on. One of the great things here is that story ideas are welcome from everywhere" (Ryan, 2004).

Involving visual journalists in the process of story generation is important for the same reasons that it's important to employ a diverse group of people in the newsroom.[8] It broadens the definition of what is newsworthy (duCille, 1991). Photographers must always be at the scene of the story in order to get the photograph. Writers often collect information from the Internet, by telephone or by email. For this reason, photographers generally have a different perspective than writers. They are frequently exposed to a greater diversity of people, and their ideas often seem more radical – edgier – because they are working in the "streets" as opposed to gathering information indirectly.

Story ideas are judged on their perceived level of "newsworthiness." The concept of "newsworthiness" is engrained in the newsroom culture. The Poynter Institute reports, "As they have for the last twenty years, US journalists still rate their journalistic training as the greatest influence on their concept of what is newsworthy.[9] In fact, the proportion saying that training is very influential (seventy-nine percent) was higher than in previous years." The study continues, "The second-most influential factor on news judgment was the journalists' supervisors, with fifty-six percent rating them very influential, followed by news sources and newsroom colleagues" (Poynteronline, 2003).

The newsworthiness of a story is generally determined by whether or not it "gives readers what they want" or by whether or not it has a "news hook."[10] I've attended many editors' meetings in which one of the editors has said, "We can't run that story because our readers aren't interested in land mines in Cambodia – in deforestation in Haiti – in malnutrition in inner-city America, etc." Jacobson calls this argument a "convenient myth" that has as a consequence "censorship 'by omission.'" He says that this strategy is not limited to the mainstream press and offers an example from the 1980s when "the acting editor of the left-of-centre *London Observer* pulled a magazine cover image by Sebastaio Salgado featuring a severe drought in Mali on the pretext that it might disturb readers enjoying themselves on the beach during August Bank holiday. . . . It was replaced with a fashion photograph" (Jacobson, 2002, p. 4). Many editors reason that readers are not interested in stories that "don't affect their daily lives," or that readers aren't patient (or smart) enough to read a story that has complexity – that demands thought (Rosenblum, 1993).

Sometimes more complex social issues are addressed through news publications when the editors and/or writers find a "news hook."[11] For example, the unusually large number and intensity of hurricanes that devastated the Gulf Coast of the United States in 2005 gave cause for a number of stories about global warming and the environment. Likewise the war in Iraq has prompted stories that begin to explain religious, cultural, national, and economic issues in the Middle East – Fallujah became familiar to American news consumers.

A story can also have a news hook if a celebrity or someone important in the news is involved. The plight of Tibet received news coverage because Richard Gere became interested. Africa found itself in the spotlight for a brief moment as Angelina Jolie (purposely to bring light on African issues) and Madonna adopted African children, and societal concerns such as "driving under the influence" and "anti-Semitism" receive periodic attention when celebrities such as Mel Gibson get into trouble. McChesney says that "for those outside power, generating a news hook is extraordinarily difficult and usually requires extraordinary action. The 1968 report of the Kerner Commission on Civil Disorders, for example, specifically cited the poor coverage and lack of contextualization by journalism of racial injustice issues as strongly contributing to the climate that led to the riots of the 1960s" (McChesney, 2004, p. 71).

Once an editor accepts a story proposal, the writer is encouraged to create a request for photographs. Editors and writers understand that having a strong photograph with the story will help move that story to a more visible part of the paper – perhaps the front page. For that reason, writers not only request photographs but many times request a specific photographer – one who they know is likely to provide a powerful image.

Despite the hierarchical nature of the traditional newsroom and the elevated status of word journalists, visual journalism has established itself as a voice in nearly all newsrooms through the assignment system. Today, photo assignment editors in most newsrooms receive "photo requests" rather than "photo orders." Writers are required to justify the need for photographs and provide all of the information that will assist the photographer in his or her work. Ideally the photo assignment editor talks with both the writer and photographer about the requested photographs. *Chicago Tribune* associate director of photography Todd Panagopoulos says, "I think that the assignment desk here influences almost all of the images in the paper based on . . . how soon you get the information, where do you think it might play in the paper, what photographer may be best. I'd say 90 percent of all the photo requests made come through our desk so we are kind of like a funnel" (Panagopoulos, 2004).

Photo assignment editors today typically receive requests electronically. Their challenges are to follow through with each request by gathering more information about the story from the editor, writer, or photographer who submitted the request, determining how much space is available, prioritizing the assignment so that the resources (photographers) are used efficiently and in some cases matching the assigned photographer with the particular assignment.[12]

Some newspapers impose a time deadline each day after which photo requests are technically not accepted. This is to allow photo editors time to get more information about the story and photographers more time to shoot the assignment. Frequently, however, writers and section editors submit the request after the deadline. "You can draw a line in the sand, but ultimately it's about the readers . . . You're going to read it [the request], and it's a great assignment, and what are you going to do? You're going to shoot it. You're just a hostage, but you're going to do the right thing" (Elbert [*Washington Post* assistant managing editor/director of photography], 2004).

Since photo assignment editors typically work with two or three sections, it's important that the editors are well-organized and good communicators. *Los Angeles Times* photo editor Kirk McKoy says:

> I go to all of the meetings for all of the sections along with the section editors, the photo section editors and designers. So my day is a nonstop marathon of meetings. And, I basically do that to keep a handle so that I know what's going on in the sections. I try to squeeze time in to talk to the photographers about assignments.
>
> Some of the section editors will come over and sort of give me an advance idea of what's coming up and ask if I have any thoughts on how to cover it. At that point I try to get an idea of who's the best photographer to do it, then I sit down with the photographer and with the designers if we have time and decide how it [the story] should be illustrated. I come up with ideas for the photographer to think about while he is shooting. And, I squeeze in some editing – a little one on one with photographers. And, I answer a lot of email. (McKoy, 2004)

Many photo requests need further discussion with the reporter or section editor. Joe Elbert says that each assignment editor at the *Post* is responsible for two sections, and he estimates that each editor looks at around 2,500 requests per year. Of that he says about 70 percent don't need work, but 30 percent need "some massaging, some attention, some dialogue" (Elbert, 2004).

Since resources (photographers) are limited not all requests become assignments. Stories are prioritized. Staff photographers are assigned to lead packages, front-page stories, section fronts, etc. Space also becomes an issue. When the assignment editor knows that space is tight, he may not assign a staff photographer to a secondary story. Elbert says that sometimes a dialogue is created between editors where for example, "the style editor may say, 'You know, this [story] is page five – I don't need a special effort. You can assign that photographer for the financial front'" (Elbert, 2004).

Sometimes a staff photographer is or isn't assigned on the basis of the subject's notoriety. *Chicago Tribune* "Features" picture editor Geoff Black says:

> I'll ask, "Who am I shooting?" Let's say it's Prince. We're going to send a photographer to shoot Prince because those photos are going to have a lot more legs [broader interest] beyond that review. If it's a local group, but they're not going to make it [become successful] then I'll determine whether or not we send a photographer. But, you have to be careful because someone who is just beginning today may be hugely successful in the future. I'm talking to the writers and the editors, asking them, "How important is this person? Is this the Ray Charles of your generation?" (Black, 2004)

Assignment editors further influence the visual reporting by determining who will be assigned to photograph the story. Sometimes writers enjoy working with particular photographers and request them specifically. Assignment editors generally try to honor those requests. Other times the selection of a photographer is influenced "by whether it's a story about African-Americans, Latinos, or Asian-Americans. And, gender can be a factor. Race and gender can make a difference. Some of our Latino photographers, for example, really want to go shoot issues that are important to Latinos" (Panagopoulos, 2004). In diverse communities language skills may also play a part in assigning a particular photographer to a story.

Assignment editors also consider the photographers when making assignments but aren't always able to accommodate their wishes.

> All of the photographers want to travel and go out on trips. But when it comes down to it there's only maybe a handful of people who can leave at a moment's notice, who have the experience so that if they need to backpack through rural Mali for a week they can do that and get the pictures back. . . . When our staff ages and has kids, there is a lot more pressure on them to avoid going to Haiti or to Iraq, places like that. (Panagopoulos, 2004)

Most assignment editors have a list of freelance photographers that they will go to when there aren't enough staff photographers to handle the assignment load. Generally, freelancers are assigned to stories of less priority. At the *Chicago Tribune*, for example, they rarely freelance news. "We freelance prep sports and feature assignments, but if the feature story is destined for A1, we would not [give the assignment to a freelancer], and we probably would not assign a freelancer to the main sports story" (Panagopoulos, 2004).

Editors, writers, and other photographers give assignment editors feedback on how the freelance photographers perform with their assignments. As director of photography at Copley Chicago Newspapers, I always had a stack of portfolios on the light table from photography students seeking internships and photographers wanting staff positions or work as freelancers. The photo editors and I quickly identified the freelance photographers we could rely on, and they were routinely assigned to stories that matched their particular strengths.

When a freelance photographer consistently completes his assignments well, he may be considered for a staff position when one becomes available. *Los Angeles Times* photographer Luis Sinco relates his story going from freelance to staff photographer:

> Being on staff makes a difference in the assignments that you get. During my whole contract and freelance career here [at the LA Times] I worked lots of nights doing a lot of calendar stuff and not necessarily big entertainment like Madonna or a lot of hot numbers like I do now. It was a lot of ballet, a lot of modern dance, a lot of symphony, so, you know, I got a really great cultural education being here as a freelancer and as a contractor because it was all this cultural stuff that you pay 100 bucks a ticket for. I looked at it as a positive experience, but at the same time I wasn't doing the Lakers' championship runs. I wasn't traveling as a freelancer. Basically, we were just filling up the rest of the paper. Every once in a while you'd get a good Metro assignment but rarely would you get a crack at an assignment that would be a fun page thing or a big sporting event like the Olympics – no way you're getting that as a freelancer. (Sinco, 2004)

Photo editors use other sources for photographs as well. The picture agencies are essential in providing photographs to the news magazines (Chapnick, 1991). Services like the *New York Times*, AP [Associated Press], AFP [Agence France Presse], Reuters, Getty Images, and Corbis are similarly indispensable to the newspapers. There are also specialty wire services like Wire Image (entertainment world) that offer photographs of specific topics. And, as newspaper ownership expands, sister papers increasingly share editorial content.

Although the photographs provided by wire services are fundamental to newspapers, it is the newspapers that act as clients and the wire services as providers. Thus, the selection process of wire stories and photographs is strongly influenced by the perceived needs and desires of the news publication clients.

To say, however, that these decisions are based entirely upon the requirements of the newspapers would be overly simplistic. The decisions at the wire services are also influenced by the need to minimize expenses. And, although the wire services will apparently not spare any expense when covering a story with great client interest such as the Iraq War the same cannot be said for more "marginal" stories such as Sudan.

Once photographers are assigned to a story they are often guided by journalistic concepts that help to define their work and perhaps discourage them from critically examining the way in which that work is produced. "Objectivity" is taught in many journalism programs and espoused by most news publications.[13] Photography in particular is thought to be objective because the camera directly captures the image. Yet, it's debatable as to whether it's possible to achieve objectivity – being able to describe or record something in a detached way without being influenced by emotions, cultural background, etc. – or if the idea of "objectivity" is even desirable. "Objectivity" suggests that there is only one way of seeing something correctly. This overlooks differences of perception and may infer that the perspective of the news media is somehow free from prejudice.[14]

The use of "official sources" is another strategy that guides journalists in shaping their stories.[15] The reliance on official sources tends to legitimize stories and allows the news media to claim political detachment. Official sources, however, are most frequently chosen from among political and economic elites. This practice, like that of "objectivity," tends to restrict the range of diversity of ideas and fosters repetitive visual reporting – photographs of the same politicians, military leaders, "experts," etc. appear repeatedly in the news media.

Photographers' work is greatly influenced by the relationships that they develop with writers and by how closely the photographs mirror the word stories. Some writers and photographers enjoy working together and appreciate the skills that the other brings to the table. While photographing one summer in Egypt for the English-language magazine, *Cairo Today*, I was fortunate to work with writer Heba Salah on two assignments. Her open-minded yet critical approach to stories and her quiet, non-judgmental attitude towards her subjects gave me the opportunity to learn a great deal about the culture, and it put her subjects at ease so that I could photograph without difficulty.

The relationship between the photographer and writer often dictates how well the words and photographs will work together to tell a cohesive story. Gail Fisher sent *L. A. Times* photographer

Francine Orr to South Africa to work with a writer after she and the writer had worked well together on another story in Africa. Fisher says:

> Words and photos really needed to go together with this, and so she went back to South Africa to work on the anniversary in Rwanda, and then went back to Ethiopia, and then went back to Kenya to work on the AIDS project some more. So, now I think we will have a really strong package of both words and photography, and that's so important that they go together. There can't be that disconnect. If you're going to have really great packages [of words and photographs], they have to marry each other in a sense. The photographer can bring a new dimension to it, but you can't be weaving somebody through the story and you don't have any images of them [the subjects]." (Fisher, 2004)

Fisher's example also demonstrates the way in which the meanings of the photographs can be influenced and even directed by the story content.

Deadlines affect both the quality and content of photographs. Photographers face several challenges in creating a "real," meaningful, and aesthetically-pleasing photograph. Making contact with the subject and/or gaining access to the subject's life can take hours, days, sometimes months. Subjects, particularly those who value their privacy for whatever reason, many times do not want intimate parts of their lives captured in photographs. Once a photographer has the subject's permission to be photographed, he or she must take the time to capture or produce a photograph that has good composition, quality light, a strong moment, and meaningful content.

Sometimes the relationships between photographers and writers help to determine how much time is available before deadlines have to be met. *Chicago Tribune* photographer Scott Strazzante explains:

> I think there was a lot of resentment at the *Herald News* among the writers in relation to the photographers because a lot of times the photographers – and I would do it a little bit too – would work

> on a story and then all of a sudden we would drop it on the writer when we were almost finished and they would have to catch up. This is kind of the opposite way that most newspapers work where the reporter does most of the work and then all of a sudden the photographer is brought in late in the process to illustrate the story.
>
> At the [*Chicago*] *Tribune* photographers almost have to hide their stories while they work on them because if you don't, all of a sudden they'll [the editors] say, "Okay, we're going to run this on Sunday whether you're done or not." We're [the photographers] allowed to pitch our own stories at the *Tribune*, but once they get into the flow of the newsroom the editors will decide when they're going to run them. It's like you have to build up a good amount of the work and then make a pitch when you're 60 percent done – then a reporter will come on. (Strazzante, 2004)

Finally, photographers are also directed in their work by a code of ethics. Photographers have been disciplined and some have lost their jobs for posing subjects and/or recreating situations. News publications allow some exceptions such as fashion, food, and editorial illustrations as long as they are labeled, "illustration." Portraits can be manipulated as long as it's obvious that the photographer has controlled the subject and the image.

Photographers are also expected to avoid situations that have been created by subjects specifically for the camera. Many photo editors will caution photographers to diplomatically ask questions of their subjects to ensure that the situation is real. And, they will instruct the photographers not to take photographs of a contrived event. This sometimes creates tension between word and photo editors as word editors are expecting a photograph and may be less concerned about the veracity of the image. Photo editors try to ameliorate the circumstances by having the photographer make portraits of key participants in the story.

Once the photographer finishes the photographic work, the images are edited. Photographers generally do the first or pre-edit whether they are transmitting a selection of photographs digitally or going through them on a computer at the publication. A photo editor may then make a final edit from the photographer's selects or might ask the photographer to show what else is available. Ideally, the editing process is one in which there is discussion and an exchange of information – photographers get critical feedback regarding the photographs and the editor finds out more about the story. Geoff Black says, "During the edit I'm listening to the photographer because they're explaining to me what they saw while they were there. And there are times when I'm looking at a photograph and I'm asking them, 'What's going on?' because it's not always clear when you just look at a photograph" (Black, 2004).

Photo editors use several criteria for the selection of photographs. They evaluate images based on composition, light, and moment. And, at most publications editors try to ensure that the content of the photograph "represents what we are trying to represent in the story" (Black, 2004). In this way the concepts conceived by the person who generated the story idea are communicated through the visuals as well as the words.

Black concludes, "I learned my job through working for seven years at *The Times* of Northwest Indiana as a photographer and as a photo editor plus the three years of working here [*Chicago Tribune*]" (Black, 2004).

Photo editors are constantly looking for photographs to offer for the front page. It's the newspaper's showcase, and it signals the story's importance (Wanta, 1988). In this way editorial preference and newsroom culture become part of the newsroom routine. And, routine, rather than direct intervention from the top editor, guides most everyday newsroom decisions.

Usually, all of the newsroom editors have an opportunity to weigh in on the selection of front-page photographs, and when there isn't a strong image for the front page, editors get nervous.[16] Colin Crawford (assistant managing editor/photography) describes the process and strategies for front-page picture selection at the *Los Angeles Times*:

> We've got a 3:30 meeting everyday where basically we're pitching photos for A1 and the national foreign section inside so it's sort of the top photos of the day. And, this meeting is attended by

> department heads or deputies, designers, graphics people, my photo editors, John [Carroll, editor of the paper], the managing editor, and the night production people.
>
> We present 12 photos, maybe on a busy day 20. There are a couple of different selections for the top story of the day and if we've got a good story that maybe isn't running on page one but it's got strong photography, we'll lobby for space and to make people aware that it's there.
>
> In pitching the page-one photos we usually show the photos that we like best first, but not always. Sometimes it's the newsiest stuff, but we give people options. There was one day where we had a ton of great photographs, and they were saying, "Space is really tight," so I said for our presentation, "Okay, run like eight photos for this story," so after seeing the photos, the editor pops up and says, "You know, that photography is great. We need to get some space for that." We play mind games sometimes – we do. But it's easier to lobby for something that people can see is great than to just tell them it's great. . . . I think that often the word editors can't differentiate between the fact that it's just a really boring photo – "But, it's an important story." "But, it's a really boring photo."
>
> There are times when there are photos that I call dull but important. For example, when the President sits down behind the desk, it's a boring photo, but if he sits down behind the desk and says, "We're going to war," we need to run the photo. And, I certainly understand that, but what we tend to do as well is to say, "That's our lead story, and here's a photo – we'll put it out there even though the photo is boring." Sometimes we'll even do things as bad as – and we've done this a few times, and it makes me crazy – "We're not going to put that story on the front page because it's not good enough, but there's a boring photo that goes with it, so we'll put that out there because that'll represent the story." Okay, so we'll take a bad photo and put it on page one because it's sort of a story you'd like people to recognize, but you won't put a bad story out there. (Crawford, 2004)

Cropping becomes part of the editing process. "Around the world, cropping is the accepted form of alteration or editing – the photographic equivalent of paraphrasing or ellipsis within the photographic narrative of a picture" (Irby, 2004). Cropping can improve both the aesthetics of an image and the content. Photographers and photo editors must weigh the advantages and disadvantages of the crop – distractions are reduced thereby better isolating the content, but crops also remove information. Photographers and photo editors must decide how much and where to crop to maximize the presentation of necessary content without eliminating important information. "You know the rule of thumb – Carol's [Guzy] famous rule – You shoot twenty millimeters loose on everything and then do the rest in the darkroom even when your darkroom is a computer" (Elbert, 2004).

Almost all newsrooms today work with digital cameras and digital editing so photographers often edit much of their work in the field. Editors may want to look at a smaller or larger edit depending on the trust that they have in any given photographer as an editor.

The digital darkroom has made it easier for photo editors to receive images from sources other than staff photographers. One could argue that this increased reliance upon freelance, agency, and wire photographers helps to decentralize, and perhaps diversify, the selection of images. It must be remembered, however, that photographers make their livings by being continually employed; they realize that their clients are the publications for which they are photographing, and they realize that there are certain expectations in terms of technical proficiency, aesthetics, content, and style. In the end, "[wire] photographers are at the mercy of editors. On the biggest of stories, the AP may transmit a dozen pictures for each twelve-hour cycle. A half-dozen photographers may be shooting non-stop, each with three motorized cameras. Someone has to pick and choose" (Rosenblum, 1993, p. 82).

Despite factors that tend to homogenize the types of photographic images produced for news publications, photographers in the field can make a difference. Many times photographers are specifically selected for their technical skills, personal style, sensitivity, language skills, etc. Sometimes photographers are simply excellent journalists.

Despite having the ability to tell stories with a camera, many photographers give their captions little thought yet captions critically affect the way in which photographs are interpreted (Berger, 1982).[17]

Carl Mydans, who, along with his wife, spent almost two years in Japanese prison camps during World War II, said of his work during that conflict:

> I made notes on everything, every roll of film I shot and, if I could, every frame on each roll, with enough background so that I could transcribe those notes into running captions of what the shipment contained, what outfit I was with, what the action was, the roll number and the frame number. . . . Many times the captions were just as important as the film. Many of us making very good pictures of action in very difficult circumstances were unable to get sufficient captions down between taking our film out of our camera and giving it to someone to take in for shipment. Then, even though the film got to New York, if someone could not make head or tail out of what you had, it was not usable, and so there was worship of captions in the field. (Fulton, 1988, p. 143)

Readers go to the caption to find out what is going on in the photograph, to give the photograph context. Sometimes the light in the photograph can indicate a time of day; the background might give information as to the setting, and the subject's expression and/or body language can suggest a mood. But, captions can clarify (or misidentify)[18] the information in the photograph and relate the photograph to the story.

At some newspapers photographers write the captions while at others photographers are responsible for the caption information, but word people – usually the copy editors – write the captions.

Caption style is pretty similar at most newspapers. For example:

> The caption style [at the *New York Times*] I don't think has changed that much. The first sentence basically describes why this picture is being run in the paper and refers to some aspect of the story –

> tying the photo and story together. The second sentence usually tells what is going on in this particular picture – basically, the "what," "where," "when," and "who." (Frank, 2004)

All editors agree that the photograph and the caption are inseparable. *Los Angeles Times* senior photo editor Kirk McKoy concludes, "It's important that words and pictures work together. It's the package, all three together, words, pictures, and design that entices you to read a story" (McKoy, 2004).

Designing the page is the final step in the photo reportage process. Many photo editors and fewer photographers begin to previsualize the page as they edit the photographs. A number of publications foster good communication between photography and design, and some photo editors take it upon themselves to bring designers into the story planning early on. Occasionally – particularly on a larger project – a team including the writer, section editor, photographer, photo editor, and designer will be formed to talk about all aspects of the story and photos, the editing, and design.

Communication between the photo, word, and design departments is extremely important to creating an effective presentation, and respect for the story-telling qualities of the photographs is critical. Joe Elbert says:

> You design for content [of the photographs] . . . When I got here [*Washington Post*] I one time worked with this designer – and it was like the worst designer I've ever worked with in my entire life. And I said, "Wow, this isn't design, this is just bizarre." I didn't understand how the pages were drawn this way and someone said, "Joe, don't you realize that wherever that person [the subject in the story] is mentioned in the story is where the picture goes?" Now think about designing a page where you go into a 50 inch jump story and the design on the page is based on the image being next to where that person is mentioned in the story. How far do you want to take something? (Elbert, 2004)

Designing for content means utilizing the photographs in ways that attract readers' attention, tell stories visually, and provide emotional impact. *Los Angeles Times* deputy design director Michael Whitley gives an example:

> Last year during the California wildfires the photography was sort of horribly stunning. It was frightening, and it was emotional, and it was a reality that you could not get from the words – just the true fright from people's faces – and, so we went up every day with huge photo spreads, and the pictures were really worth it. (Whitley, 2004)

The process of working with the wildfire photographs was made easier because photographers were using digital cameras. They were able to edit photographs in the field, send them back to the newsrooms using their cell phones and continue to cover the fires. Digital photography and digital darkrooms have made work less stressful for photographers and photo editors. Photographers now have the freedom to file from anywhere in the world via satellite phones and communicators that are getting smaller and smaller. Luis Sinco says:

> The digital cameras allow you to stay busier photographing. You don't have to drive back and forth to the newsroom. I live in Long Beach, and I remember a few years back when I was still shooting film – late 90s – Greenpeace had this thing where they were blockading a ship full of paper out of Long Beach Harbor. I was coming in here from like a 2 o'clock assignment. I was working until 5, and while I was driving in, I was listening to the radio news, and they said, "Okay, this whole operation has started, they're moving the ship in. If any Greenpeace people get in their way, they're just going to move them out with coast guard."
>
> I thought, "Holy Cow, I'd better get down there!" I drove out of the parking lot, called my editors on the cell phone and said, "I'm on my way to Long Beach to check out this Greenpeace thing." But, when I got there, the whole thing just dragged on and on. It was already 6:30 by the time anything happened. Some guy jumped off of one the Greenpeace boats and tried to chain himself to the piling of the pier where the ship was going to go. Some Coastguard men jumped right in after him, and I photographed that.

> Then, I was thinking, "I'd better get out of here because I've got to go all the way to downtown Los Angeles and process the film and get an edit." By the time I got back to the newsroom it was like 7:30 and the deadline was 8, and I still had to process the film, edit it and scan it in – we scanned negatives back then – and you feel yourself developing ulcers while you're driving back.
>
> Now, it would simply be a matter of transmitting from the boat. I think it makes it a lot easier – you worry less about peripheral stuff like driving and really concentrate more on what you're doing as a photographer. But, I also think it makes you work harder because you're able to respond immediately and not worry about having to come back. I think it's easier for the people at the desk too. Everything is a lot faster now. (Sinco, 2004)

Digital photography has accelerated the process for the photographer in the field and the photo editor in the newsroom, but the overall procedure from story idea to seeing the images on the page remains the same. Writers and word editors, who learn "what is news" through journalism training, initiate most story ideas. Photographers are generally assigned to illustrate concepts developed by word journalists, and photographers know the types of photographs that are accepted and appreciated by their publications. Photo editors use several criteria for selecting photographs including aesthetics and content. Photographic content is usually matched with the content of the word story, and captions provide the link between the words and pictures. Finally, newsrooms take on the personalities of the top editors. These editors set the tone for the individual newsroom culture, and newsroom culture largely defines what is news and how that news is presented.

Notes

1 The *Lexington* [Kentucky] *Leader* and the *Lexington Herald*, following the orders of Fred Wachs, the papers' general manager and publisher, failed to cover the 1960s Civil Rights movement despite the fact that it was local news. Wachs, it is said, "generally supported desegregation but favored a cautious approach. . . . Many

experts agree that the decisions made at the *Herald* and the *Leader* hurt the Civil Rights movement at the time, irreparably damaged the historical record and caused the newspapers' readers to miss out on one of the most important stories of the 20th century" (Blackford & Minch, 2004).

2 During a 1992 interview *New York Times* news editor Bill Borders said of executive editor Max Frankel, "Nobody pretends that this is a democracy around here. And, if he wants to rule something, even if everybody in the room is against him, he can do it" (Borders, 1992).

3 Eddie Adams' photograph of General Nguyen Ngoc Loan shooting Viet Cong suspect, Nguyen Van Lem, during the Viet Nam war won a Pulitzer Prize for AP in 1969. Adams later apologized to Loan because the photograph ruined Loan's reputation and complicated the rest of his life. Adams wrote in a eulogy for Loan, "The General killed the Viet Cong; I killed the General with my camera. Still photographs are the most powerful weapon in the world. People believe them; but photographs do lie, even without manipulation. They are only half-truths."

4 While I was the director of photography for Ecuador's *El Universo* the managing editor and section editors frequently urged me to select photographs other than those that I had chosen for publication. Most often they wanted a more literal photograph that in my opinion lacked emotional impact. I rarely altered my decision. The owner/publisher, Carlos Perez, however, only asked me to change my selection once. It was a one-and-a-half column photograph of Ecuadorian President Jamil Mihuad. During the election campaign Mihuad's opponents had suggested that he was homosexual – political poison in the conservative atmosphere of 1990s Ecuador. Carlos Perez asked me if I didn't think that the photograph that I had picked made the president look "a little feminine" and that perhaps we should find another. I told him that I thought that the photograph made the president appear like a politician under pressure. Nevertheless, I changed the photograph, partially because it was the only time that Carlos requested a change so I knew that it was important to him; partially because he knew his own culture better than I did and finally because I was aware that as the publisher of the paper he would make any changes that he felt necessary – and that particular photograph was not worthy of a confrontational discussion.

5 In 1993 Muller became the Editorial Director of Time Inc. and served in that capacity until 2000.

6 Visual journalists Denis Finley at the *Virginian-Pilot* and Maggie Steber at the *Miami Herald* became assistant managing editors as well as section editors, and Finley is now editor of the *Virginian-Pilot*, but these are rare cases.

7 After observing the *El Universo* newsroom for a week before assuming the role as director of photography in 1998, I wrote a proposal to owner/publisher Carlos Perez. In it I highlighted three stages of change. The short-term changes empowered the photography department to do the daily photo edits and allowed the director of photography to consult with the managing editor and the design director regarding front-page photo usage and design. The medium-term changes addressed working with the photographers to improve their overall photography skills and the long-term (and in my mind the most important) changes created a team approach to initiating and developing story ideas. Photographers were held accountable for generating story ideas, and section editors were obligated to listen to and evaluate stories proposed by photographers. In addition writers and photographers were required to work together at developing the stories.

8 In explaining the failure of *Washington Post* editors to initially detect the deceit in Janet Cooke's "Jimmy's World" story, Pamela Newkirk says that the story is credible to white editors. "That is not to say that Cooke's deceit was instantly detectable (even though many in the newsroom did, early on, find her story implausible), but it is to suggest the images she created already resonate with enough people to render them credible. The fascination with black pathology pervades the news industry, and reporters quickly learn that stories like 'Jimmy's World' are a quick ticket to page 1" (Newkirk, 2000, p. 167).

9 Journalists have all heard the slogan, "dog bites man is not news; man bites dog is news." This journalistic mantra sometimes skews the portrayals of individuals or groups. While director of photography for Copley Chicago Newspapers I attended a news meeting during which an editor read a letter from a Hispanic woman who lived in the suburb that the newspaper served. The letter referred to a story the newspaper had published that featured a parent in the community who accused organizers of a beauty pageant for Hispanic girls of rigging the results. The author of the letter was

angry because the contest only became news after the controversy. The newspaper hadn't published anything about the contest before the accusation. After the allegation, the story was front-page news. The editor laughed and said, "People just don't understand what's news and what's not news." I told him that I thought the woman had a good point. His response was, "How did you ever become a journalist?"

10 There are of course major exceptions to this, particularly in some of the environmental stories that have been published by newspapers in the past several years.

11 McChesney believes that news organizations are intimidated and influenced by the "political right." The news hook allows editors and writers to justify stories by framing them within the news event. He says, "The average American cannot help but be exposed to the noticeable double standard in the treatment of politicians and issues in the media, depending upon party and ideology. The fate of Bill Clinton and George W. Bush reveals the scope of the conservative victory. A Nexis search, for example, reveals that 13,641 stories focused on Clinton avoiding the military draft but a mere 49 stories featured Bush having his powerful father use influence to get him into the Texas Air National Guard instead of the draft." McChesney continues, "Rick Kaplan, former head of CNN, acknowledged that he instructed his employees to provide the Lewinsky story with massive attention despite his belief that it was overblown; he knew he would face withering criticism from the Right for a liberal bias if he did not pummel it. 'I think if you look at the way Clinton's been treated,' former Christian Coalition director Ralph Reed said, 'you'd be hard-pressed to say that the personal liberal ideological views of most reporters . . . have somehow led to a free ride for Bill Clinton'" (McChesney, 2004, p. 118).

12 "We have photographers who have particular strengths, and we try to play to those strengths. We have some photographers who are good in the studio, for example, and we try to play to that strength when we assign. That's not to say it's favoritism, it's just that if someone expresses a desire and does well in it and satisfies all of the people who care about photography, then we'll just play to that strength" (Wells [*L. A. Times* photo editor], 2004).

13 "The concept of journalism as politically neutral, nonpartisan, professional, even 'objective,' did not emerge until the twentieth century. During the first two or three generations of the republic

such notions for the press would have been nonsensical, even unthinkable. Journalism's purpose was to persuade as well as to inform and the press tended to be highly partisan. A partisan press system has much to offer a democratic society – as long as there are numerous well-subsidized media providing a broad range of perspectives. . . . By the early twentieth century newspaper concentration was on the rise, but almost nowhere were new dailies being launched successfully in existing markets. For journalism to remain partisan in this context, for it to advocate openly the interests of the owners and advertisers who subsidized it, would cast severe doubt on its credibility" (McChesney, 2004, pp. 58, 60).

14 Chomsky suggests that what "objectivity" really means is viewing and reporting on the world from the ideological perspective of the mass media. "The mass media are capitalist institutions. The fact that these institutions reflect the ideology of dominant economic interests is hardly surprising" (Chomsky, 1979, p. 78).

15 "Among news sources, there is no order or logic. Head-of-state interviews are treasured by editors, most of whom refuse to let correspondents quote taxi drivers because they sound too easy. In fact, cabbies usually reveal more" (Rosenblum, 1993, p. 105).

16 There were several days during my tenure at *El Universo* when the managing editor, design director and I waited for a photographer to return from a late-afternoon assignment hoping that he would have a strong photograph for the next day's front page.

Todd Heisler says, "They [the *Rocky Mountain News* editors] have two meetings every day, an 11 o'clock meeting and a 3 o'clock meeting. The 11 o'clock meeting is like a progress meeting for the day. They get all of the word and photo editors together in a room and say, 'What's our big story for today? What's our potential page one? What are we working on today?' They'll say, 'This afternoon we're doing this; we already shot this; we're putting all our efforts on A1.' Then at 3 o'clock they'll say, 'Okay, what worked out and what didn't work out?' I joke that the 11 o'clock meeting is the 'optimist meeting' and the 3 o'clock is the 'pessimist meeting' because at 11 they're like 'all this stuff's going to work out,' but then people get out in the streets and either they can't get access or it wasn't really a story or they couldn't get the story yet – by 3 o'clock – they're still trying to get in touch with the people or the people won't call them [the photographers] back. There are a lot of different issues that come up that ruin the plans for A1" (Heisler, 2006).

17 "Accuracy in captions is critical to the success of photo departments. We want to call ourselves journalists, but we don't write factual captions; we don't even write complete sentences" (Rasmussen [*Florida Sun Sentinel* director of photography], 2004).

18 "My favorite caption story – it was my previous beat, I covered higher education – there was a tribute being made at UC Berkley to Mario Savio. They put in a room or a coffee shop or something in one of the libraries. Now, to most people they'd hear Mario Savio, so what? Mario Savio was the leader of the free-speech movement in 1963. . . . The university detested this fellow – he was a troublemaker in their minds. And now, this was in the late 90s, years later and they're naming a damn section of the library after him. We said, 'This is unnatural,' so we did this story. I didn't go to the event, but we had a photographer go. Now, Mario Savio was dead which made it easier for the university to embrace him, but his son and his widow were there. I wrote in the story that the event was attended by his son and the widow. And, the photo – I don't know if it was taken by a staff photographer or a stringer – had the son and the widow, and the copy desk wrote in the caption, 'The son and his mother' . . . The next day I get a call and this woman says, 'I'm demanding a correction, I want to tell you that that woman is not his mother.' And, I said, 'Okay, just so that we don't have to correct this twice, how do you know that's not his mother?' And she says, 'I'm his mother. That's his second wife.' So, this was a classic case of assumption. They [the copy desk] assumed the widow was this boy's mother, and it wasn't" (Weiss [*L. A. Times* staff writer], 2004).

References

Berger, J. (1982). Appearances. In J. Berger & J. Mohr (Eds.), *Another way of telling*. New York: Pantheon.

Black, G. (2004). *Interview by author* [cassette recording] June, Chicago.

Blackford, L. & Minch, L. (2004). Front-page news, back-page coverage, the struggle for civil rights in Lexington. *Lexington Herald Leader*, July 4, p. A 1.

Boeth, R. (1992). *Interview by author* [cassette recording] March, New York.

Borders, B. (1992). *Interview by author* [cassette recording] March, New York.

Carroll, J. (2004). *Interview by author* [cassette recording] June, Los Angeles.

Chapnick, H. (1991). *Interview by author* [cassette recording] November, New York.

Chomsky, N. (1979). Ideological conformity in America. January 27.

Crawford, C. (2004). *Interview by author* [cassette recording] June, Los Angeles.

Crocker, R. R. (1992). *Interview by author* [cassette recording] March, Washington, D.C.

Davis, M. (2006). *Telephone interview by author* [digital recording] May, Miami.

Downie, L. (1992). *Interview by author* [cassette recording] November, Columbia, MO.

duCille, M. (1991). *Interview by author* [cassette recording]. November, Washington, DC.

Elbert, J. (2004). *Interview by author* [cassette recording] June, Washington, DC.

Fisher, G. (2004). *Interview by author* [cassette recording] June, Los Angeles.

Frank, D. (2004). *Interview by author* [cassette recording] June, New York.

Fulton, M. (1988). Bearing witness: The 1930s to the 1950s. In M. Fulton (Ed.), *Eyes of time: Photojournalism in America* (pp. 105–172). New York: Little, Brown and Company.

Gans, H. (1980). *Deciding what's news*. New York: Vintage.

Heisler, T. (2006). *Telephone interview by author* [digital recording] May, Miami.

Huppke, R. (2004). *Interview by author* [cassette recording] June, Chicago.

Irby, K. (2004, March 29). Beyond taste: Editing truth. *poynter.org*.

Jacobson, C. (2002). Introduction. In C. Jacobson (Ed.), *Underexposed: "Pictures can lie and liars use pictures."* London: Vision On Publishing.

Jones Griffiths, P. (2002). Death of the photographer. In C. Jacobson (Ed.), *Underexposed: "Pictures can lie and liars use pictures."* London: Vision On Publishing.

McChesney, R. W. (2004). *The problem of the media*. New York: Monthly Review Press.

McKoy, K. (2004). *Interview by author* [cassette recording] June, Los Angeles.

Muller, H. (1992). *Telephone interview by author* [cassette recording] October, Columbia, MO.

Newkirk, P. (2000). *Within the veil*. New York: New York University Press.

Panagopoulos, T. (2004). *Interview by author* [cassette recording] June, Chicago.

Poynteronline (2003). Training is the biggest influence on news judgment. *poynter.org*, April 10.

Rasmussen, T. (2006). *Telephone interview by author* [digital recording], May, Miami.

Rosenblum, M. (1993). *Who stole the news*. New York: John Wiley & Sons.

Ryan, K. (2004). *Interview by author* [cassette recording], June, New York.

Sinco, L. (2004). *Interview by author* [cassette recording] June, Los Angeles.

Smith, M. (2004). *Interview by author* [cassette recording] June, New York.

Strazzante, S. (2004). *Interview by author* [cassette recording], June, Chicago.

Wanta, W. (1988). The effects of dominant photographs: An agenda setting experiment. *Journalism Quarterly*, *64*, 107–111.

Weiss, K. (2004). *Interview by author* [cassette recording] June, Los Angeles.

Wells, H. (2004). *Interview by author* [cassette recording] June, Los Angeles.

Whitley, M. (2004). *Interview by author* [cassette recording] June, Los Angeles.

5

Economics

In addition to newsroom culture, corporate ownership influences the framework within which journalists work. News publications have become increasingly corporate owned during the past several decades. As a result decisions are routinely made to appease shareholders and advertisers – sometimes at the expense of news consumers. “The content of the press is directly correlated with the interests of those who finance the press” (Altschull, 1987, p. 254).

Shareholders demand increased profits, and publications deliver through lowering expenses and/or increasing income. The Tribune Company’s 2005 Annual Report says, “Our operating strategies focus on what we can control. This means listening to customers and responding to their needs; finding innovative ways to grow revenue and expand audience reach; and practicing aggressive cost management. These objectives are top priorities in every area of our business” (Tribune Company, 2005, p. 2).

Typically, news media costs are controlled by trimming the number of employees; managing employee salaries and benefits; cutting the amount of space dedicated to editorial content (the news hole) versus advertising; restraining the use of freelance work; limiting travel expenses, and “peeling back circulation in remote or low-income areas of less interest to advertisers” (Meyer, 2004, p. 41). Each of these cost-cutting strategies can have consequences for the news product.

“Downsizing the workforce” has become a mantra for today’s corporate management. Layoffs and early retirement offerings are routine. The Tribune Company says, "While operating revenues for the year rose 2 percent to $5.7 billion, operating profits were down 11 percent, largely because of two charges recorded by the publishing group – $90 million related to anticipated settlements with *Newsday* and *Hoy* advertisers,[1] and $41 million for the elimination of about 600 positions at our newspapers" (Tribune Company, 2005, p. 5). The elimination of 600 jobs was a large budget expense for 2005, but presumably would begin to have strong economic rewards thereafter.

In July 2006 The New York Times Co. announced that it would consolidate printing operations, eliminating about 250 jobs (CNNMoney.com, 2006). The 1992 Washington Post Company's Annual Report noted that the company responded to overall declining revenues by assuring shareholders that cost control "remains a top priority." More specifically, the company told shareholders that they (the company) "worked hard to keep the number of employees low" during the preceding year and that they will do even more in the future because, they say, "a low cost base gives us the leverage to realize substantial profit growth when economic conditions improve" (Washington Post Company, 1992, p. 4). And, a 2002 report noted, "[Knight Ridder's] stated goal in response to the economic downturn that began toward the end of 2000 was to trim news staffs by 10 percent" (Meyer, 2004, p. 192).[2]

Despite corporate denials, some believe that reducing the number of employees at news organizations affects the news product.[3] When Knight Ridder's *San Jose Mercury News* staff was significantly downsized in 2001, publisher Jay Harris resigned. During a speech to the American Society of Newspaper Editors Harris said:

> What troubled me, something that had never happened before in all my years in the company, was that little or no attention was paid to the consequences. . . . There was virtually no discussion of the damage that would be done to the quality and aspirations of the *Mercury News* as a journalistic endeavor, or to its ability to fulfill its responsibilities to the community. (Meyer, 2004, p. 192)

Hollinger International went about reducing expenses after purchasing Fox Valley Press, Inc. in Illinois by orchestrating mass layoffs[4] and by attempting to lower employee benefits.

> When Canada-based Hollinger International bought the *Herald News* in Joliet, IL last December in an asset sale, it was not legally bound by any contracts negotiated by seller Copley Press [Fox Valley Press] Inc. But as part of its purchase agreement, Hollinger did agree to honor virtually all of the terms Copley had negotiated with the Chicago Newspaper guild less than a year earlier – all that is, except for the employee pension program and an employer 401 (K) match.
>
> That may have assuaged Copley's corporate conscience, but it didn't sit well with employees. "We negotiated these benefits in good faith over an eight-month period with Copley," says *Herald News* reporter and unit chairman Charles B. Pelkie. "Then Hollinger wails in the door and tells its new employees that they really aren't worth that much." (The Guild Reporter, 2001)

Although management and employees might suggest that financial negotiations and journalism are kept separate – that employee bitterness doesn't intrude on newsroom professionalism, it's difficult to determine the effects that employee rancor could have on the news product. And, community perceptions of their news provider may well have been influenced by the highly visible feud.

Decreasing the size of the news hole is another cost-control strategy increasingly employed by news publications. Sometimes this means fewer stories and fewer photographs; other times the stories are shorter, and/or the photographs are sized smaller. During my final year with Copley Chicago Newspapers there were frequent discussions (sometimes heated) regarding the lack of space for word and visual stories – in previous years the space was generally available for stories that the senior editors felt were important. In 2000, however, management trimmed costs before selling the papers.[5]

Large metropolitan newspapers are also experiencing reductions in available space. The *Los Angeles Times*' Gail Fisher says:

> They [projects that photographers and writers at the *L. A. Times* are working on] will absolutely be affected by budget cuts, and a lot of these [stories] are serious – I'm really worried at this point. I think the very-very best won't be affected that much just like we came up with space for the Reagan funeral. . . . [And] I don't think it's [financial pressures] going to change the way that we aggressively cover news in stories, but I do think we'll do less quantity – space is an issue. (Fisher, 2004)

Hal Wells, also at the *Los Angeles Times*, observes that the reduced amount of space has affected the way in which *Times* photo assignment editors use freelance photographers. He believes that because there is less space available for photographs, editors must now think about the wisdom of paying a freelance photographer four hundred dollars for a photograph that only runs two columns. Wells says that in the past when a writer requested a photograph to go with a story and the photo desk didn't have a staff photographer available, the photo editor generally hired a freelancer without hesitation. Now, he says, the photo editor thinks more about the cost versus the amount of space available. "We're noticing that what was usually a 10 or 12 page section going down to an 8 or 10 page section." And, he continues, "I think readers notice these things [too]. You know, they're receiving lots of editorial content and then suddenly it's crammed in and not as easy to read – I think it takes its toll on readership" (Wells, 2004).

Assignment editors feel the effects of budget constraints in other ways as well. Immediately after Ronald Reagan's death *Chicago Tribune* editor Todd Panagopoulos tried to get a *Tribune* photographer assigned to the press pool covering the "lying in state" event at the Rotunda in Washington, DC. Staff photographer Pete Souza was working full-time in Washington and was Reagan's photographer, but Panagopoulos says that when the *Tribune* hired Souza they made an agreement allowing him to continue working on the Reagan archives during the week after Reagan's death. The *Tribune* sent staff photographer John Lee to Washington who was unable to get a pool position. Panagopoulos admits, "I didn't push really hard for the Rotunda because we only had one guy there [in Washington, DC] – which was a decision I did not agree with – we should have sent two photographers. Then we can put someone in the pool and still have someone going around and getting other kinds of shots – so I didn't push really hard [to get Lee into the Rotunda] because we decided to go with one person to save money" (Panagopoulos, 2004).

The fact that the *Chicago Tribune* did not have photographs from the Rotunda taken by one of its own staff photographers seems like a small issue, particularly when pool photographers as well as the wires and other sources for photographs could be used by the *Tribune*, but a multitude of changes necessitated by cost management cumulatively affect news reporting. A 2004 survey conducted by the Pew Research Center for the People & the Press concluded, "Journalists are growing more concerned that bottom-line financial pressures are 'seriously hurting' the quality of news coverage. . . . [And] More than half of the executives at national news organizations said greater business pressures are 'just changing the way news organizations do things'" (Associated Press, 2004a).

Cost management is half of the equation for maximizing profits. The other half is "growing revenue." Revenue is overwhelmingly generated through advertising.[6] "Industry-wide, advertising accounted for 82 percent of newspaper revenue in 2000 and circulation was the other 18. That was a shift from a 71–29 division in mid-century" (Meyer, 2004, p. 37). Advertising issues help to determine, both directly and indirectly, the framework within which news is produced.

Occasionally, the editor's perspective comes into direct conflict with the corporate perspective. In most cases when this happens, the corporate perspective prevails. For example, in 1991, *Newsweek* magazine picture editor, Guy Cooper, talked about the difficulties in putting together the Pearl Harbor issue. In response to the question, "Was Japanese advertising a criterion for the omission of any photographs in the 'Pearl Harbor' issue?", Cooper responded: "There were discussions about certain photographs in the prison camps, etc. and whether they were really germane. And, we decided they weren't. We're just talking about an event that happened 50 years ago, so yes, there were discussions" (Cooper, 1991). In this case *Newsweek* possibly preempted reprisals from Japanese advertisers through self-censorship.

Photographer Peter Essick (1991) suggests that most times the editor's perspective and the corporate perspective are in harmony. He cites as examples *Time* and *People* magazines. Both, he says, used reader demographics as an excuse for not putting people of color on their covers. In that way the choice of covers became justified as a business decision but probably coincided with editorial preference as well.[7]

Advertisers routinely withdraw ads when they disagree with a publication's editorial content (Kaufman, 1991). Advertisers less directly influence the way in which news is framed by demanding large audiences and/or audiences with particular demographics.

For example, *Lexington Herald* and *Lexington Leader* general manager and publisher Fred Wachs ordered the papers' editors to largely ignore the 1960s Civil Rights movement. (On July 4, 2004 the *Lexington Herald-Leader* apologized for its lack of reporting the Civil Rights movement. Documentary photographs by African-American photographer Calvert McCann accompanied the front-page apology.)[8] His defenders say that he was concerned about the welfare of his community. But, Thomas Peoples, the former NAACP leader, said that when it came to excluding civil rights coverage, Wachs wasn't protecting his town so much as his papers' bottom lines. "They catered to the white citizenry, and the white community just prayed that rumors and reports would be swept under the rug and just go away," he said (Blackford & Minch, 2004).

Occasionally the lines between advertising and editorial content are blurred. Many of the editorial photographs that appear in today's news publications are created illustrations while advertisers employ photographers to document real life and then use the photographs to promote their products. Readers are often forced to look carefully for the small print that declares, "Paid for Advertisement."

Some newspapers have gone even further to confuse the distinction between editorial and advertising. Tim Rasmussen recalls a discussion with the editor and publisher that led to his departure from the Fredericksburg *Freelance Star*:

> The publisher and the editor pulled me into a meeting and said we're going to try to make a new revenue stream. We want all of the [editorial] photographs turned over to the advertising department so that they can show them to advertisers so that advertisers will buy ads based on the photographs that we took for the paper. That one set me back, and I said let me think about that for a minute. And then they said, we also need the photographers to start shooting advertising and marketing.
>
> I said, well first of all, we're never going to turn our photographs over to advertising, we can't. We go out to these assignments. We tell readers that we're here for the newspaper; they understand what that means. It's a completely different thing. Legally it's questionable. Ethically, to turn them over to an advertiser to make money off of photographs, I won't do it. And, as far as shooting advertising, I won't do that either. I was actually very diplomatic in the way that I said it. It got a little heated and at one point the publisher said, "Well then pick one of your photographers for me to fire." So, I said, "You can have my job right now before I'll fire one of the photographers." At that point the editor said, "Why don't we stop here and revisit it tomorrow?" So that night I went online to check job openings. (Rasmussen, 2006)

Newspapers in a corporate environment seek higher profits to placate the demands of stockholders. Former Knight Ridder executive editor Lee Hills says, "It isn't always easy as a public company in America today. . . . Many big traders in the stock market and their advisors decide to buy or sell depending on how this quarter's results compare with the previous quarter and the last year" (Meyer, 2004, p. 200). As a consequence publishers find themselves explaining to shareholders the reasons for poorer than expected economic results and trying to assure them of future economic gains. The 2005 Washington Post Company Annual Report asserts:

> 2005 was a somewhat disappointing year. Our newspapers, TV and magazine businesses turned in poorer results than their managers expected when the year began. . . . These are the facts, and I'll set them out for you in detail. You need to know them.

> You also need to know this; all of us at the Washington Post Company feel we have a chance to be a significantly more valuable business a few years from now. That's a chance, not a certainty (certainty departed the media business some time ago) . . . The stopping power of the newspaper page and the newspaper preprint work as well as ever. Readers go to the paper to find ads, and the ads also work, in a distinctly un-Google way: they reach people who aren't consciously searching for a shirt, a bottle of wine, a cell phone network or a movie – and they lead them to buy one. We haven't taught our advertisers to use our high-traffic websites as effectively. (Graham, 2006)

Increasingly, media owners face mandates from shareholders to either increase profits or find new ownership.[9] For example, in 2007 the Tribune Company "under pressure from key shareholders to boost its stock price," sought new ownership and subsequently accepted a buyout offer from real estate investor Sam Zell (Heher, 2007). Zell then joined the Tribune board of directors. William Osborn, a Tribune director who led the review process, explains, "The strategic review process was rigorous and thorough. . . . We determined that this course of action provides the greatest certainty for achieving the highest value for all shareholders and is in the best interest of investors and employees" (Heher, 2007). One might also ask, "Is it in the best interest of the readers?"

The story of Knight Ridder Newspapers, Inc. provides a good example of a newspaper company going from private to public ownership and eventually selling its newspapers to another corporation. The Knight and Ridder newspaper companies went public in 1969 and merged in 1974. During the early years of corporate ownership the families were able to maintain control of the papers because they owned a majority of the stocks.

> [But], by 2002, institutional and outside investors controlled about 90 percent of Knight Ridder stock, according to P. Anthony Ridder who became CEO in 1995. Contacts with investors and analysts became more intense. "Since I have been CEO," said Ridder, "the number of meetings has increased dramatically, and institutional investors expect you to call on them." (Meyer, 2004, p. 175)

In response, Ridder aggressively lowered the Knight Ridder budget through personnel cuts. Nevertheless, Knight Ridder's largest shareholder, Private Capital Management, pressured the publisher to seek new ownership.[10]

> If Knight Ridder's board does not accede to the demand, the firm [Private Capital Management] added in a securities filing, it would "strongly consider" supporting efforts by other unnamed investors to replace the board and managers, take over the company or "take other action to maximize shareholder value." (Siklos, 2005)

In June 2006 the Knight Ridder chain of 32 daily newspapers was sold to The McClatchy Company. In less than 40 years the Knight and Ridder newspapers had gone from being family owned to corporate owned to non-existent, casualties of shareholder expectations.

Corporate ownership provides a major context within which news is reported. In an editorial about Hollywood, *Miami Herald* columnist Leonard Pitts suggests that despite "the talk about Hollywood as a bastion of liberalism, the truth is, this business – like any other – is conservative. People are generally conservative when it comes to their money" (Pitts, 2007). The same can be said for the news business. Journalists (and particularly photojournalists who are frequently working "in the streets") are often liberal in their politics, but those liberal ideals are moderated through newsroom filters, and the stories are told (or not told) within the corporate context. Pitts continues, "That's what the cultural crusaders never seem to get. Whether Hollywood is pushing the boundaries of acceptability (*Brokeback Mountain*) or rolling down the middle of the mainstream (*Spider-Man 3*), it all grows out of the same calculation: The investment will produce a return" (Pitts, 2007). News media operate within conservative parameters. Stockholders expect a handsome return on their investments.

Despite the efforts of some media critics to draw attention to the way in which the news media influence public opinion from a corporate perspective (Parenti, 1986) or the way in which corporate cutbacks influence news production (Epstein, 1974), the news media themselves seldom suggest possible effects of corporate ownership on the way in which news is reported (Lee & Solomon, 1990). In 1989, for example, Time Inc. was taken to court by Paramount in a challenge to Time's $14 billion buyout of Warner. Although the case attracted heavy media coverage, "most of the press covered the entire ordeal simply as a business story without dwelling on the social and political consequences of such a merger" (Lee & Solomon, 1990, p. 70).

Journalists, those participating daily within the newsroom environment, expressed their opinions regarding corporate news media priorities through a Poynter Institute survey published in 2003. Although a solid majority felt that good journalism was important to the owners, it ranked third among what they perceived to be ownership priorities.

> We asked journalists a number of questions about the presence of business values in their newsrooms, and the results were mixed. The value most important to their companies' owners, they felt, was keeping the audience as large as possible (89 percent felt this was very important to the owners or senior managers). Ranking second was "earning high, above-average profits" (77 percent), but 73 percent also felt that "producing journalism of high, above-average quality" was very important to owners as well. Conspicuous in this grouping was the low number (32 percent) feeling that "maintaining high employee morale" was very important to the owners. (Poynteronline, 2003)

The corporate model of the news media that has evolved during the past several decades alters the definition of a free press from one that allows the freedom to express in the name of public discourse to one that allows the freedom to express in the name of financial gain. Media critic Robert McChesney says, "The turn to a more market-based notion of a 'free press' came gradually with the emergence of powerful private, profit-driven media. Nothing in the First Amendment mandated this interpretation" (McChesney, 2004, p. 30). McChesney calls this the "commercial interpretation of the press."

> Proponents assert that this right is absolute, because the First Amendment says "no law." Therefore capitalists can do as they please in the realm of media and they need answer only to their bottom lines; the market will prove to be a superior regulator of the press. (McChesney, 2004, p. 30)

The strategy of "giving the public what it wants" permeates newsroom thinking. I have attended many news meetings during which editors have said, "Our readers don't want to read about . . ." or, "Our readers aren't interested in . . ." or worse yet, "Our readers won't understand this story." Likewise, I've many times heard, "This photograph is too complicated for our readership." Many news publications rely on surveys to tell them what's of interest to readers. This approach to journalism and freedom of the press facilitates financial gain but underestimates the intelligence and sophistication of readers and undercuts the principle of public discourse.

Many believe that it runs counter to the intentions of the First Amendment. Supreme Court Justice Hugo Black "in his famous opinion in the 1945 *Associated Press v. U.S.* case . . . [said], 'That [First] Amendment rests on the assumption that the widest possible dissemination of information from diverse and antagonistic sources is essential to the welfare of the State'" (McChesney, 2004, p. 31). And:

> In the Supreme court's seminal 1927 *Whitney v. California* case, Justice Louis Brandeis concluded: "Those who won our independence believed that the final end of the State was to make men free to develop their faculties . . . that the greatest menace to freedom is an inert people; that public discussion is a political duty; and that this should be a fundamental principle of American government." (McChesney, 2004, p. 30)

During a speech to the American Society of Newspaper Editors, John Carroll, former editor of the *Los Angeles Times* and Knight Visiting Lecturer at Harvard University "said that the current ownership models simply aren't working. 'Restoring a balance at newspapers between financial performance and public duty is probably impossible under this form of ownership'" (Knight Foundation, 2006).

Corporate owners, says Carroll, "care nothing about the practice of journalism. . . . What they care about 'could not be simpler: money. That's it. . . . Gone is the notion that a newspaper should lead, that it has an obligation to its community, that it is beholden to the public'" (Knight Foundation, 2006).

Change may be difficult since the newspaper industry and its shareholders have become accustomed to high profit margins. Ironically, the recent struggles by newspapers to meet shareholder profit expectations may present an opportunity for change in the news media ownership model. Carroll is somewhat optimistic about the possibility of a revitalization of the locally owned newspaper. "I'm seeing a new phenomenon: Local people seeking to buy the paper back from the corporations. I've spoken with several of them. These are serious people – sophisticated people with real money. Perhaps this is a trend."

These sorts of owners, Carroll said, "talk about the importance of the paper to the community. They talk about restoring its pride. . . . They see the newspaper as a fallen angel, and they say they'd be willing to accept a lower financial return, which would allow the paper to breathe again" (Knight Foundation, 2006).

This kind of transformation would require a monumental change in the way that newspaper owners view their mission – a change from serving the stockholder to serving the readership and the citizenry at large. Because newspapers have lost some of their economic luster, the time may be right for such a sea change.

Notes

1 In 2004 Tribune-owned newspapers *Newsday* and *Hoy*, both of New York, overstated their circulation figures to advertisers. Short-term this resulted in higher rates collected by *Newsday* and *Hoy*, but when advertisers were made aware of the inflated numbers, The Tribune Company was forced to compensate them. The Tribune Company reported in its 2004 Annual report, "The discrepancies

resulted from unethical conduct by a small group of employees who were subsequently terminated" (Tribune Company, 2005, p. 4).

2 In June 2006 the Knight Ridder chain of 32 daily newspapers was sold to The McClatchy Company.

3 In 2006 *Los Angeles Times* publisher, Jeffrey M. Johnson, was fired because he objected to staff cuts ordered by the Tribune Company. One month later Dean Baquet, the editor of *The Los Angeles Times*, was forced out because he refused to carry out the cuts mandated by the Tribune Company. In January 2008 Baquet's successor, James O'Shea, refused to cut $4 million from the newsroom budget and was subsequently fired.

4 In 2005 Hollinger announced that it would eventually eliminate 300 jobs from its Chicago group of newspapers (10 percent of its workforce). "The reorganization will add $16 million to $20 million to annual operating income after 2006, Hollinger said" (Fitzgerald, 2006). Hollinger also blamed an increase in workers' compensation as one reason for a "disappointing" 2005 operating income.

5 In December 2000 Hollinger International Inc. bought Fox Valley Press, Inc. This acquisition included Copley Chicago Newspapers (four daily newspapers in the suburbs of Chicago) and Sun Publications (11 community weekly newspapers in the Chicago suburbs). "David Radler, President and Chief Operation Officer of Hollinger International Inc., said, 'These assets are highly additive to our existing Chicago Group of newspapers. We are all delighted to add them to our portfolio'" (writenews.com, 2000).

Hollinger Inc. became the story not long after its purchase of Fox Valley Press, Inc. when Conrad Black, the chairman of Hollinger International, faced charges of racketeering, mail and tax fraud, money laundering, and obstruction of justice. He was subsequently found guilty of obstruction of justice and three counts of mail fraud.

6 In 2006 the *Wall Street Journal* began selling advertising on its front page for the first time in more than 50 years. Ads are now being placed in the lower right-hand corner of the front page as well as in a banner along the bottom of the front page. "'The front page of the *Wall Street Journal* will provide the greatest opportunity available anywhere, in any medium, for advertisers seeking to reach a large, affluent, and influential audience' [said L. Gordon Crovitz, executive vice president of Dow Jones and *Wall Street Journal* publisher]" (CNNMoney.com, 2006).

7 Writer and director David Mamet calls this "censorship" in the name of "concern for commercial viability" (Mamet, 2002, p. 64).

8 "The [July 4, 2004] notice accompanied a series of stories titled 'Front-page news, back-page coverage' and decades-old black-and-white pictures taken by an independent photographer [McCann who was working as a janitor and film processor in a private photography store]. 'It has come to the editor's attention that the *Herald-Leader* neglected to cover the civil rights movement,' the clarification read. 'We regret the omission'" (Associated Press 2004b, 2004).

Although the *Herald* and the *Leader* relegated much of the civil rights movement to a column called, "Colored Notes," the movement was reported extensively by the *Louisville Defender*, a black newspaper, and the *Louisville Courier-Journal*.

9 Rupert Murdoch aggressively pursued the purchase of the *Wall Street Journal* during the summer of 2007. A deal was agreed to on July 31, 2007 and closed in mid-December 2007. Negotiations had been complicated by the reticence of the previous owners of Dow Jones (the Bancroft family). They were fearful that Murdoch would use his position to influence the editorial content of the paper. But Murdoch prevailed largely due to the company's weak stock price. Upon taking control of the paper Murdoch almost immediately brought in his own group of executives to run the paper.

10 "Private Capital Management, which is run by the portfolio manager Bruce S. Sherman, is a subsidiary of the brokerage firm Legg Mason. The firm has increased its holdings of newspaper stocks since 2000, a period of considerable uncertainty in the industry . . .

Private Capital Management is also the largest outside shareholder in The New York Times Company and has large positions in Belo, Gannett, Media General, McClatchy, Journal Register and Lee Enterprises. With $32 billion in assets under its direction as of June 30, Private Capital Management was ranked by Nelson Information as the second-best money manager, based on its returns over 10 years" (Siklos, 2005).

References

Altschull, J. H. (1987). *Agents of power.* New York: Longman.

Associated Press. (2004a). Effects of cuts concern journalists. May 24, *Author.*

Associated Press. (2004b). Paper apologizes for civil rights coverage. July 5, *washingtonpost.com.*

Blackford, L. & Minch, L. (2004, July 4). Front-page news, back-page coverage, the struggle for civil rights in Lexington. *Lexington Herald Leader*, p. A 1.

CNNMoney.com. (2006). Wall Street Journal to run front page ads. July 19, *money.cnn.com*

Cooper, G. (1991). *Interview by author* [cassette recording] November, New York.

Epstein, E. J. (1974). *News from nowhere.* New York: Vintage.

Essick, P. (1991). *Interview by author* [cassette recording] August, New York.

Fisher, G. (2004). *Interview by author* [cassette recording] June, Los Angeles.

Fitzgerald, M. (2006). Hollinger: Sun-Times cluster results "disappointing," may cut 10% of workforce. January 19, *nevadathunder.com*

Graham. D. E. (2006). *2005 Washington Post Company Annual Report.* Washington, DC: Washington Post Company.

The Guild Reporter (2001). Byline strike challenges loss of pension package. April 20, *newsguild.org*

Heher, A. M. (2007). Tribune accepts $8.2B offer from Zell. April 2, *Yahoo News.*

Kaufman, M. (1991). *Interview by author* [cassette recording] November, New York.

Knight Foundation. (2006). Newspaper industry needs new owners, says former LA Times editor. April 26, *Knight Foundation News Release.*

Lee, M. A. & Solomon, N. (1990). *Unreliable sources: A guide to detecting bias in the news media.* New York: Lyle Stuart.

Mamet, D. (2002). Making choices: Confronting or avoiding the issue In C. Jacobson (Ed.), *Underexposed: "Pictures can lie and liars use pictures."* London: Vision On Publishing.

McChesney, R. W. (2004). *The problem of the media.* New York: Monthly Review Press.

Meyer, P. (2004). *The vanishing newspaper: Saving journalism in the information age.* Columbia, MO: University of Missouri Press.

Panagopoulos, T. (2004). *Interview by author* [cassette recording] June, Chicago.

Parenti, M. (1986). *Inventing reality: The politics of the mass media.* New York: St. Martin's.

Pitts, L. (2007). Movies mirror our culture, like it or not. *The Miami Herald*, May 14, p. 1B.

Poynteronline. (2003). Journalistic values persist despite profit pressures. April 10, *poynter.org*

Rasmussen, T. (2006). *Telephone interview by author* [digital recording] May, Miami.

Siklos, R. (2005). Shareholder demands that chain be sold. *The New York Times*, November 2, p. C 6.

Tribune Company. (2005). *2004 Tribune Company Annual Report.* Chicago: Author.

Washington Post Company. (1992). *1991 Washington Post Company Annual Report.* Washington, DC: Author.

Wells, H. (2004). *Interview by author* [cassette recording] June, Los Angeles.

writenews.com. (2000). Hollinger International acquires Copley's Chicago newspapers. October 23, *Poynter.org.*

6

Ethics

> *Photojournalists operate as trustees of the public. Our primary role is to report visually on the significant events and on the varied viewpoints in our common world. Our primary goal is the faithful and comprehensive depiction of the subject at hand. As photojournalists, we have the responsibility to document society and to preserve its history through images. (National Press Photographers Association, 2004)*

Many believe that the news media have a credibility problem. Yet, most journalists seem to have a clear idea of their profession and its demands for fairness, honesty, and believability.

> We [photo editors and photographers] all operate within a continuum of documentary, portrait, and illustration photography, and we know what is acceptable in a news photo and what is not acceptable. Manipulation is not acceptable; anything that changes the meaning of a photo is not acceptable. You can change an aesthetic but not the content. I don't think that we need to carry around a code of ethics in our pockets. Most people are familiar with the ethical issues. (Wells, 2004)

Nevertheless, breaches in ethical behavior do occur. To maintain the trust of news consumers, news media generally deal swiftly and decisively with journalists who cross the line. *Chicago Tribune* features picture editor Geoffrey Black says, "Something that is very important in journalism is honor and trust because yes, the *Tribune* is 150 years old and there's a whole lot there, but more important than that, our whole business is based on what people believe" (Black, 2004). Credibility is paramount to the news business.

Some journalists refer to the concept of "objectivity" to demonstrate their unbiased presentation of the news. Many, however, believe that objectivity is not possible and instead contend that the goals of journalism should be fairness, truthfulness, and thoroughness. Despite public criticism of journalism my experience has been that most journalists work hard to get things right and have a profound sense of fairness. This suggests something different from being "objective." Journalists, word and visual, bring their own life experiences and biases to every story that they tell, but their professionalism urges them to gather information from a wide variety of sources and to present that information in the most honest way possible. Black says that a large part of getting it right is each person taking the responsibility to ask questions and to have discussions.

> I think that it's important that you do your little part. I mean, somebody says, "You're a photo editor, how important is that?" Well, those photos have to be accurate. The caption information has to be accurate. The way the information was gathered has to be above board. All of those things have to be taken into consideration when you're putting out the work. And, it's important that you ask questions and that you communicate the whole way through [the process]. It's not about a single-minded, monolithic vision that somebody has. It's about the story and getting the story right.
>
> For example, there was a discussion in a meeting about getting [and reporting] quotes from people. The main idea was, "Do you clean up the quote?" I'll use Daley as an example. Mayor Richard Daley of Chicago will make a statement, and it may not be grammatically correct. The writer might end up writing, "This is what Daley said – quote." This is the quote – what was said – the writer's not going to fix it. Then, depending on the quote, the writer may write, "He (Daley) might have been saying – may have been meaning this." But, you leave what Daley said as is. At least that's the way that we deal with it in our section.

> You have discussions about quotes; you have discussions about everything from "Does this appear to be racist?" "Does this appear to be taking sides?" "Does it appear that we're being gender biased?" "Are we being equitable and fair in how we're portraying the situation?" You don't want to take sides so you have those discussions. (Black, 2004)

News ownership and top editors demand that journalists maintain high ethical standards because they know that the trust of news consumers is critical to the life of the business. *The New York Times* code of ethics states:

> Reporters, editors, photographers, and all members of the news staff of the *New York Times* share a common and essential interest in protecting the integrity of the newspaper. As the news, editorial, and business leadership of the newspaper declared jointly in 1998: "Our greatest strength is the authority and reputation of the *Times*. We must do nothing that would undermine or dilute it and everything possible to enhance it."
>
> At a time of growing and even justified public suspicion about the impartiality, accuracy, and integrity of some journalists and some journalism, it is imperative that the *Times* and its staff maintain the highest possible standards to insure that we do nothing that might erode readers' faith and confidence in our news columns. (*New York Times*, 2003)

While ownership views ethics as a business imperative, most journalists appear to uphold ethical principles from a sense of professionalism. *Miami Herald* director of photography Luis Rios led an effort in which all of the *Herald*'s photographers and photo editors wrote their opinions on why it is important to never change any of the content in a photograph and why it's vital to maintain the integrity of photography. The photo department's opinions were published on the *Herald*'s Op-Ed page (Steber, 2004).

An ethical approach to photojournalism requires the photographer to go beyond ensuring the integrity of the photograph. Photographs need to be put into context. Photographers should be able to get a sense of the situation, the moment, the mood, and then be able to convey that sense to the photo editors. And, photo editors are required to discuss the assignments with the photographers to gather information that will provide context. Ideally the photo editor will have an opportunity to talk with the writer as well. Black says, "You want to get as many different opinions and ideas as possible about a particular photograph before you decide, 'Okay, this is going to be the one'" (Black, 2004).

Most newsrooms today have guidelines that address ethical issues in photojournalism – usually dealing with the digital alteration of photographs and the treatment of subjects. Ethical standards in photojournalism have evolved in part as a response to changing technology but also as a result of the more informed expectations of news consumers. In the early twentieth century photographs began to be "taken for granted as the standard of truth" (Jussim, 1988, p. 53), yet news publications spent little or no time tackling ethical questions about the use or abuse of photographs. Photo historian Michael Carlebach says:

> Photographs printed in newspapers and magazines [in the early twentieth century] were often altered in order to make them more palatable to the public or to enhance their effect. Graphic artists added filigrees and bold-type, pictures were cropped, gerrymandered, and stuffed into dense pictorial layouts. However accurate the original image, what actually appeared on the printed page sometimes bore only the most tenuous connection to fact. (Carlebach, 1997, p. 32)

Photographers also began faking photographs more than a century ago so that newspapers and magazines could publish images that "confirmed" the (many times sensational) stories. For example,

> Photographers desperate to describe the war [World War I] but restricted to secure areas far behind the lines did bend the truth; most of them felt they had no choice. Their editors back home demanded photographs, and so they did what they could, using diplomacy and military connections to construct realistic and believable situations. (Carlebach, 1997, p. 92)

Today news photographers are fired for faking photographs, but the practice still exists. Photojournalists face constant pressure to make aesthetically outstanding photographs that contain the content demanded by their editors. Many times editors see images from events on television and want to know why the photographers from their publications don't have the images. Yet, "in an era of dubious 're-enactments on network newscasts'" (Lacayo, 1995, p. 169), still photographers may not be able to "document" the event in the same way (or perhaps not at all) as the television reportage. In addition, photographers rarely have sufficient time to find and make a strong photograph or group of photographs.

On one occasion while editing a photographer's assignment for the "Vida y Estilo" ("Life & Style") section at *El Universo*, it became obvious to me that the photographer had "staged" the photographs. I confronted the photographer, and he told me that he had only 10 minutes to make two photographs (one portrait and one "real" photograph) to go with a story about an artist. We had a frank conversation about setting up photographs; I destroyed the faked negatives and told the section editor that he would have to either use the portrait by itself or push back the publication date for that story. The section editor initially protested but eventually found a substitute story for that week and submitted a new request for a photograph of the artist.

Photo director Tim Rasmussen talks about the pressures to set up work during his early years as a magazine photographer.

> I was quite disheartened by the whole magazine gig. The ethics were so different from what I had been taught and what I believed in strongly. Everybody I worked for in New York, bar none, at one point or another hinted or directly told me that if I didn't come back with the photographs that I needed to set them up to bring them back, that it wasn't acceptable to take an assignment and to not deliver. That's an enormous amount of pressure on a young photographer . . .
>
> I think that the guys out doing news are pure. It's when you get an assignment – I mean I would get an assignment to go to Lowell, Massachusetts for a week to cover immigration. There's no way that I was going to pull off a story in that time frame. I had no

> contacts, no subjects – I had nothing. I had a draft of a story written by a reporter and then I'm trying to make real pictures out of it – that was really difficult. I'm not saying that magazine photographers don't hold ethics to be high, but I think that they're under enormous pressure to deliver the pictures and some of them have no problem with this [setting up photographs]. (Rasmussen, 2006)

In 1994 veteran *Los Angeles Times* photographer Mike Meadows was fired for staging a photograph that was disseminated nationwide.[1] Meadows' photograph of a firefighter splashing himself with water from the swimming pool of a burning house was being nominated for the Pulitzer Prize when the firefighter in the photo told the *Times* that he had been directed by Meadows. Fellow *Times* photographer Luis Sinco says:

> Mike Meadows was a nice guy. He had an abrasive personality, but we got along fine. I was very disappointed that he would do something like that because that's all the guy did. He was like a big newshound. He would get all the spot news that he would see or he would hear about on the scanner. I think that's how he got hired on staff . . . because he was this big newshound. So, I don't know what his thinking was when he had been doing it for so many years. (Sinco, 2004)

Newspapers frequently make distinctions between their news and feature sections regarding the way in which photographs may be used ethically. Photo editor Hal Wells says that at the *Los Angeles Times* they never use photo illustrations or cutouts in the "A" or "California" sections, but that those techniques are used in the features sections. "By keeping high visual standards that reflect truth and honesty in a news section, I think readers begin to understand, 'Oh this is the "A" section, I'm not going to see any hanky panky here'" (Wells, 2004).

Many readers, however, are skeptical of photographs today because they know the power of computerized software tools such as Photoshop that can digitally alter images while leaving few traces of the changes. Photo retouching has existed since the beginnings of photography but may be more dangerous now because of the almost seamless nature of digital manipulation.

> Conventional forms of retouching [pencil, airbrush, whiteout, spot tone] were always detectable by experts; they were often detectable by anyone. The computerized reworkings are different. It is virtually impossible to tell whether such pictures have been altered, leaving open the possibility that photographs will be able to lie in ways unimaginable in the past. (Lacayo, 1995, p. 168)

Los Angeles Times photo editor Kirk McKoy explains:

> I think Photoshop has created a virtual nightmare for editors. They are afraid people are altering images to get a better picture or they're darkening, really darkening down the edges of the frame to emphasize the subject. I think we started that back in the old darkroom by creating the "Hand of God" [a phrase used among photojournalists for burning or darkening all areas of the frame that are to be deemphasized. In this case the darkening is extreme and creates an artificial-looking image], which was allowed, but now all of a sudden we're slapped on the hand [or worse] for using it.
>
> At an earlier time in photojournalism [before Photoshop], newspapers would have retouchers who would just come in and literally manipulate the whole photograph. All of that leads to mistrust as to what photography is.
>
> One of the biggest examples is after 9/11 happened, a photograph that ran on a website with a guy standing on the observation platform with the plane coming at him in the background. It was passed around saying, "This is a camera that was found, and someone processed the film, and there is the plane coming into the building." But, then everyone realized that the guy is wearing a heavy overcoat in the summer with a big wool-knit cap, and the light on the guy is coming from this way and the light on the plane is coming from another way." (McKoy, 2004)

McKoy explains another example when a freelance photographer that he hired used the "Clone" tool ("Clone" is a tool in Photoshop that allows one to copy one part of a photograph and paste that into another part of the same or a different photograph) to digitally put a cigarette into the hand of the subject. McCoy noticed that the cigarette appeared more than once along the edge of the frame. He subsequently telephoned the photographer and asked him for the raw (original) file. The photographer admitted to "cloning" the cigarette into the image and began to give his reason for doing so, but McCoy told him to just send in the raw file because the digital addition of an element into the photograph violated the *Times* ethical policy. "The most important thing is that we go through a painstaking process to show our readers the truth, and we try not to bend the rules. I guess we fire people who break rules, and we're very serious about that" (McKoy, 2004).

Los Angeles Times photographer Brian Walski was fired in 2003 for "breaking the rules" while photographing the war in Iraq. Walski, a long-time photographer who had worked for the *Times* since 1998, digitally created one photograph by combining parts of two others. Unfortunately for Walski his photograph was shared by the *Times* with other Tribune Company papers. The *Hartford Courant* published Walski's photograph on its front page. Thom McGuire, the *Courant*'s assistant managing editor for photography and graphics, was responsible for the decision to use Walski's photo. "'It was a great image,' McGuire says, 'and I missed the manipulation, and I feel bad for everyone involved.' Others did not miss it. A *Courant* employee was looking through images for a friend and noticed what appeared to be duplication in the picture" (Irby, 2003a).

After McGuire was informed of the transgression he contacted Colin Crawford, the *Los Angeles Times*' assistant managing editor for photography. *Los Angeles Times* editor of the paper John Carroll says, "Colin got that call in the nighttime, I think Tuesday, and didn't tell me about it until Wednesday morning. And I looked at it – honest to God it took me a while to see it" (Carroll, 2004). Later that day Crawford was able to speak to Walski who admitted to the wrongdoing. Carroll continues:

> I talked about it with Colin. I talked about it with Dean [Baquet], the managing editor, maybe others and decided that he had to be

fired. There was just no way around it. And I decided that we might as well do it now, rather than later. I've never fired anybody without having him in the office, so Colin told him to come back and told him that he was off the staff.

The next day inside the paper we published the three images, the combined [image], then the two images from which it was made, with an explanation of what happened. And on page one, we published an editor's note saying basically what had happened. We had to protect the reputation of the paper, that's why we fired him so quickly. You know, the minute it was discovered we made a statement that this is just totally unacceptable to us, and we're not going to do this to our readers, and we're going to be very open about it. Brian came back and to his credit, he came in and talked to me, looked me in the eye and said, "I did it. I'm very, very sorry. It was the mistake of a lifetime. I know I'll probably never work in a newspaper again," and I was impressed that he acknowledged what he had done, that he had done the wrong thing, so I wished him well.

We got some public feedback; it wasn't an outcry. You know, we are under scrutiny by people on the Internet and talk shows all the time, and they'll always try to read something into it, like we're slanting the news, but I think to anyone who looked at what happened, it was quite clear what happened. This was just a photographer frustrated at not being able to get the image he wanted and creating it on the computer screen.

Everybody here knew that this wasn't a matter of Brian not knowing that what he did was wrong. But, the main educational thing that we did was to fire him. Everybody knows that. And, you do this as a message to your staff that this is unacceptable. You do it as a message to your readers that this doesn't meet our standards. (Carroll, 2004)

Los Angeles Times photographer Luis Sinco says:

[Walski] was getting all the great assignments; he was single; he was a good photographer; he was very technologically savvy. Why would somebody do that? Now, you're not working here anymore, and you're not doing these great assignments. If you look at Walski's stuff – the next day we ran this correction with a panel of the three frames, and I thought any one of the frames really would have done well. (Sinco, 2004)

And Walski in an apology to the *Los Angeles Times* photography staff writes:

> This was after an extremely long, hot, and stressful day but I offer no excuses here. I deeply regret that I have tarnished the reputation of the *Los Angeles Times*, a newspaper with the highest standards of journalism, the Tribune Company, all the people at the *Times* and especially the very talented and extremely dedicated photographers and picture editors and friends that have made my four and a half years at the *Times* a true quality experience.
>
> I have always maintained the highest ethical standards throughout my career and cannot truly explain my complete breakdown in judgment at this time. That will only come in the many sleepless nights that are ahead. (Irby, 2003b)

Miami's Spanish-language newspaper *El Nuevo Herald* provided another example of unethical digital manipulation when on June 25, 2006 two photographs were digitally combined to form one. Although Walski's motivation for manipulation was to aesthetically improve the image, *El Nuevo Herald*'s treatment of the photographs was politically inspired. The photograph of four prostitutes propositioning a foreign tourist while policemen, a woman and a little girl stand next to them ran five columns in the "A" section of the paper. The headline read, "Jineteras: la triste carne del dólar" ("Prostitutes: the sad meat of the dollar"). In this case the photographer was not responsible for the offense and in fact urged editors to refrain from using the manipulated images.

> It [the published image] pushed an anti-Castro agenda in a newspaper advertised by its new owners, McClatchy and Co., as the "most-honored, highest-circulation Spanish-language newspaper in the continental United States."
>
> And, perhaps worse, higher-ups at *El Nuevo* overrode the objections of veteran photographer Roberto Koltun, who snapped both pictures several years ago in Cuba (and didn't return a call seeking

> comment). "Two things were put together," commented photo coordinator Orlando Mellado. "[Koltun] expressed concern about it for that reason and others. He basically didn't want it used."
>
> So why did the newspaper print it?
>
> "That's a decision that was made by another editor," Mellado responded before referring me to Luis Garcia, an *El Nuevo* artist.
>
> "I remember putting together something for that section," Garcia said when I phoned him. "I'll go get it and call you back." He never called. Three follow-up messages weren't returned. Nor were two messages left with Andrés Reynaldo, who edits the section in which the photo appeared, Séptimo Día (Seventh Day).
>
> I also left multiple messages with Humberto Castelló, the paper's executive editor; and Gloria Leal, the associate editor. They weren't returned either.
>
> "You expect this kind of thing from a Communist newspaper," commented one local photographer. "But from a legitimate news organization, this is unacceptable." (Strouse, 2006)

El Nuevo Herald's explanation appearing on page 6A on July 27, 2006 declared that a mistake had been made by not identifying the digitally composed photograph as a "fotomontaje" (photo illustration), thus leaving readers with the impression that the photograph was a real photograph (Shoer Roth, 2006).

Rules regarding other forms of digital manipulation such as "dodging" (making selected areas of the image lighter) and "burning" (making selected areas of the image darker) are a little less explicit than those governing the use of the "clone" tool. Even the rules that pertain to the digital correction of color are not precise. The Associated Press, for example, writes:

> Only the established norms of standard photo printing methods such as burning, dodging, toning and cropping are acceptable. Retouching is limited to removal of normal scratches and dust spots.
>
> Serious consideration must always be given in correcting color to ensure honest reproduction of the original. Cases of abnormal color or tonality will be clearly stated in the caption. Color adjustment should always be minimal. (Associate Press, 2003)

Charlotte Observer photographer Patrick Schneider was suspended in 2003 for over-burning award-winning photographs of firefighters. Schneider offered to present his work as an educational tool in ethics at various conferences and seminars. Poynter Institute's Kenny Irby says,

> During the presentation [at NPPA's 14th Annual Women in Photojournalism Conference], Schneider shared his Photoshop technique, using the dodge and burn tool and the cropping tools, exclusively. These were not sophisticated techniques, just very basic adjustments that led to the removal of secondary background information that may have helped – or been central to – the viewers' understanding of content and context. And that is where I draw the line.
>
> As an industry, now is the time to accept the power of accuracy. There is little amnesty for those who break the sacred trust of credibility. (Irby, 2003b)

After the 2003 incident Schneider declared, "'I will no longer tone my background down that far'" (Visual Editors, 2006). But, in 2006 Schneider was fired from the *Observer* for digitally changing the colors of another firefighter photograph. In a letter to the readership *Charlotte Observer* editor Rick Thames writes:

> Accuracy is among our most sacred journalistic values. That goes for the photographs, as well as the words, that we publish.
>
> So, it is with much regret that I inform you that the color in a photograph in Thursday's editions was inappropriately altered before it was published.
>
> The photo, taken by *Observer* photographer Patrick Schneider, appeared on the front of the Local & State section. It depicted a Charlotte firefighter on a ladder, silhouetted by the light of the early morning sun.
>
> In the original photo, the sky in the photo was brownish-gray. Enhanced with photo-editing software, the sky became a deep red and the sun took on a more distinct halo.
>
> The *Observer*'s photo policy states: "No colors will be altered from the original scene photographed."

> Schneider said he did not intend to mislead readers, only to restore the actual color of the sky. He said the color was lost when he under exposed the photo to offset the glare of the sun . . .
>
> We apologize for this misstep. Your trust is important to us. We will do all we can to ensure the integrity of all of our photos going forward. (Thames, 2006)

While the digital technique of combining two photographs into one clearly violates the ethical mandates of photojournalism, the digital alteration of the colors is somewhat more subjective. The *Observer*'s photo policy says, "No colors will be altered from the *original scene* photographed" (my italics). Schneider says, that he wanted to "restore the *actual color* of the sky" (my italics). It's hard to imagine how Schneider could recall the exact or "actual" color of the sky after he finished the assignment. At the same time, colors are "altered" from the original scene by the reproduction capabilities and settings in the camera. The colors in Schneider's original file may well have differed from those that his eyes "saw" while taking the photograph.

Photographers and photographs can deceive readers in ways other than through digital manipulation. As was presented in Chapter 3, journalists begin with a concept and then find symbols to represent the concept. Photographers are frequently sent on assignments to create images that will symbolize concepts suggested by writers and editors. This can lead to confusion or even dishonesty.

For example, a February 16, 1992 *USA Today* front-page story about Los Angeles gangs was illustrated with a photograph of gang members brandishing guns. The story was about the potential for violence in Los Angeles if the four police officers accused in the Rodney King case were acquitted on federal charges. The subjects in the photograph were led to believe that the photograph would illustrate a story about a planned program in which gang members would exchange guns for jobs. In the aftermath *USA Today* acknowledged the deception, but this example illustrates the way in which photographic symbols can be misapplied to concepts.

I recall a photograph that we published while I was director of photography for Copley Chicago Newspapers. The story was about the presence of casual betting in everyday life – how people bet on everything from sporting events, to how much a newborn will weigh, to who will receive a higher grade. The section editor, design editor, and I discussed the possibilities for a photograph to go with the story, and it was decided the photographer would go to the local golf course and photograph golfers from behind and from afar so that their faces would not be visible. The photographer took the photograph as we had envisioned it, and the next day it was published along with the story.

Later that day I received a telephone call from one of the golfers in the photograph. Friends and family members had been able to recognize him and his fellow golfers in the photograph because of the clothing, body language, etc. He was rightfully outraged that he had been associated with the "Betting" story through his presence in the photograph. I apologized, and we prominently published an apology in the next day's newspaper. I had failed to consider all of the possibilities and consequences of making a photograph of random people to symbolize a particular concept.

In a similar way photographs are sometimes selected to reinforce the words in the headline. This practice can also be problematic. *Los Angeles Times* deputy design director Michael Whitley says:

> Our desire is to always reflect the matter of the situation and not automatically marry the picture exactly with what the words are going to say. For example, if we have a picture of a moment when someone made an angry face, and then we say, "That person messed something up," then we've chosen to put those two together. We may be marrying the photograph and the words, but we may not be reflecting the reality of the situation, and that really concerns me.
>
> In fact, this week our Lakers lost to the Pistons, and we published a photograph – a very nice photograph, but I think it was inaccurate. It was a picture of Kobe wiping sweat off his face with his jersey (see Photo 11). He lifted his jersey up to wipe the sweat

Photo 11. End of an Era? Kobe Bryant, who scored 21 points on seven-of-21 shooting during the Pistons' win, might have played his final game as a Laker after eight seasons, which included three championships. Photograph by Wally Skalij. Copyright, 2004, *Los Angeles Times*. Reprinted with permission.

off his face, and the photographer caught him at the moment that his shirt was pulled all the way over his face, and the photograph looks like he is hiding his face in shame.[2] Well, that isn't what happened at all, but we published this photograph at six columns and that's sort of what it implies. There was a headline that said, "Rout of Order." It was a huge headline with Kobe sort of hiding his face underneath.

I think it was sort of a little shell game with readers. I think that we didn't really give them a very honest reality of the situation. We probably had lesser photographs – less visually appealing – but that had genuine emotions. The picture that we published is aesthetically more pleasing, but he is wiping sweat off his face, he's not hiding his face. It's the middle of the game. Those sorts of things I think can hurt your photographic credibility. You don't

> always have to look for an image that literally matches the words. The best thing to do is sort of take a step back and say, "How do we reflect the reality of this situation, and is this particular photograph doing it," because that's why you're using the photograph – to give readers some sense of what it was like to be there. (Whitley, 2004)

Newspapers sometimes resort to using archive photographs to accompany a story. This practice has its dangers as *Chicago Tribune* picture editor Geoffrey Black explains:

> We did a story on the "Hall of Fame Highway." We called it the hall of fame highway because there are many halls of fame that are clustered around this one particular highway. There was a photo that ran of the [Pro Football] Hall of Fame in Canton, Ohio that was taken by a photographer of ours in 1999. The problem with that photo was that they had updated the interior of the Hall of Fame.
>
> The photo was taken in 1999 – five years ago, and it's changed now. So I ended up writing an explanation on it and that we regret that there was an error because it was a file photo. We didn't indicate that it was a file photo and that was the thing – we should have. (Black, 2004)

One of the most difficult ethical dilemmas for editors is the decision to publish a photograph that contains the graphic consequences of violence. The problem is two-fold. Friends and relatives of the victim(s) are likely to see the photograph – in a sense they are forced to relive the tragedy. Many times editors will take into consideration whether or not the victim is a local resident thinking that the families of non-local residents are less likely to view the photograph. At Copley Chicago Newspapers I was one of a group of editors that made the decision to publish a photograph of an automobile accident in which three people were killed. A shoulder and arm of one of the victims was visible in the photograph, and there was a lengthy discussion as to whether readers really needed to see the explicit details. In favor of publishing the photograph was the fact that the accident took place in a dangerous intersection – the scene of several other accidents – and the occupants of the car were from out of town. Although I was one of the editors in favor of using the photograph, I still use that front page as part of an ethics discussion, and I'm not convinced that we did the right thing.

On April 16, 2007 a Virginia Tech student killed 32 people on the Virginia Tech University campus. He then committed suicide. The *Virginian-Pilot* published a powerful photograph of a wounded survivor being carried from a building (see Photo 12). The photograph ran six columns across the top of the *Virginian-Pilot*'s front page and contained tough details of the victim's condition and a feature that to some looked like the man's penis. Many of the *Virginian-Pilot*'s readers reacted strongly to the photograph and to the paper's decision to publish it on the front page. On April 17 *Virginian-Pilot* editor, Denis Finley, used the paper's blog to describe to readers and employees the decision-making process. He explains:

> The complaints revolve around two things:
>
> 1 The choice of the photo for the front page, that it was too graphic and disrespectful.
> 2 That the photo showed the man's penis.
>
> First I'll address question two. The shooting victim's penis was not visible in the photo. The photo was taken by Alan Kim of our sister newspaper in Roanoke. Alan and Dan Beatty, Roanoke's director of photography, have looked through other images that were shot in sequence around that image, and it's clear to them that it's a piece of clothing or part of a tourniquet. They, too, have gotten calls because they used the picture as well.
>
> Now question one. This was a tough call. We had a lot of discussion about using this photo at our 6:15 p.m. front-page meeting. We have very strict standards when it comes to publishing a graphic photo such as this. We asked a lot of questions.
>
> Was the person dead? No, according to Alan Kim, who said that police were carrying out survivors and leaving the dead behind. Did he die later? We did not know that [the victim in the photograph was Kevin Sterne, a Virginia Tech senior who survived]. Was

The Virginian-Pilot TUESDAY, APRIL 17, 2007 · 142ND YEAR · NO. 148 · 50 CENTS

MASSACRE

SHOOTER KILLS 32 AT VA. TECH IN NATION'S WORST RAMPAGE

ALAN KIM/THE ROANOKE TIMES

THE HORROR UNFOLDS An unidentified person is carried out of Norris Hall at Virginia Tech in Blacksburg on Monday. A gunman killed 32 people on the campus before fatally shooting himself.

On campus: Mayhem, panic, frantic calls

Question of security Students, parents and the media raise questions about how the campus police handled events after the initial report of a shooting. **Page A12**

Reaching out Students turn to the Web to share information quickly with each other and their parents. **Page A12**

Local reaction Old Dominion students had one question on their minds: Are my friends and family OK? **Page A14**

Commentary

We all share in the grief The deadly rampage on Va. Tech's campus binds Virginians. **Editorial, Page B14**

Security is a concern Columnist Kerry Dougherty says security moved up on the checklist in her daughter's college search. **Page A14**

More online

Follow the story Get updates, see video and more photographs or join a discussion at **pilotonline.com.**

"As the death toll kept going up, you could hear the silence coming over Blacksburg." – MALISSA BRADSHAW

HOKIE NATION STUNNED BY CARNAGE ON CAMPUS

BY MATTHEW BOWERS
THE VIRGINIAN-PILOT

Geology test completed, Chris Sherman was walking across the Drillfield at Virginia Tech on Monday morning when he heard two bangs.

The freshman from Virginia Beach looked up to see his roommate "running at me, yelling, 'They're shots! They're shots! They're telling people to get down!' "

Sirens wailed. Police cars flew across the campus.

The pair hustled back to their dorm room, slid a dresser and television in front of their door and watched the school's nightmare unfold on the news.

Monday's shooting deaths of 33 people – including the gunman – on the rural Blacksburg campus of more than 25,000 struck hard in South Hampton Roads, home to about 1,200 of its students and more than 6,000 alumni.

Phone lines jammed and e-mails flew as students and their frantic

Please see **Shock,** *Page* **A13**

STEVE HELBER/THE ASSOCIATED PRESS

ON 'TRAGIC DAY,' 30 ALSO HURT BEFORE GUNMAN KILLS HIMSELF

Two hours between shootings raises questions on security

FROM STAFF AND WIRE REPORTS

BLACKSBURG — A gunman massacred 32 people at Virginia Tech in the deadliest shooting rampage in U.S. history Monday, cutting down his victims in two attacks more than two hours apart before the university could grasp what was happening and warn students. The bloodbath ended with the gunman committing suicide, bringing the death toll to 33.

The shooter, whose name was not released Monday night, carried two 9 mm semiautomatic handguns and wore blue jeans, a blue jacket and a vest that carried additional ammunition, law enforcement officials and witnesses said. Witnesses described him as a young man of Asian descent – a silent killer who was calm and showed no expression as he pursued and shot his victims.

He left two dead at a dormitory and 30 more at a science and engineering building, where he executed people taking and teaching classes and even shot at a custodian who was helping a victim. Witnesses described scenes of chaos and grief, with students jumping from windows to escape gunfire and others blocking their classroom doors to keep the gunman away.

Continued on Page A15

Photo 12. *The Virginian-Pilot*, April 17, 2007. Reprinted with permission of *The Virginian-Pilot*.

> he local? We didn't know that because no names were released yesterday. We are VERY sensitive to publishing photos such as this, especially if we think the family lives here. We knew we risked the fact that the man was local and could have died after the photo was taken. Was he recognizable? No. That usually helps when we consider publishing a photo like this.
>
> After discussing the photo and looking at the other choices, we decided to publish this photo because it so perfectly captured the horror of the event that unfolded just hours away from us. We thought we would be irresponsible to try to sanitize this story. It is the second worst mass shooting in the history of the world, not the U.S., the world. To be squeamish at a time like this would not serve our readers. Did we outrage and disgust some readers and some of you? I am sure we did. But we felt like it was our obligation to capture the outrage and horror of this event.
>
> These decisions are never easy. But there are times when the circumstances trump any urge we have to protect our readers from the brutal realities of life, and we are compelled to publish such realities. To do anything less would be to shirk our responsibility to tell the truth.
>
> Thanks for listening. We would be happy to field any comments.
>
> Denis Finley, Editor, the *Virginian-Pilot.* (Finley, 2007)

Finley's letter received a mostly positive response from readers on the blog. They seemed to appreciate being "let in" on the decision-making process and to know that the decision was made after substantial discussion and thought.

Photo ethics expert Bob Steele says, "While writing to readers to explain past decisions is a legitimate approach, editors might consider being more proactive in explaining their decision-making process. When possible they can explain their reasoning in a column or sidebar at the same time the story and/or photo runs so that readers would have the context of the decision in relation to the product itself" (Steele, 2004). He offers another photograph published by the *Virginian-Pilot* as an example, "When the *Virginian-Pilot* ran a picture of the body of an American soldier being dragged through the streets of Mogadishu, Somalia,

Managing Editor Cole Campbell wrote a same-day explanation to the readers about the paper's decision" (Steele, 2004).

Not all ethical issues are black-and-white or defined explicitly in a code of ethics. Some need discussion among a broad and diverse group of people. This is one of the reasons that newsroom diversity is vital, and why an open line of communication with the community is also important. When there are difficult ethical decisions to be made almost certainly some individual or group will be unhappy with the results. What is important is that there is a process in place by which the issues can be discussed fully and openly so that a fair and conscientious decision is made.

> [The process must reflect] attention to journalistic principles, a genuine concern for ethical issues, a recognition of the consequences of the decision on various stakeholders, and a willingness to explore alternative approaches to maximize truth-telling and to minimize harm to vulnerable individuals.
>
> News organizations that value ethical decision-making hone their skills at this process in the same way that they develop their skills in reporting, writing, and editing. A newsroom that is practiced in this skill of ethical decision-making is much more able to resolve dilemmas quickly and effectively even on deadline. (Steele, 2004)

Appendix

From the *New York Times* Code of Ethics

Images in our pages that purport to depict reality must be genuine in every way. No people or objects may be added, rearranged, reversed, distorted or removed from a scene (except for the recognized practice of cropping to omit extraneous outer portions). Adjustments of color or gray scale should be limited to those minimally necessary for clear and accurate reproduction, analogous to the "burning" and "dodging" that formerly took place in darkroom processing of images. Pictures of news situations must not be posed. In the cases of collages, montages, portraits, fashion or home design illustrations, fanciful contrived situations and demonstrations of how a device is used, our intervention should be unmistakable to the reader, and unmistakably free of intent to deceive. Captions and credits should further acknowledge our intervention if the slightest doubt is possible. The design director, a masthead editor or the news desk should be consulted on doubtful cases or proposals for exceptions (*New York Times*, 2003).

Associated Press Statement of Policy

The following statement of our policy on electronic handling of photos was issued in 1990, the infancy of high-speed photo transmission and digital picture handling. It is as valid today as it was then.

Electronic imaging raised new questions abut what is ethical in the process of editing photographs. The question may have been new, but the answers all come from old values.

Simply put, the Associated Press does not alter photographs. Our pictures must always tell the truth.

The computer has become a highly sophisticated photo-editing tool. It has taken us out of a chemical darkroom where subtle printing techniques, such as burning and dodging, have long been accepted as journalistically sound. Today these terms are replaced by "image manipulation" and "enhancement." In a time when such broad terms could be misconstrued, we need to set limits and restate some basic tenets.

The content of a photograph will NEVER be changed or manipulated in any way.

Only the established norms of standard photo printing methods such as burning, dodging, toning and cropping are acceptable. Retouching is limited to removal of normal scratches and dust spots.

Serious consideration must always be given in correcting color to ensure honest reproduction of the original. Cases of abnormal color or tonality will be clearly stated in the caption. Color adjustment should always be minimal.

In any instance where a question arises about such issues, consult a senior editor immediately.

The integrity of the AP's photo report is our highest priority. Nothing takes precedence over its credibility. (Associated Press, 2003)

National Press Photographers Association Code of Ethics

Preamble

The National Press Photographers Association, a professional society that promotes the highest standards in photojournalism, acknowledges concern for every person's need both to be fully informed about public events and to be recognized as part of the world in which we live.

Photojournalists operate as trustees of the public. Our primary role is to report visually on the significant events and on the varied viewpoints in our common world. Our primary goal is the faithful and comprehensive depiction of the subject at hand. As photojournalists, we have the responsibility to document society and to preserve its history through images.

Photographic and video images can reveal great truths, expose wrongdoing and neglect, inspire hope and understanding and connect people around the globe through the language of visual understanding. Photographs can also cause great harm if they are callously intrusive or are manipulated.

This code is intended to promote the highest quality in all forms of photojournalism and to strengthen public confidence in the profession. It is also meant to serve as an educational tool both for those who practice and for those who appreciate photojournalism. To that end, The National Press Photographers Association sets forth the following Code of Ethics.

Code of Ethics

Photojournalists and those who manage visual news productions are accountable for upholding the following standards in their daily work:

- Be accurate and comprehensive in the representation of subjects.
- Resist being manipulated by staged photo opportunities.
- Be complete and provide context when photographing or recording subjects. Avoid stereotyping individuals and groups. Recognize and work to avoid presenting one's own biases in the work.
- Treat all subjects with respect and dignity. Give special consideration to vulnerable subjects and compassion to victims of crime or tragedy. Intrude on private moments of grief only when the public has an overriding and justifiable need to see.
- While photographing subjects do not intentionally contribute to, alter, or seek to alter or influence events.
- Editing should maintain the integrity of the photographic images' content and context.
- Do not manipulate images or add or alter sound in any way that can mislead viewers or misrepresent subjects.
- Do not pay sources or subjects or reward them materially for information or participation.
- Do not accept gifts, favors, or compensation from those who might seek to influence coverage.
- Do not intentionally sabotage the efforts of other journalists.

Ideally, photojournalists should:

- Strive to ensure that the public's business is conducted in public. Defend the rights of access for all journalists.
- Think proactively, as a student of psychology, sociology, politics and art to develop a unique vision and presentation. Work with a voracious appetite for current events and contemporary visual media.
- Strive for total and unrestricted access to subjects, recommend alternatives to shallow or rushed opportunities, seek a diversity of viewpoints, and work to show unpopular or unnoticed points of view.
- Avoid political, civic and business involvements or other employment that compromise or give the appearance of compromising one's own journalistic independence.

- Strive to be unobtrusive and humble in dealing with subjects.
- Respect the integrity of the photographic moment.

Strive by example and influence to maintain the spirit and high standards expressed in this code. When confronted with situations in which the proper action is not clear, seek the counsel of those who exhibit the highest standards of the profession. Photojournalists should continuously study their craft and the ethics that guide it. (National Press Photographers Association, 2004)

"Guiding Principles for the Journalist" by Bob Steele

SEEK TRUTH AND REPORT IT AS FULLY AS POSSIBLE

- Inform yourself continuously so you in turn can inform, engage, and educate the public in a clear and compelling way on significant issues.
- Be honest, fair, and courageous in gathering, reporting, and interpreting accurate information.
- Give voice to the voiceless.
- Hold the powerful accountable.

ACT INDEPENDENTLY

- Guard vigorously the essential stewardship role a free press plays in an open society.
- Seek out and disseminate competing perspectives without being unduly influenced by those who would use their power or position counter to the public interest.
- Remain free of associations and activities that may compromise your integrity or damage your credibility.
- Recognize that good ethical decisions require individual responsibility enriched by collaborative efforts.

MINIMIZE HARM

- Be compassionate for those affected by your actions.
- Treat sources, subjects, and colleagues as human beings deserving of respect, not merely as means to your journalistic ends.
- Recognize that gathering and reporting information may cause harm or discomfort, but balance those negatives by choosing alternatives that maximize your goal of truth-telling.

ASK GOOD QUESTIONS TO MAKE GOOD ETHICAL DECISIONS

- What do I know? What do I need to know?
- What is my journalistic purpose?
- What are my ethical concerns?
- What organizational policies and professional guidelines should I consider?
- How can I include other people, with different perspectives and diverse ideas, in the decision-making process?
- Who are the stakeholders-those affected by my decision? What are their motivations? Which are legitimate?
- What if the roles were reversed? How would I feel if I were in the shoes of one of the stakeholders?
- What are the possible consequences of my actions? Short term? Long term?
- What are my alternatives to maximize my truthtelling responsibility and minimize harm?
- Can I clearly and fully justify my thinking and my decision? To my colleagues? To the stakeholders? To the public? (Steele, 2004)

The Society for News Design's Code of Ethical Standards

(Adopted Aug. 30, 2006)

Preamble

As members of the Society for News Design, we have an obligation to promote the highest ethical standards for visual journalism – for all journalism – as they apply to the values of accuracy, fairness, honesty, inclusiveness, and courage.

Accuracy

Accuracy is the indispensable value in journalism and must not be compromised. We must deliver error-free content, across all our media platforms. We must ensure that our content is a verifiable representation of the news and of our subjects. We promise never intentionally to mislead those who depend upon us for public service. We will correct errors promptly and prominently. We must be as accurate with our colleagues as we are with our audiences.

Honesty

We value original thought and expression. Our work will be free from fraud and deception – that includes plagiarism and fabrication. We will attribute content and honor copyrights. We will strive to keep news content free of special interests, inside or outside the news organization. We embrace the value of transparency, disclosing the thinking behind key decisions – from a credit line up to an editor's note on the front page.

Fairness

We must be scrupulously fair. We recognize that our work can have great impact on the subjects we cover and therefore we must respectfully balance that against the public's need to know. Even when it is impossible to avoid harm in the pursuit of truth telling, we will work hard to minimize that harm. We will listen to our critics. Our judgment in these matters must be based on our sense of right and wrong in a manner consistent with our professional values.

Inclusiveness

We will remain vigilant in our quest to combat prejudice and lead needed reforms. We will avoid stereotypes in reporting, editing, presentation, and hiring. Diversity, broadly defined, will be a hallmark of our work.

We accept the responsibility to understand our communities and to overcome bias with coverage that is representative of the constituent groups in the community. Over time, many groups, lifestyles, and backgrounds should see themselves and their values represented in the news.

Courage

Journalists need moral and, at times, physical courage to fulfill their responsibility to serve the public. It takes courage to stand behind values such as accuracy, honesty, fairness and inclusiveness. Such courage is necessary to achieve personal integrity and build credibility. This includes the courage to step beyond rigid boundaries. We must test conventional thinking and explore innovative story-telling to help changing audiences understand an increasingly complex world.

Logic and literalness, objectivity and traditional thinking have their important place, but so must imagination and intuition, responsible creativity and empathy.

Notes

1 "Only starting with the Vietnam War is it virtually certain that none of the best-known photographs were set-ups. And this is essential to the moral authority of these images. . . . Technically, the possibilities for doctoring or electronically manipulating pictures are greater than ever – almost unlimited. But the practice of inventing dramatic news pictures, staging them for the camera, seems on its way to becoming a lost art" (Sontag, 2003, pp. 57, 58).

2 Photographer Wally Skalij's caption read, "Lakers Kobe Bryant wipes his sweat against the Pistons in Game 5 of the NBA Finals at the Palace in Auburn Hills Tuesday." The published caption read, "END OF AN ERA? Kobe Bryant, who scored 21 points on seven-

of-21 shooting during the Pistons' win, might have played his final game as a Laker after eight seasons, which included three championships."

References

Associated Press. (2003). Associated Press: Letter on photo editing policy. September 25, *poynter.org*

Black, G. (2004). *Interview by author* [cassette recording] June, Chicago.

Carlebach, M. L. (1997). *American photojournalism comes of age.* Washington, DC: Smithsonian Institution Press.

Carroll, J. (2004). *Interview by author* [cassette recording] June, Los Angeles.

Finley, D. (2007). About the Tech "massacre" on the front page. April 17, *hamptonroads.com*

Irby, K. (2003a). *L.A. Times* photographer fired over altered image. April 2, *poynter.org*

Irby, K. (2003b). Suspended photographer focuses on ethics. September 25, *poynter.org*

Jussim, E. (1988). "The tyranny of the pictorial": American photojournalism from 1880 to 1920. In M. Fulton (Ed.), *Eyes of time: Photojournalism in America* (pp. 36–73). New York: Little, Brown and Company.

Lacayo, R. (1995). Resurgence: 1980–1995. In R. Lacayo & G. Russell (Eds.), *Eyewitness* (pp. 165–189). New York: Time Books.

McKoy, K. (2004). *Interview by author* [cassette recording] June, Los Angeles.

National Press Photographers Association (2004). NPPA board adopts new "modernized" code of ethics. July 10, *nppa.org*

New York Times (2003). New York Times: Guidelines on our integrity. September 25, *poynter.org*

Rasmussen, T. (2006). *Telephone interview by author* [digital recording] May, Miami.

Shoer Roth, D. (2006). Una aclaración necesaria para el lector. July 27, *miami.com*

Sinco, L. (2004). *Interview by author* [cassette recording] June, Los Angeles.

Sontag, S. (2003). *Regarding the pain of others.* New York: Farrar, Straus & Giroux.

Steber, M. (2004). *Interview by author* [cassette recording] August, Miami.

Steele, B. (2004). Covering victims: Storytelling with power and respect. March 31, *poynter.org*

Strouse, C. (2006). Listen up, McClatchy. July 27, *miaminewtimes.com*

Thames, R. (2006). Observer photo was altered improperly. July 28, *charlotte.com*

Visual Editors (2006). Doctored photo costs photog a newsroom job. July 28, *visualeditors.com*

Wells, H. (2004). *Interview by author* [cassette recording] June, Los Angeles.

Whitley, M. (2004). *Interview by author* [cassette recording] June, Los Angeles.

7

Relationships: Photographer and Subject

My name is Rob Finch, and I'm a newspaper photographer for the Beacon News in Aurora, Illinois. This year I was lucky enough to win the 1999 Photographer of the Year award sponsored by the University of Missouri. . . . I would just like to say, "Thank you, thank you to all the subjects of my pictures because if it wasn't for them sharing their lives with me, none of this would be possible." (Finch, 2000).

Photojournalists frequently use the word "shooting" when referring to photographing people.[1] It elicits thoughts of stalking or hunting prey. And, indeed, many photographic assignments are "quick hit" encounters in which the photographer looks for an interesting (or famous) face, decides whether she wants a simple or more complex photograph[2] and waits for a "peak" moment of expression or activity. Most often the subject is aware that he's being photographed, but there are also times when the photographer might feel that knowledge of her presence will distract the subject or keep him from acting natural. Or, the subject might make it clear that he won't allow photographs of himself. In these cases the photographer may use a longer lens or even sneak "shots" from a hidden camera.

Immediately after leaving graduate school, I was invited to participate in the "Homeless in America" project as an intern. I spent a month living and photographing in a homeless shelter and on the streets of Asheville, North Carolina. Every day many of the homeless would gather on the benches of a downtown park and bus stop. The area was an island surrounded by one-way streets and traffic lights. One day I watched as a small car drove around the park again and again. Each time the car stopped for a traffic light, a long lens would appear from the driver's window. When the light turned green, the lens would disappear, and the circuit would be repeated. It bothered me. I felt like that person was stealing and wondered if the photographs could possibly convey any emotional connection with the subject.

I also thought about my own motives for participating in the homeless project. I found it difficult to be around one of the subjects, Cleveland O'Neil, because of his cantankerous nature as well as his racist and sexist beliefs. Nevertheless, I spent time with him every day, getting to know him better and taking photographs that I hoped would be successful. I had been given the opportunity to participate in a project with some of the world's top photographers, and I wanted my work to be included in the book.[3] I knew that O'Neil was an engaging subject, and I hoped to make the most of my access. For his part, I think that O'Neil (see Photo 13) was a lonely man who found some joy in my companionship.[4] On some level I was aware of that loneliness and used it to my benefit. At the same time, I believed that the project was an honest effort to raise public awareness regarding homelessness, and I felt strongly about the issue.

All photographers seek some level of access to their subjects. As Rob Finch says, "If it wasn't for them sharing their lives with me, none of this would be possible." But, as in all professions, photographers are individuals with diverse personalities, educational backgrounds, and life experiences. Every photographer has his own way of cultivating relationships and his own standards of ethical behavior. As a graduate student, I attended a presentation by a famous guest photographer who when asked a question about working with subjects said, "You've got to get the bastards to do what you want them to do." And, Janet Malcolm in her book, *The journalist and the murderer* says:

> Every journalist who is not too stupid or too full of himself to notice what is going on knows that what he does is morally inde-

Photo 13. Cleveland O'Neil approaches an Asheville, North Carolina policeman to ask for a ride to his home in Newport, Tennessee. The officer called a squad car that took O'Neil back to the Asheville Homeless Shelter. Photograph by Loup Langton. © Loup Langton, All Rights Reserved.

fensible. He is a kind of confidence man, preying on people's vanity, ignorance, or loneliness, gaining their trust and betraying them without remorse. Like the credulous widow who wakes up one day to find the charming young man and all her savings gone,

> so the consenting subject of a piece of nonfiction writing learns – when the article or book appears – *his* hard lesson. Journalists justify their treachery in various ways according to their temperaments. The more pompous talk about freedom of speech and the "public's right to know"; the least talented talk about Art; the seemliest murmur about earning a living.
>
> The catastrophe suffered by the subject is no simple matter of an unflattering likeness or a misrepresentation of his views; what pains him, what rankles and sometimes drives him to extremes of vengefulness, is the deception that has been practiced on him. On reading the article or book [or viewing the photograph] in question, he has to face the fact that the journalist – who seemed so friendly and sympathetic, so keen to understand him fully, so remarkably attuned to his vision of things – never had the slightest intention of collaborating with him on his story but always intended to write [or photograph] a story of his own. (Malcolm, 1990, p. 3)

Although there is some truth to what Malcolm says, she has oversimplified the issue of relationships between journalists and their subjects. During the same semester in which the guest urged students to "get the bastards to do what you want them to do," I audited a class with Melissa Farlow.[5] She had a very different idea of how photographers should interact with their subjects. "Above all," she would say, "be honest with the people you are photographing and treat them with respect."[6]

Photographers attempt to gain intimate access to subjects so that their photographs will reveal multiple levels of information and have strong emotional impact. Subjects allow access to their personal lives for a myriad of reasons – a need for companionship, a desire to be understood, a search for fame or recognition of a cause.[7] There's a kind of dance that takes place in which the photographer seeks to photograph everything, good and bad, and the subject attempts to exercise control over how he is visually portrayed. Many times the photographer or the subject (sometimes both) is left dissatisfied.

Most subject–photographer relationships begin solely for the purpose of the story and end once that story is finished.

Photographers often focus on getting their photographs while remaining emotionally outside the relationship. Some photographers, however, become more engaged with their subjects. For example, "[James Nachtwey][8] talks about the times when he has stopped photographing; when it is more important to actually do something to help rather than to take pictures. . . . Unlike some photographers he puts the needs of those he is photographing or comes across when photographing above the need to take pictures" (Marshall, 2001).

Professional organizations like the National Press Photographers Association (NPPA) and individual newspapers offer ethical guidelines to help ensure that subjects are treated fairly. For example, the *Austin American-Statesman*'s guidelines declare, "*Statesman* staff or those representing the newspaper should not mislead subjects of their photos in order to obtain permission to photograph them. They should not break the law to obtain photos or promise subjects access to their photographs without prior permission or agreement with supervisors."

The cautions against misleading subjects "in order to obtain permission to photograph them" and breaking the law are straightforward. The admonition that staff, "should not . . . promise subjects access to their photographs without prior permission or agreement with supervisors," is a bit more complex in that it contains three separate concepts. First, photographers should not mislead subjects into thinking that they will be able to see the photographs before publication. To permit all subjects to preview their photographs is impractical in terms of time and labor. Second, the newspaper maintains control of the photographs and therefore the image or portrayal of the subject. To cede control to the subjects could have the effect of turning newspapers into nothing more than public relations' vehicles. Finally, the subject is implicitly allowed access to the photographs with "prior permission or agreement with supervisors." This allows photographers, their editors, and the newspaper flexibility during sensitive situations.

I spent the summer of 1997 as a guest photo editor for the *Austin American-Statesman*'s "Life & Arts" section. Director of photography, Zach Ryall, allowed me to make all decisions regarding the section's photographic work. One story was particularly sensitive. It was about a teenage girl who suffered from a back problem that required her to wear a brace every day. The parents approved of the story and photographs about their daughter, but the photographer (a woman) assigned to the story was concerned about the girl's feelings. She sensed that the teen was uncomfortable with the thought of having her photograph (with back brace) in the newspaper. The photographer asked me if she could show the girl the photos before they were published. I agreed that the family could preview the photographs and decide whether or not they wanted them published. In the end, the teen and her parents felt comfortable with the photographs, and one was selected by the photographer to be printed along with the story.

Newspapers also create guidelines that prohibit photographers from "staging" or "setting up" photographs.[9] *Chicago Tribune* photo assignment editor, Todd Panagopoulos, says,

> Our policy for photographers is that if they get into a situation where the assignment is not real [the situation is created for the photographer by the subject], we want our photographers to diplomatically ask questions, figure out when there will be some real moments, shoot some portraits. . . . We ask that they [the photographers] call the assignment desk to tell us, "This is not real. The subjects are recreating this for the camera. I made some portraits." Then the assignment desk will go to the requesting writer or editor and say, "This didn't work out. If you do need to run the story tomorrow, it will have to be a portrait or sometimes there won't be a photo. There have been times when the photographer has come back and later realized, "Wow, this [whatever activity was photographed] was done for me [the camera]." And at that point we will erase the disks. We have done it. (Panagopoulos, 2004)

Although credibility demands that news photographers refrain from setting up photographs, many newspapers create a conundrum for photographers by not allowing them sufficient time to develop a relationship with the subject or to allow things to unfold naturally. The Missouri Photo Workshop, one of the oldest and most respected photojournalism workshops in the United

States says in its online statement, "Photographers' success depends on forming trusting, comfortable relationships with their subjects. It may take several days and many hours a day for the subject of a photo story to forget about the photographer's presence and just get on with their life" (University of Missouri, 2006). Not all stories demand "several days," but every photographer knows that it takes time to create a relationship and to capture a "real" photograph that has story-telling qualities and strong aesthetics.

Photographer P. F. Bentley was given the luxury of working for a long period of time behind the scenes of the Clinton Presidential primary campaign in 1992. His photographs are "real" and well executed. Many of them are award winners.[10] Yet, some question the nature of the photographer–subject relationship because while Bentley was on assignment for *Time* magazine, he became a member of the Clinton campaign team.

Bentley had photographed several previous New Hampshire primaries for *Time*, so he was accustomed to the routine. *Time* associate picture editor Richard Boeth, however, exhorted Bentley to find a fresh approach to his 1992 New Hampshire coverage. The "fresh approach" for Bentley was to take a cue from the past when photographers were sometimes given intimate access to the President. He wondered if it would be possible to gain that kind of access with any of the 1992 candidates, and although there were no clear-cut favorites at the time, Bentley felt that Clinton "had the look" of a front-runner.

Bentley had to "sell" his idea to the editors, to the Clinton campaign people, and, ultimately, to Clinton and his family. He flew from New Hampshire to New York to make his pitch to the editors in person, first approaching his picture editor (Boeth) and the top picture editor Michele Stephenson. They bought into the idea and formed a strategy for bringing managing editor, Henry Muller, on board. Muller was intrigued by the idea and after some discussion over whether it would be in color or black and white,[11] approved the project.

Shortly after receiving Muller's go-ahead, Bentley talked with Dee Dee Myers, Clinton's press secretary. The conversation was not as difficult as it might seem since both were speaking the same language – Bentley was responsible for gaining access to public officials; Myers was responsible for controlling the news media's access to her particular public official. Bentley explains the discussions this way:

> We [Bentley and Myers] were on a flight from New Hampshire to New Jersey, and we sat in the back of the plane, and I told her the whole idea. Later that day we flew back to New Hampshire together and continued the discussion. She said, "I'll get you a dinner with Clinton."
>
> A few days went by and then Clinton and [campaign aides] George Stephanopoulos, Paul Begala, Bruce Lindsey and I head out to eat at the Crock Pot or Stock Pot, and I had about a half hour to talk with Clinton about the idea. He liked it; he was headed home to Arkansas for two days, and he said he had to talk it over with Hillary. I told him the hardest part was going to be that we had to instantly be oldest and best pals even though we didn't really know each other, and we had to trust each other. So, he heads home, and at the end of the dinner George [Stephanopoulos] pulls me aside and says, "It'll be okay."
>
> Two days later Clinton comes back; I hand in the [press] pool pass, and I'm handed a [Clinton campaign] staff pass. I knew that I was still part of the press, but it was good to hear that they were comfortable with me, which is all that I really cared about. . . . By the third day I had just become part of the campaign. I remember George and Paul after New Hampshire telling me on the plane, "P. F., you can't ever go back; you're one of us now." (Bentley, 1993)

Bentley's description of the "deal" prompts at least two questions: How could he move between being a member of the press and a member of Clinton's staff and why would Clinton allow a photographer inside the campaign? Perhaps the answers to both questions are related.

As part of his pitch to the Clinton campaign Bentley made a promise that *Time* would not use any information that he obtained while working on the project. After seeing the first set of photographs, Boeth was convinced that Bentley's Clinton project was a photographic coup for *Time* (*Time* published edits of Bentley's photos in three separate issues during the 1992 Presidential race). Boeth was also, according to Bentley, "disturbed that he couldn't use them that week as a news item since of course I had all of the exclusives – I'm in on the [Gennifer] Flowers thing, the draft issue. He [Boeth] was shocked about what really happens" (Bentley, 1993).

By making Bentley a staff member the Clinton campaign made certain that potentially embarrassing inside information didn't get published.[12] At the same time Clinton received media attention in which the "behind the scenes" nature of the photographs helped to create an image of him as a "real person," not just a political candidate.[13] This type of portrayal is valuable in the symbolic arena; as Barthes (1972) observed, photographs of candidates show voters their own likenesses, but these likenesses are "clarified, exalted, superbly elevated." Art and photography critic Charles Hagen elaborates further:

> In the mix of actions, ideas and pageantry that makes up a Presidential race, two parallel campaigns vie for voters' attention. One is the explicit campaign of issues, while the other, equally important, deals with images and symbols. . . . Using a complex mix of media . . . candidates [of the 1992 campaign] have presented themselves and their families, in an effort to convince voters of their character, and their ordinariness. (Hagen, 1992)

Bentley's photographs helped introduce Clinton and his family to the American public in a way that said, "They're a lot like us." In exchange, Clinton allowed Bentley exclusive photographic access behind the scenes. In this case both the subject and the photographer benefited from the relationship.

Relationships between photographers and subjects, however, are frequently less accommodating and more stressful. The case of South African photographer, Kevin Carter, provides an extreme example of how personal ambition sometimes collides with more humane instincts to create a tragic ending.

> In 1993 Carter headed north . . . to photograph the rebel movement in famine-stricken Sudan. . . . [H]e wandered into the open bush.

Photo 14. March 1, 1993, Sudan – Vulture Watching Starving Child. Photograph by © Kevin Carter/Corbis Sygma. "Megan Patricia Carter Trust" Copyright Corbis. All Rights Reserved.

> He heard a soft, high-pitched whimpering and saw a tiny girl trying to make her way to the feeding center. As he crouched to photograph her, a vulture landed in view (see Photo 14). Careful not to disturb the bird, he positioned himself for the best possible image. He would later say he waited about 20 minutes, hoping the vulture would spread its wings. It did not, and after he took his photographs, he chased the bird away and watched as the little girl resumed her struggle. (MacLeod, 1994, p. 72)

The next year, Carter's photograph of the girl and the vulture won the Pulitzer Prize for feature photography. He was a star among his peers and "wrote to his parents in Johannesburg saying, 'I swear I got the most applause of anybody. I can't wait to show you the trophy. It is the most precious thing, and the highest acknowledgment of my work I could receive'" (MacLeod, 1994, p. 71). Yet, shortly after receiving the Pulitzer he committed suicide. Although several factors may have contributed to Carter's decision to end his life,[14] the incident with the girl in Sudan clearly haunted him. His friend and colleague, Joao Silva says:

"He was depressed afterward. . . . He kept saying he wanted to hug his daughter" (MacLeod, 1994, p. 72). Photojournalists physically move on after they have finished their assignments, but moving on emotionally can sometimes be more difficult.

Journalists are often criticized for the way in which they work with people who are suffering or grieving from personal tragedy. The criticism seems to be particularly acute during times of war as families confront the deaths of loved ones and journalists yearn to tell their stories. Nevertheless, there are numerous examples of journalists providing comfort to the bereaved. Jay Price, military reporter for the *Raleigh* (N.C.) *News and Observer* says, " 'Families almost always want to talk, and you should view this as a positive thing, not [as] being a vulture. Their son or daughter was a hero, and they don't want to be just a number any more than we do' " (Scanlan, 2006).

The "Final Salute," published by the *Rocky Mountain News*, serves as an outstanding example of a tragic story told with sensitivity and commitment. And, it serves as a model for journalist–subject relationships. The journalists, Jim Sheeler (writer) and Todd Heisler (photographer),[15] created and maintained a close relationship with Marine Major Steve Beck.

Heisler had been sent to Iraq to cover the war while Sheeler had been assigned to write about the war from the home-front perspective. As part of that work, Sheeler reported on a number of Marine funerals and began to see many of the same faces in attendance. He initially thought about doing a story on the Marines who were members of the Honor Guard that was always present at the funerals. He hoped to write a story that would reveal individual personalities rather than present a group persona. To gain the access that he would need, Sheeler approached Beck who was responsible for all of the family notifications and for making the funeral arrangements. Beck was cautious and asked Sheeler what he had previously written regarding the Marines. As so often happens, the journalist and the subject already shared some background.[16] Heisler explains:

> Jim [Sheeler] had done a story about two tombstones. They were the tombstones for Marines Sam Holder and Kyle Burns who were

> killed in the same engagement in Fallujah. The person who made the tombstones at Fort Logan cemetery was a Marine as well, and Jim wrote the story through his [the tombstone maker] eyes – how he got to know the Marines that he was making the tombstones for. It turns out that Major Beck had done the notification for one of those families so that he had been seeing the same things that were in Jim's story, so that was when he [Major Beck] opened up a little bit. (Heisler, 2006)

Beck decided to help Sheeler with his new idea of following a Marine who had been killed in Iraq from the point that his body touched ground at home until the moment that he was buried. And, shortly after the conversation between Beck and Sheeler, Heisler was brought on board.

Heisler says that almost immediately another Marine was killed in Fallujah, but the family wasn't interested in talking to Sheeler or allowing Heisler to photograph except from a distance. What did happen, however, is that Sheeler and Heisler began to bond with Beck and gained a better understanding of the story. At the same time Sheeler and Heisler came to an agreement between themselves that the story would not be over until both of them felt satisfied with the words and photographs.

While the two journalists could not immediately complete their in-depth story, the *Rocky Mountain News* still expected them to file daily stories about the local service members who were killed in Iraq. This allowed them more time to continue their discussions with Beck.

Three critical points emerge as a result of the time that Sheeler and Heisler spent with Major Beck. First, Beck observes their commitment to the project. Second, Sheeler and Heisler learn about the Marine way of doing things and gain some understanding of their subjects and third, their newspaper begins to have more confidence in the eventual success of the story. Heisler says:

> Major Beck called us and said he was going to visit the Burns family in Wyoming to deliver their son's personal belongings. He said, "I think you should meet this family, and I think that they'd like to meet you. Why don't you ride up with us?" So then I went

to my editors and said, "Hey, we're going with Major Beck, can you take me off the schedule?" And, they did. The way a story evolves I think is that when you start, it's a little harder to convince your editors to cut you loose [from the daily schedule] because they don't know what you have or are going to have. As you start getting deeper into the story and getting more images so that you can show them where you're going, then they become much more willing to let you go out and do what you need to do. By the time I got to August where I needed to go to Reno to follow Katherine [another subject], I said to [director of photography] Janet [Reeves],[17] "I have to go to Reno," and she said, "Go." There wasn't even a question about schedule or anything else.

By this time Major Beck was kind of onboard. I mean there is getting access and there is keeping access. Obviously, this was a story that was important to Major Beck but whether he was going to let us tell the whole story was a different matter. Every time that we worked on something with him, there was a discussion about access, about what we wanted to do, about "what's this story going to be?" It was hard to answer that question, the story was very young at that point. Really it was a matter of getting to know him and him getting to know us.

I think that you do that with any long-term project – you have to get to know each other. He told us later on that he just wanted to be able to do his job and didn't want to have to worry about us, whether we were going to stand in the wrong place, especially me [because of the cameras], whether I was going to stand too close to somebody. He was very protective of the families. He wanted to be comfortable knowing that we knew the process inside and out so that when something did happen we knew how it was going to work. (Heisler, 2006)

As the story progressed, Beck showed great trust in Sheeler and Heisler. For example, he allowed them onto the tarmacs as caskets were removed from commercial flights (see Photo 15). Although there is a general ban on photographing caskets on military bases, there is no rule regarding commercial airlines. Nevertheless, Beck took a personal risk in allowing the journalists such access. In return, Heisler says that he felt obligated to tell the story

Photo 15. Passengers aboard the commercial flight bringing home the body of 2nd Lt. Jim Cathey watch as his casket is unloaded by a Marine honor guard at Reno-Tahoe International Airport. Photograph by Todd Heisler. Copyright, 2005, *Rocky Mountain News*. Reprinted with permission.

thoroughly and to the best of his ability to repay the Major for his trust in them.

The photograph on the tarmac was one of about 80 images that Heisler showed to a group of editors during a progress meeting. While the images were being projected, Sheeler read a list of quotes from subjects. Heisler says of the meeting, "Our editor and publisher, John Temple, said it was the only news meeting he ever attended where everybody was in tears" (Heisler, 2006).

The only obligation that Beck performed and did not allow the journalists access was notifications. After the notification, however, Beck would tell the family about Sheeler and Heisler and the story that they were doing. Later, Sheeler or Heisler or both would call the family and make whatever arrangements the family was comfortable with. One of the most moving stories was of Katherine Cathey who while pregnant received notice that her husband, Jim, had been killed in Iraq.

Heisler says that when he and Sheeler went to Reno to meet Cathey they went to her house and talked with her until about midnight. As they talked she spread out all of the photographs that she had of her husband and her and later said, "You know, this is going to sound strange, but you guys made my night." Heisler continues, "Jim [Sheeler] is a great reporter, but he's also a great person and a great listener. He really knows how important it is to get all of this information right. These stories are very important to the families. These are their obituaries, but they are also memorials" (Heisler, 2006).

That same night Heisler and Sheeler explained to Cathey that they wanted to follow her through the process until her husband was buried. She agreed to their proposal and felt comfortable enough the next day to allow them to ride with her in the limo that took her to the airport to receive her husband's body. In the end, she gave them access to every part of the process. Heisler says, "I think that we established a good relationship and she wanted us to be there. This was something that I discovered along the way and something that Major Beck agreed with, that to really do this story right, to do it so that it wasn't superficial, we had to get close" (Heisler, 2006).

Like Kevin Carter, Heisler (and Sheeler) won a Pulitzer Prize for his work. Cathey visited the *Rocky Mountain News*' newsroom after the Pulitzer was awarded. Heisler says of Cathey's appearance:

> She said that we took the time to get it right. "They let me talk about my husband. I can't think of two other people more deserving of this." That meant a lot to me. It's one thing to know that they liked the story and they're happy with that, but it's another thing for them to be okay with it winning lots of awards and you getting notoriety for it. That was something I had a hard time with, and I didn't even know how to approach it with them. You have a good relationship but that's a totally different relationship. It actually was a huge weight off my shoulders to hear how she felt about the Pulitzer. (Heisler, 2006)

Heisler says that the relationship with Major Beck became a very close one after eight months of working together. While talking to me about that relationship during a phone interview, Heisler became quiet at one point and then said:

> I'd read it to you, but I don't think that I'd be able to get through it. If you go online on our webpage, there's a speech that he [Beck] made in our newsroom [pause] actually I'll read it to you. Beck explained why stories like "Final Salute" are important. "They have an element of perfection to them," he said. "It's kind of like the perfect chord or the perfect pitch that you hear from three feet away that gives you goose bumps. That touches your imperfect soul and reminds you of your humanity, who you are as an individual, who you are as a people and who you are as a nation."
>
> There was another thing that he did for us. We did a brown bag lunch like many newspapers do. Somebody works on a project or they go on a trip. They come back and give a presentation for all the other reporters and editors so that they can learn more about the project. So Jim [Sheeler] and I were talking about this project with about 50 people from the newsroom, and Major Beck walks in about halfway through the presentation. And we were like, "what's he doing here?" He had his uniform on and he said, "I don't

> want to take up too much of your time, but I want to make a presentation." He had this flag box that he had made and there was a flag in it. It was actually his father's. His father was a Marine, and when his father died he [Beck] had arranged the honor guard for him so it was actually his father's flag that he gave to us. He etched on the glass, "The Final Salute, 11 November, 2005." That explains what it meant to him. (Heisler, 2006)

Clearly Major Beck did not feel as though a "deception had been practiced on him" by Sheeler and Heisler. There are several points to be made in the creation and nurturing of relationships in "Final Salute." First, the journalists were honest with the subjects from the beginning. Second, the journalists took the time to get to know the people they were covering, and they respected their wishes. Third, the newspaper gave the photographers that time and support. Heisler recalls editor and publisher, John Temple saying to others in the newsroom:

> "There's this scene in the story where Major Beck is teaching the Marines how to fold the flag for their friend the day before the burial and he says, 'This is the last time this flag is ever going to be folded so it has to be perfect. It's for Jim [Cathey].'" Temple then says, "We need to treat this project with the same amount of respect. We have to respect what Todd [Heisler] and Jim [Sheeler] have been through in this experience and this is how it has to be treated." (Heisler, 2006)

Finally, Sheeler and Heisler's relationships with the subjects didn't end when they knew they had their story. They continued to care about Beck, Cathey, and the others and how they might feel about Sheeler and Heisler winning Pulitzer Prizes.

Relationships between photojournalists and their subjects are similar to other relationships in life.[18] Regardless of a photographer's experience, it is often a struggle for the photographer to ask a subject if he can become a part of her life by hanging around and photographing for hours, days, or even more. Although some photographers only want to take what they can get from their subjects without any regard for their wellbeing, others care deeply about their subjects. Relationships are generally nurtured through time spent together and through commitment to the relationship. And, trust is something that is earned and sometimes betrayed – by either party.

Newspapers influence the relationships that are formed between photojournalists and their subjects by allowing or not allowing the photographers the time to develop those relationships. When Heisler and Sheeler began their project, the *Rocky Mountain News* didn't know what they were going to get from the "Final Salute" story. They showed confidence in the journalists and gave them the time necessary to develop meaningful relationships with their subjects. The paper was rewarded with a number of awards, including two Pulitzer Prizes, but even more importantly, they published an important and underreported story in an intimate and sensitive way.

Ultimately, it is up to the photographers in the field to work with subjects in a fair, honest, and compassionate manner. The stories should always be about the subjects, not the photographers.

Notes

1 While at the World Press Photo offices in Amsterdam in 2006, I attended a presentation by Poynter Institute's Visual Journalism Group Leader, Kenny Irby. One of his opening comments was, "I refuse to call photographers, 'shooters.' We should not think of ourselves as hunting people."

2 Simple photographs concentrate on one element within the photographic frame. This is often accomplished by using a longer lens and/or a larger aperture creating a narrow depth of field. The narrow depth of field limits the number of distractions as well as the amount of information in the photograph. Simple photographs are generally composed more narrowly as well.

Complex photographs include more information (and potentially more distractions) via greater depth of field and broader composition. A complex photograph can offer multiple layers of information and provide more context, but is more difficult to create successfully.

3 *Homeless in America.* (1988). Washington DC: Acropolis.

4 In 1987 with the help of the Veterans Administration I was able to find Cleveland O'Neil's nephew who was then living in Baltimore. He gave me background information on O'Neil but did not want O'Neil to know how to contact him. O'Neil apparently had no other family or friends and died alone in an Asheville motel room a year after I photographed him.

5 Melissa Farlow is a contributing photographer for *National Geographic* magazine. While working in Louisville, Kentucky, she was part of a newsroom team that won a Pulitzer Prize, and Farlow has won a number of other prestigious awards for her newspaper and magazine work.

6 Commenting on a story that was published in the Hartford *Courant* involving heroin addicts, staff photographer, Brad Clift, gives an example of treating subjects with respect. He says that he was "'worried that these people who entrusted their life stories to us, that it [having their photographs published] would put them at risk. Even in extreme worlds, people have dignity.'" (McBride, 2002).

7 The film, "Capote," offers an excellent example of the hopes, expectations, manipulations, disappointments, etc. that are part of a subject–artist relationship. During one phone conversation with his friend Harper Lee, Capote says of his subject who has been accused of murder, "He trusts me. He's given me absolutely everything. He wants so badly to be taken seriously, to be held in some esteem." When Lee asks Capote if he (Capote) holds him in esteem, Capote answers, "Well, [pause] he's a gold mine."

8 James Nachtwey has won the Robert Capa Gold Medal (5 times), Pictures of the Year International's Magazine Photographer of the Year Award (8 times) and the International Center of Photography's Infinity Award (3 times).

Nachtwey, who photographs war and its effects, says about his own relationships with subjects, "In a war the normal codes of civilized behavior are suspended. It would be unthinkable in so-called normal life to go into someone's home where the family is grieving over the death of a loved one and spend long moments photographing them. It simply wouldn't be done. Those pictures could not have been made unless I was accepted by the people I'm photographing. It's simply impossible to photograph moments such as those without the complicity of the people I'm photographing, without the fact that they welcomed me; that they accepted me; that they wanted me to be there. They understand that a stranger whose come there with a camera to show the rest of the world what is happening to them, gives them a voice in the outside world that they otherwise wouldn't have" (Nachtwey, 2001).

9 In 1994 *Los Angeles Times* photographer, Mike Meadows, was fired for a photograph of a Los Angeles County firefighter splashing his head with water from a back-yard swimming pool while a house burned in the background. The photograph was going to be entered for Pulitzer Prize consideration, but rumors of staging led to a conversation with the fireman who said that the photographer suggested he pour water on his head. Meadows said, "'I deny categorically asking or telling any fireman to pose for me in front of a pool. I may have been guilty of saying this would make a nice shot, but to the best of my recollection, I did not directly ask him to do that . . .'" (Kurtz, 1994, p. D 1).

10 Bentley won first and second-place awards as well as six awards of excellence for his photographs of the Clinton campaign in the fiftieth Pictures of the Year competition. He also published a book, *Clinton: Portrait of victory*, based upon his photographs taken during the Clinton campaign.

11 Bentley insisted that he be permitted to use black-and-white film since he was trying to "be a fly on the wall," capturing real moments without using artificial lighting, and black-and-white film was more accommodating to that type of photography. The use of black-and-white images might have also coincidentally made Clinton seem more a part of history since documentaries about US historical figures traditionally include black-and-white film footage. Muller, with some reservation, gave his approval for the use of black-and-white film.

12 It might be argued that this is another form of "embedding." The journalist accompanies the subject and is given an insider's view of the action while at the same time becoming part of the team.

13 The "behind the scenes" content of the photographs seems a bit disconnected from the "not behind the scenes" word text. For example, a *Time* magazine story titled, "Bill's Big Bash," was published on July 27, 1992. It contained six pages (two spreads and two single pages) that were devoted to the story's word text written by Margaret Carlson and seven photographs by Bentley. Although the photographs are intimate – Clinton in a hotel steam room, playing

the saxophone on the balcony of his Santa Monica hotel room and watching Al Gore practice for a joint press conference in Little Rock – the text is limited to reporting the Democratic convention in Madison Square Garden. *Time* editors attempt to link the photographs to the words through the captions by pointing out that Clinton is trying to "soothe and moisturize his ragged vocal cords" the day before the convention in the steam room photograph and that "Gore's smooth performance at the convention showed what an asset he could be on the campaign trail" in the caption of a photograph showing Clinton and Gore together at the Governor's mansion in Little Rock.

14 In his September 12, 1994 *Time* magazine story titled, "The life and death of Kevin Carter," writer Scott MacLeod says that Carter and other photojournalists working in the South African townships took drugs to "relieve tensions and partly to bond with gun-toting street warriors." The drug issue ultimately caused a breakup with his girlfriend. Carter also told friends of his unhappy childhood. Perhaps most damaging was the constant dangers that he and his colleagues faced as well as the horrific scenes that they witnessed.

15 Sheeler (feature writing) and Heisler (feature photography) won Pulitzer Prizes for their work on "Final Salute" which was published as a 24-page special section in the *Rocky Mountain News* and appeared on the newspaper's website. Heisler also won numerous awards in the Pictures of the Year International contest, the National Press Photographers Association's "Best of Photojournalism" competition and the World Press Photo contest in Amsterdam.

16 While living in Austin, Texas, I was working on a photographic story about children in the Latino community. The local school principal had suggested one boy in particular. When I approached his mother, she was naturally cautious. We talked for some time, and she told me that she was attending night classes, including one on photography. She also told me about an interesting book that she had found in the library called *Homeless in America*. I asked her if she had the book at home, and when she produced it, I showed her my name and photo in the book. She invited me to photograph her son, Jimmy, and the rest of her family any time I wished.

17 Pictures of the Year International named Reeves 2006 "Newspaper Picture Editor of the Year." In the same contest Reeves won first

place for "Editing a Special Section" for her work with "Final Salute."

18 The relationships between writers and photographers are also critical. John Temple says, "[Sheeler and Heisler] went on a journey together, an emotional journey. Together, they could take readers on the same journey. Alone, they couldn't. The partnership extended right to the end. When Jim wrote, he surrounded himself with Todd's photographs. When it was time to write the captions, he pulled out quotes and ideas that hadn't fit in his narrative. Together, they wrote poignant captions that provided another strand through the story, one that wasn't repetitive of the narrative and that added understanding to the pictures" (Temple, 2006, pp. 2, 3).

References

Barthes, R. (1972). *Mythologies* (A. Lavers, Trans.). New York: Hill and Wang.

Bentley, P. F. (1993). *Interview by author* [cassette recording] November, Columbia, MO.

Finch, R. (2000). *Rob Finch: 1999 newspaper photographer of the year* [video] March, Copley Chicago Newspapers.

Hagen, C. (1992). Photographs and political families. *The New York Times*, October 25, p. H 28.

Heisler, T. (2006). *Telephone interview by author* [digital recording] May, Miami.

Kurtz, H. (1994). *L. A. Times* gets burned by disaster photograph. *Washington Post*, February 2, p. D 1.

MacLeod, S. (1994). The life and death of Kevin Carter. *Time Magazine*, September 12, pp. 70–73.

Malcolm, J. (1990). *The journalist and the murderer*. New York: Vintage.

Marshall, P. (2001). James Nachtwey (1948–). September 24, *photography.about.com*

McBride, K. (2002). Shooting up on A-1: A controversial photo and a small New England town. November 25, *poynteronline.org*

Nachtwey, J. (2001). *War photographer* (Documentary film, Christian Frei, producer), Icarus.

Panagopoulos, T. (2004). *Interview by author* [cassette recording] June, Chicago.

Scanlan, C. (2006). June 7, *Poynteronline.org*

Temple, J. (2006). The power of collaboration. April, *digitaljournalist.org*

University of Missouri (2006). Missouri photo workshop. *mophotoworkshop.org*

8

Iraq Wars

The transformation of everything into images has had an unsettling effect on perception, as Roland Barthes noted in Camera Lucida. While the omnipresent photograph may not have served to "de-realize the human world of conflicts and desires" to the extent this author suggests, there is no question that it has affected responses to pain, suffering, and pleasure in real life, making these facets of human experience seem somehow commonplace, less intensely felt, and less urgent. (Rosenblum, 1984, p. 507)

The Navy jet carrying President George W. Bush on May 1, 2003 landed on the deck of the aircraft carrier USS Abraham Lincoln. The President, dressed in a green flight suit and carrying a white helmet, emerged from the jet, waved to sailors on the observation deck and saluted crew members on the flight deck. The event, captured by still photographs and live television, allowed the President to present an image of an engaged wartime leader. The jet's landing and the President's triumphant interaction with crew members in front of a banner that declared, "Mission Accomplished," provided an excellent opportunity to visually define his role as "Commander in Chief" and to control the visual symbolism of his presidency (although even many Bush supporters came to view the "Mission Accomplished" images as politically naïve and even embarrassing).

From the same flight deck President Bush would later that evening proclaim the end of major combat operations in Iraq.

Nevertheless, the fighting continued and other symbols supplanted those created on the deck of the USS Abraham Lincoln.

Government and military leaders aggressively pursue various strategies to control photographers' mobility and access, selection of images (censorship) and sense of patriotism. Despite these efforts, "it is most often reality, caught randomly in the lens of a photographer or cameraman, that helps determine what we think" (Kifner, 2003).

Many believe that although the Vietnam War afforded photojournalists unprecedented freedom to document the horrors of war, it was an anomaly. Veteran photographer, Catherine Leroy,[1] says,

> "We rode in military planes, did helicopter assaults during operations, walked with units, everywhere, anytime. . . . We were not subjected to censorship. It was unprecedented, and it will never be repeated again. We have now entered 'the brave new world' where disinformation and censorship are being implemented and access reduced to photo opportunities" (Lang, 2006c).

Nevertheless, each war seems to provide a handful of images that define that particular war and many times the images are disturbing and run counter to the wishes of the government and the military. A David Turnley photograph from the first Gulf War offers an excellent example. Photo historian and critic Paul Lester explains:

> Turnley's helicopter filled with medical personnel and equipment touched down about 100 yards from a frantic scene. An American military vehicle had just taken a direct hit. Soldiers on the ground were upset as they said it had mistakenly been struck by a US tank. The wounded were quickly retrieved from the vehicle and carried to the helicopter. Sgt. Ken Kozakiewicz, suffering from a fractured hand, slumped into the helicopter. The body of the driver of Kozakiewicz's vehicle was placed on the floor of the helicopter inside a zippered bag. A medical staff member, perhaps thoughtlessly, handed the dead driver's identification card to Kozakiewicz. Turnley, sitting across from the injured soldier, recorded the

> emotional moment with his camera when Kozakiewicz realized that his friend was killed by the blast.
>
> Later at the hospital, Turnley asked the soldiers their names. He also asked if they would mind if the pictures were published. They all told him to get the images published.
>
> The rules of combat enforced by the military required that Turnley give his film to military officials for approval for publication. A day after the incident, Turnley learned that his editors had not yet received his negatives from the Defense Department officials. Military officials insisted that they were holding on to the film because the images were of a sensitive nature. They also said that they were concerned about whether the dead soldier's family had been informed of his death. Because of Turnley's argument that the family must have been informed by then, the officials released his film.
>
> His photographs were eventually published in Detroit and throughout the world. The picture of Kozakiewicz crying over the loss of his friend was called the "Picture of the War" on the cover of *Parade* magazine. Several months after the war, Turnley spoke to Kozakiewicz's father, who had been in one of the first American military units in Vietnam. Reacting to the censorship of images by military officials, David Kozakiewicz explained that the military was "trying to make us think this is antiseptic. But this is war. Where is the blood and the reality of what is happening over there? Finally we have a picture of what really happens in war." (Lester, 1994)

Other examples of photographs that became disturbing symbols of recent conflicts include the incinerated body of an Iraqi tank soldier on the "Highway of Death" and an American soldier's body being dragged through the streets of Mogadishu. Each of these images captured moments of horror that upset viewers' sensibilities, and by all accounts the Mogadishu photograph hastened the United States withdrawal from Somalia.

But, contemporary war journalists face difficult challenges from the government and the military while pursuing their stories.

During the first Gulf War, dubbed "Desert Storm" by the US military, journalists were tightly controlled through the institution of a military press pool. Sontag suggests that the concept of a pool has been around for about a century. "There had always been censorship, but for a long time it remained desultory, at the pleasure of the generals and heads of state. The first organized ban on press photography at the front came during the First World War; both the German and French high commands allowed only a few selected military photographers near the fighting" (Sontag, 2003, pp. 64, 65).

The pool created during the first Gulf War manipulated reporting from the front in several different ways. It limited the overall number of pool journalists to about one hundred; it controlled access to the front, and once at the front, journalists were assigned "military escorts." In addition journalists were required to sign Department of Defense rules that "prohibited reporting that would in any way endanger the troops. A journalist had to get approval before attempting any story. Once the piece was completed, the story and pictures were subject to US and allied military censorship" (Lester, 1994).

Despite the threat, many journalists believe that outright censorship was minimal. The problem, they say, was that access to real people and events was greatly limited by the pool system. Instead, the military provided the media with overwhelming amounts of information and photo/video "opportunities."

Post Gulf War analyses were critical of the media's performance for three reasons: first, the news media (particularly the major mainstream media) did not combat military press restrictions in any significant way; second, the news media became almost a cheerleader for the US military actions, and third, the news media allowed the Gulf War to completely dominate the news, pushing other important national and world events out of the picture (Gannett Foundation, 1991).

By not challenging the system, but rather accepting and publishing managed news prepared by the military, the news media in many ways became a component of the war effort. This included demonizing the enemy and celebrating the wonder of high-tech war machines. It also included a virtual disregard for the enormous number of civilian casualties. Former NBC news and PBS president Larry Grossman says:

> There is no question that in war, reporters tend to be cheerleaders for their own side and their own country. They are patriots like everybody else and tend to have very conventional views of what is going on. But certainly in this war, which lasted for such a short time and was so intense, I think there was no question that we saw an unusually patriotic, supportive journalistic corps. . . . This was the ultimate in the cheerleading war. (Gannett Foundation, 1991, p. 65)

At the start of the second Gulf War teams of editors at newspapers across the United States prepared for the task of covering the war by lining up freelance help, planning special sections and requesting additional space (Theo, 2004). Meanwhile, the US military announced that a program of embedding journalists into military units would replace the pool policy. Embedded journalists travel with the soldiers and share their experiences. *Los Angeles Times*' assistant managing editor Colin Crawford says, "I think they [US military command] were ultimately really smart because what happened is that these journalists got shot at and were suddenly able to tell the story of what war is like and what the men and women were going through out there. I think there were situations where, for example, a reporter would say, 'Hey, no, this guy was shooting at us that's why that busload of people got killed'" (Crawford, 2004). New technology has made it possible for a photographer, equipped with a digital camera, computer, and satellite phone, to make, edit, and transmit photographs while accompanying troops virtually anywhere in the world.

In general, journalists and news publications seem pleased with the (embedded) arrangement.[2] It allows journalists access to combat situations and facilitates extraordinary photographs from the viewpoint of a frontline soldier. At the same time journalists run the risk of telling their stories from a very limited perspective. They not only share experiences with the soldiers, they are also dependent upon them for their protection. Photographer, Toby Morris, relates his experience after being shot:

> I just fell on my face. I didn't even know what happened . . .
>
> A sergeant (Patrick Meyer) from the same Humvee I was in, he ran over and grabbed me by the strap of my flak jacket. He started

> dragging me to the other side, between this wall that was maybe four or five feet away and the Humvee. You assume there's no way you could get shot there because you're between the wall and this Humvee. He was about to throw me in the Humvee then he gets shot in the leg. He fell into the Humvee.
>
> I was still lying on the ground trying to figure out what to do. Five seconds had elapsed, maybe. And then I get shot again in the ankle. It's sort of weird because you don't actually hear it. But, at that point I could hear the guy in my mind recharging his weapon. Like, click, click, click, click. And I was like, "OK, I'm about to die." I sort of used my right leg to push myself up and into the Humvee. And I fell on top of this poor sergeant who was bleeding everywhere. The turret gunner got down out of the turret and into the driver's seat and started driving . . .
>
> I'm 28 and a lot of the guys there are my age or a little younger. They're young guys, and a lot of them have these really great qualities. They're what I think of as old-school Americans: uncynical, having really strong beliefs in freedom, liberty." (Lang, 2006b)

In effect, the military has attempted to recruit journalists to tell the story from the soldier's perspective. In exchange the military allows the journalists near total access to the fighting and looks after their welfare (Colombo, 2005). This does not mean that all embedded journalists report in a way that monolithically espouses the military's viewpoint. There is a distinction between the soldier's perspective and that of the military – they are not always one and the same. Nevertheless, journalists who eat, sleep, drink, laugh, and cry with the soldiers, who endure the same privations and dangers and who depend upon the soldiers for their safety are more likely to see these soldiers as young men and women who have "these really great qualities." Embedded journalists are part of the unit and as such cannot help but have a team mentality.

To acknowledge the brilliance of the military's strategy of embedding journalists in no way denigrates the professionalism or bravery of journalists working in Iraq (Committee to Protect Journalists, 2007). As Susan Sontag says:

> We – this "we" is everyone who has never experienced anything like what they went through [the experience of war] – don't understand. We don't get it. We truly can't imagine what it was like. We can't imagine how dreadful, how terrifying war is; and how normal it becomes. Can't understand, can't imagine. That's what every soldier, and every journalist and aid worker and independent observer who has put in time under fire, and had the luck to elude the death that struck down others nearby, stubbornly feels. And they are right. (Sontag, 2003, pp. 125, 126)

Whereas word journalists can seek sources to provide story information, photographers must not only be present as the story develops but must also have the presence of mind to compose the image and capture a moment – many times while under fire (Rosenblum, 1993).[3] Crawford says, "It's really a fine line [on deciding who to send], and it's a scary thing, and I certainly don't take it lightly. But, I don't shy away from it because although Iraq is a nasty place to be right now, that's what we do" (Crawford, 2004).

Crawford sent *Times* photojournalist Rick Loomis to Iraq in 2003, and Loomis has continued to work in Iraq for more than four years. Loomis, a multi award-winning photographer, embodies everything that an editor (and news consumer) would want in a journalist covering war. He's intelligent, brave, compassionate, and introspective. He has pursued the effects of the war on Iraqi civilians but admits that as an embedded photographer, it's become difficult to gain access.[4] He says:

> I guess one of the things that's hard to get at as a Western journalist is the toll the war has taken on Iraqi civilians. As a journalist that's what you're compelled to do, I want to tell both sides of the story, if you will. There have been times when you've been able to do it. Right after the war you could do whatever you wanted. Then after Fallujah the opportunities started closing down for the ability to tell those stories from that standpoint.
>
> After the battle of Fallujah I went into Baghdad and tried to work on several stories that talked about how civilians didn't have power, how civilians didn't have jobs, how civilians were lacking

> in security and stability, sort of the hardships that they had. For a nation that produces oil, these people were waiting in line for twelve hours to get gas in their car. They'd basically line up miles long, push their cars along, eat meals there and finally get to the gas pump and get a full tank of gas. Those things sort of seemed ridiculous to me at that point.[5] (Loomis, 2007)

Photographers who photograph war come from a variety of backgrounds and like people in any profession, they pursue their careers for a variety of reasons. The photographers that I know who have been to Iraq (either sent by a publication, agency, or wire service or who have gone there on their own) are uniformly bright, incredibly hard-working, and care passionately about the quality and credibility of their work. They talk about trying to create fair and accurate photographic reports of the war. Nevertheless, "objectivity" does not exist. Each photographer chooses to stand or kneel, etc. from a particular vantage point, he chooses a specific lens, adds some flash (or doesn't) and presses the button at a chosen moment. All of these "tools of the trade" are used to convey a message. One can logically believe that the embedded photographer uses the tools to portray his fellow Americans – those protecting him – in a positive way while portraying those that he perceives are trying to do harm to him and his military-unit buddies in a negative way.

Some photographers have chosen to be "unembedded" while covering the war in Iraq. Photographer Thorne Anderson[6] made five trips to Iraq, spending a total of close to ten months between 2002 and 2004. He was in Baghdad during the "shock and awe" campaign in the winter of 2003 before being evicted by the Iraqi secret police.

He went back in May 2003 after the fall of Saddam Hussein's government. He says that he knew that Iraq would be a target of the US after the September 11 terrorist attacks so with the help of a group called "Voices in the Wilderness" he was able to secure a visa to work on a story about the effects of UN sanctions on the average Iraqi months before the US invasion.

He says that although most journalists who were in Iraq before the war were sponsored by Iraq's Ministry of Information and tended to stay in the same hotel as their colleagues, he remained on his own. He believes that because of that he "had the luxury of working more freely and developing closer and more sympathetic relationships with Iraqi people" (Anderson, 2007). After the invasion, however, he spent more time working with other journalists both unembedded and embedded. He recalls the differences he observed between the various groups of journalists:

> It was interesting to see the different perspectives of journalists as they converged on Baghdad just after the US invasion. There was a great gathering in Baghdad of journalists who had been, for the most part: a) unembedded in Baghdad during the bombing; b) embedded with US troops coming up from Kuwait to the south; c) following the advance of Kurdish forces from the north; and d) waiting for the borders to open up from Jordan (and mostly seeing the war as reported on television). It was as if each of those four groups had seen four different wars.
>
> Speaking in broad generalities, those who had been in Baghdad, with whom I felt the most affinity, were the most likely to have felt the impact of the war on Iraqi civilians and to have a pessimistic view of where the conflict was headed in the future. Those who had been in Jordan or had been embedded with US forces invading from the south seemed most likely to view the invasion through the prism of a "war of liberation," though those who had come up from the south seemed somewhat more aware of the devastation that this had required. Those who came from the north were also similarly swayed by the Kurdish euphoria over the toppling of Saddam, but had already seen (primarily in the chaos of the fall of Mosul) some foreshadowing of the civil conflict that had already been unleashed.
>
> Even the simple semantics were revealing. I remember encountering reluctance among some of the embedded journalists with describing the invasion as an "invasion . . ." Similarly, I perceived an early reluctance of many embedded journalists to use the word "occupation."
>
> As time went on I began to see (at least for the first two years) an increasing gulf in the perceptions of journalists who worked primarily unembedded versus those who primarily embedded with the foreign occupation forces. Unembedded journalists were much quicker to recognize the disintegration of Iraqi society and civil

> security. They were quicker to recognize the early signs of an enduring rebellion against the occupation (see Photo 16).
>
> The most striking difference between embedded and unembedded journalists was the easiest to explain. Embedded journalists, by definition, traveled in the protective company of armed soldiers and had much less access to the lives of ordinary Iraqis. So it is no surprise that their stories about Iraq emphasized the day-to-day activities of foreign occupation forces, while unembedded journalists were better at chronicling the lives of ordinary Iraqis as they struggled with the massive shifts their society was undergoing. Photographically, it worked the same way. It's quite simple really. Unembedded photographers had much greater access to honest and candid interactions with Iraqi people. (Anderson, 2007).

As was suggested in Chapter 4, photographers are often the most liberal journalists, and despite the influences of embedding, many photographers still pursue the stories that explore the more human side of life. Documenting the horrors of suicide bombings; creating visual stories that show the effects of war on civilians, and making strong photographs of soldiers under fire – generating photographs that have emotional impact and that have strong story-telling qualities, however, is only half of the equation. Editors, not photographers, select the photographs to be published. In an essay written during the early stages of the second Gulf War, photographer Peter Howe[7] points out that people often rely on still photographs to get a sense of events during times of crisis, yet most photographs of the second Gulf War appearing in magazines and newspapers seem, with few exceptions, to be "sanitized":

> I do not believe that more graphic photographs haven't been taken. Given the intensity of the fighting and the fact that under the stress of being shot at the average photographer, or at least this average photographer, is hard put to make aesthetic and often even ethical decisions, these images must exist. The last thing in your mind when your life is in real and immediate danger is whether or not the readers of the Hometown Times will be offended by what you're shooting. What I think we're seeing here is a selection

Photo 16. A young boy watches his relatives repair a rocket propelled grenade launcher in the home of a fighter for the Mahdi militia in Sadr City during a lull in the fighting between the miltia and American forces. Photograph by Thorne Anderson. © Thorne Anderson, All Rights Reserved.

> process that is the result of internal media company censorship rather than the military kind. Rumors are surfacing of directives to picture editors to only choose photographs that make the US military forces look heroic, and to spare the American public the distress of seeing dead or badly wounded personnel. Of course this also spares the advertisers the same suffering as the reader, which is a fortunate coincidence.
>
> Unfortunately the media companies are right. Not only do most advertisers not want images of death and mutilation to spoil the promotion of their products, but also most readers don't seem to want that either. Wounded Iraqi children and the corpses of US soldiers may be your tax dollars at work, but don't put them on the American breakfast table. Whenever they have appeared, even if they show the corpses of the enemy, angry letters to the editor follow in their wake. During the Vietnam War Walter Cronkite, (you remember him, the Most Trusted Man in America) was criticized for showing bodies at breakfast. His response was that not only should the American public see them at breakfast, but at lunch and dinner as well, and once again before they went to bed. While on the surface this may seem arrogant and insensitive it serves the nation well. (Howe, 2004)

Editors take extreme care with their decisions when the country is at war (Irby, 2004). All of the factors discussed earlier in this book are maximized. The hierarchical newsroom structure becomes even more obvious as senior editors involve themselves more closely in the day-to-day editing decisions. Likewise, less-senior editors assiduously take their cues from the top editors and the ruling concept of "good taste." Sontag says, "[N]ewspaper and magazine photo editors make decisions every day which firm up the wavering consensus about the boundaries of public knowledge. Often their decisions are cast as judgments about 'good taste' – always a repressive standard when invoked by institutions" (Sontag, 2003, p. 68).

The rules of "good taste" are called upon to protect the publications from alienating readers and advertisers (Carter & Steinberg, 2004). This, of course, is a strategy aimed at both economics and ethics. The tactics include merely eliminating disturbing photographs from the edit or sometimes placing the troubling images inside and publishing them smaller and in black and white (Dotinga, 2004).

Editors often refer to their measure of "good taste" as the "Cheerios factor" – how would a reader react to the photograph while eating a bowl of Cheerios? Editors, trying to balance "taste" with news value, work within a framework established by their publications and media institutions such as the Poynter Institute (Irby, 2004). Although the framework assists them in making decisions about whether or not to publish a particular photograph, not all editors come to the same conclusions.

For example, several professionals and researchers from the Poynter Institute gave their opinions on what to do with the photographs showing the mutilated bodies of Qusay and Uday Hussein. President of the Poynter Institute Jim Naughton says that he would support using the photographs but he would publish them on the inside of the paper with a warning on the front page.

Former newspaper editor and current Poynter Distinguished Fellow in Journalism Values, Gregory Favre disagrees. He believes that using the photographs would be outside the framework of good taste and that they would only provide "shock value." And, Jill Geisler, the Group Leader for Leadership at Poynter, says that the photographs should be used but with "extreme respect for the dead" (Tompkins, 2003).

What most editors won't initially acknowledge is that many decisions about the selection, placement, and sizing of war photographs are at least indirectly made to protect the financial interests of the publications. As business entities with a premium on profits, news publications seek to give the customers (both advertisers and readers) what they want. They try to ascertain what readers want through surveys such as the Monitor/TIPP poll that asked whether people approved or disapproved of the release of Abu Ghraib prison-abuse photos. Perhaps surprisingly the poll found that many people weren't particularly moved one way or another:

> Ombudsmen at five daily newspapers – in Houston, Sacramento, San Francisco, Seattle, and Tucson, Ariz. – report[ed] that the most graphic images from Iraq spawned only mild to moderate interest among readers. There's much more uproar when papers tinker with TV listings, the comics, or the crossword puzzle. (Dotinga, 2004)

In another example a mass email survey was conducted by 29 news organizations. Readers were asked for their opinions regarding a photograph of charred bodies hanging from a bridge in Fallujah. A majority of the respondents favored publishing the photograph, posting comments such as, "The important thing is to give readers a sense of the brutality of the enemy we face in Iraq" (Shook, 2004). In choosing to publish photographs of the hangings, *Memphis Commercial Appeal* editor, Chris Peck says, "Memphis community standards were considered in making the decision, as well as ethics guidelines established by The Poynter Institute" (Shook, 2004).

Interestingly, although readers don't appear to be overly sensitive to graphic photographs appearing in their newspapers, they do seemingly react strongly to photographs that depict Iraqi suffering. In April 2003 the *Oregonian* published on its front page a photograph of an Iraqi man responding to the deaths of his wife, six children, two brothers and his parents (see Photo 17). Stories of Pfc. Jessica Lynch's rescue and the death of a soldier from Oregon were published in the left-hand column of the front page, subordinate to the dominant photograph of the grieving Iraqi. *Oregonian* ombudsman, Dan Hortsch says, "A handful of readers called the paper to say thanks . . . maybe four or five. By contrast, more than 50 people called, emailed or wrote to express dismay with the photo" (McBride, 2003).

Readers' feedback to the *Oregonian* included comments such as, "'I found the picture on today's . . . *Oregonian* to be a great attempt to give sympathy and support to a merciless enemy,' [and] 'The picture of the Iraqi mourning the death of his family is a perfect example of why I gave up my free subscription to your rag. It is war . . . too bad but it is true'" (McBride, 2003). Finally, one reader offered:

WEDNESDAY
April 2, 2003

The Oregonian

SUNRISE EDITION

PORTLAND, OREGON — 2001 PULITZER PRIZE WINNER FOR PUBLIC SERVICE — 35¢

FIGHTING: U.S. forces begin drive on outer defenses of the Iraqi capital

PRISONER: U.S. troops rescue Pfc. Jessica Lynch, a POW since March 23

Baghdad battle begins

U.S. Forces enter 'Red Zone' to take on the Republican Guard

ALI HEIDER/ASSOCIATED PRESS

Karem Mohammed weeps Tuesday over the bodies of his six children, his wife, two brothers, and his parents in Hillah, Iraq. Hospital officials said at least 33 people died and more than 300 were injured in airstrikes by allied forces.

By MICHAEL R. GORDON
NEW YORK TIMES NEWS SERVICE

CAMP DOHA, Kuwait — The battle for Baghdad began Tuesday night as U.S. ground forces entered the "Red Zone."

U.S. Army and Marine ground forces advanced on separate axes into the swath of territory around Baghdad defended by the Republican Guard. It has been characterized by U.S. commanders as the most strategically vital and treacherous of the war.

Although 50 miles or more from the capital, the attack brought the U.S. military one step closer to its ultimate objective: capturing Baghdad and toppling the government of President Saddam Hussein.

It also ushered in a period of heightened risk for U.S. forces.

ANALYSIS

If the Iraqis plan to unleash chemical weapons, the entry of U.S. forces into the Red Zone is expected to be the trigger, U.S. commanders say.

The Iraqis are defending the area with extended-range Frog rockets, artillery and other relatively short-range missiles that can carry chemical weapons.

The first indication that Tuesday might be the day for the Red Zone attack came at a meeting of land war commanders, linking far-flung units through a classified video television conference.

Lt. Gen. David McKiernan, the land war commander, signaled the plan.

"We are starting a big maneuver fight in the Red Zone," McKiernan said. "It is a significant close fight."

The attack south of Baghdad involved the Army's 3rd Infantry Division and the 1st Marine Expeditionary Force.

During the attack, some U.S. units crossed the Tigris River. Commanders

Please see **IRAQ**, Page B6

U.S. prisoner rescued by U.S. Special Operations

By JOHN M. BRODER
NEW YORK TIMES NEWS SERVICE

DOHA, Qatar — In a daring midnight mission on Wednesday, U.S. Special Operations forces rescued Army Pfc. Jessica Lynch from An Nasiriyah, Iraq, where she had been held captive since March 23.

Lynch, 19, of Palestine, W.Va., was found in the Saddam Hospital in An Nasiriyah, which also was being used as an Iraqi military facility, a Central Command official said. She was one of 15 members of the 507th Ordnance Maintenance Co., which was attacked by Iraqi forces after taking a wrong turn off a highway in southern-central Iraq as U.S. troops advanced toward An Nasiriyah on the first Sunday of the war.

LYNCH
Missing since nine days ago

"Coalition forces have conducted a successful rescue mission of a U.S. Army prisoner of war held captive in Iraq," Brig. Gen Vince Brooks, Central Com-

Please see **POW**, Page B6

Sherwood man dies in copter crash in Iraq

By DANA TIMS
THE OREGONIAN

Family and friends Tuesday mourned the death of a U.S. Marine captain from Sherwood, who was killed Sunday when his UH-1 Huey helicopter crashed after takeoff in southern Iraq.

CONTRERAS
Marine dreamt of flying as boy

Capt. Aaron Contreras, a father of three, was 31. He was a member of the Marine Light Attack Helicopter Squadron 169, Marine Aircraft Group 39, based in Camp Pendleton, Calif.

Contreras, the second-youngest of five sons and a 1990 Sherwood High School graduate, was remembered as a devout family man.

"He loved God, he loved his wife and children, and he lived the kind of life he

Please see **DEATH**, Page A6

Inside

◆ Turkey finds itself at odds with Europe, in disfavor with the U.S. and in desperate need of mending fences/**News Focus, B5**

Photo 17. *The Oregonian*, April 2, 2003, Copyright, 2003, *The Oregonian*. Reprinted with permission.

> I am sickened by your front page today! How can you put that poor G.I. that died in a side column, yet make the Iraqi man who lost his family the main theme? Are you not American? You can bet I will be speaking with my husband this evening, and may be canceling our subscription. Perhaps you should reconsider your stance on producing newspapers – it does NOT look as if you are objective, but ANTI-AMERICAN, ANTI-WAR, yet PRO-PROTESTORS!! (McBride, 2003)

Some time later the *Oregonian* published a photograph of an Iraqi man begging US soldiers not to shoot him. A handful of readers complained that the "newspaper's coverage of the war was 'too negative,' they wanted the 'positive side of the war'" (McBride, 2003).[8]

News publications face a myriad of ethical and economic pressures to avoid publishing "offensive" photographs. In addition, the government and military attempt to influence reporting,[9] and pressure by conservative groups has subdued media criticism of the war.[10] Despite these factors, a number of photographs have been published that emphasize the war's failures and consternate the military and government.

For example, although many readers seem not to be moved by the Abu Ghraib photographs, the consequences have been significant for the reputation of the US military – they eliminated any sense of innocence in the American occupation of Iraq – and they continue to haunt the United States' image internationally (Reynolds, 2006; Sector, 2006).

Many believe that they have become a disturbing symbol of the war (Winn, 2004). In a National Public Radio report journalist Ari Shapiro compares the Abu Ghraib photographs to other images that have become national icons:

> Photos of police dogs loosed on black civil rights protesters in Birmingham, Ala.; a naked Vietnamese girl cries in horror after a napalm attack; and the famous flag-raising on Iwo Jima during World War II are seared in the collective memory.
>
> Hal Buell, former photography director for the Associated Press and author of *Moments: Pulitzer Prize winning photographs*, says: "Words are the tools of someone who sees something and then describes it. Pictures . . . describe something that actually happened." (Shapiro, 2004)

Because photographs "describe something that actually happened," people react to them more viscerally than they do to words, but emotional responses can change as circumstances are altered. Returning to the example of the *New York Times*' photograph of Marylou Whitney in Chapter 3, the way in which photographs are "read" depends upon the backgrounds of the various viewers. Photographs from the war in Iraq may be read in different ways depending upon the political bias that each reader brings to the viewing (Thompson, 2004). And, a changing political climate can also affect the way in which a particular image is interpreted from one point in time to another. Furthermore, the political environment may influence the decision of whether or not to publish a particular photograph.

For many Americans the photograph of the burned bodies hanging from a bridge in Fallujah may have initially evoked a feeling of rage and a desire to publicize the "brutality of the enemy." As support for the war diminishes, however, some of those same people may view that photograph as a symbol of war's tragedy and as a reminder of an ill-advised decision to invade Iraq. In addition, the changing political climate may also have influenced the decision to publish the Fallujah photograph.

> [T]he news media have had thousands of photographs of the war in Iraq that were equally graphic, if not more so, and they have forsworn publishing them. So why did editors choose to use these? The answer, I think, is quite simple: It was convenient, and it was time. A newspaper could not have published similar pictures of American soldiers, because there remains a taboo on showing explicit images of our own military dead. And it would not have published similar pictures of dead Iraqis, because there remains a disinclination to show detailed images of the effects of our own military campaign. But these victims were American civilians working in the private sector and therefore unprotected by such sanctions. What's more, support for the war is waning, and we're approaching a moment of transition, so it's more in keeping with the public mood, and more revealing of the problems that lie ahead, to show evidence that things aren't going well. (Lewis, 2004)

Are the news media only willing to publish difficult and disturbing photographs when they perceive that public sentiment is turning against the war effort and that the political climate is "right" for publishing such images? Will critics in retrospect criticize the news media's reportage during the second Gulf War? The answers to both questions are probably, "yes," at least in a general sense. Clearly the George W. Bush administration and the United States military (like every other wartime government and military) are very aware of the influence and importance of visual symbols and have tried with varying success to control those symbols.

By and large, the images published during the early stages of the conflict – at a time when the public was clearly behind the invasion – were positive, affirmative of the government's decision to invade. News publications that published "negative" images – like those of the suffering Iraqi father and husband – came under fire from readers and risked economic consequences. Even worse, their "patriotism" was questioned.

As the popularity of the war (and the administration) diminished the news media (like many opposition political candidates) became emboldened. Thorne Anderson says, "Editors and reporters in the US were inundated with official spin, and it took a long time for them to shake their ideological blinders" (Anderson, 2007). But, perhaps the reasons behind editorial timidity are a little more complex than simple ideology.

Editors and reporters (word and visual) work within a framework that includes newsroom culture and routines, ethical standards, US interests, relationships with subjects, and perhaps above all, economic concerns.

Advertising dollars provide more than 80 percent of newspaper revenue. Advertisers pay according to the numbers and demographics of readers that a particular newspaper can provide. Accordingly, newspapers do all that they can to attract and maintain readers, and many readers clearly want their newspapers to be patriotic cheerleaders during times of crisis.

As early as 1938 Henry Luce considered the consequences of journalism driven by economics and the popular demands of readership:

> [Luce] warned about the popular publishing strategy that he characterized as "the give-the-public-what-it-wants theory." He saw the danger of this as not giving "the people what they must have – what

they will perish without. . . . The present [1938] crisis in world affairs may be described as a crisis in journalism. . . . Modern dictatorships are unspeakable [because] they corrupt the mind from within. They suppress the truth. They lead men by lies and fraud to desire and acquiesce in their own enslavement. And how is this corruption brought about? By the destruction of journalism." (Fulton, 1988, p. 140)

Notes

1 Catherine Leroy died in 2006. In 1976 she became the first woman to win the Robert Capa Gold Medal Award for conflict photography from the Overseas Press Club in New York.

2 The embedded-journalists policy created controversy in some newsrooms. The *Washington Post*, for example, declined to embed during the early stages of the war.

3 "For the third year running, Iraq was the world's most dangerous country for the media, with 24 journalists and 5 media assistants killed. Seventy-six journalists and media assistants have been killed there since the start of fighting in March 2003" (Reporters Without Borders, 2006).

4 Some journalists were initially able to move back and forth between being embedded and being free from military association. *Washingtonpost/Newsweek Interactive* senior video journalist Travis Fox says, "I covered the initial war, the war, not the aftermath. I think that if I were going to go back now – and I'm not planning on it – you'd have to be embedded, but at the time it was better to be on my own. You could travel anywhere, you had free movement, but then if there were security concerns you could hook up with a certain unit for a few days or you could sleep in your car at the entrance of a base – which now would be a horrible place to stay but at the time was a very secure place to stay. So, I found that I was able to cover a range of stories, both military stories and Iraqi civilian stories. I think it was very good. I think I covered much more ground than if I was with any given unit" (Fox, 2006).

5 The story by David Zucchino on kcet.org gives a sense of the dangers that photojournalists like Loomis face in Iraq. The story also provides some insight into a committed photojournalist's work ethic, professionalism and self-initiative (Zucchino, 2007).

6 Though he originally enrolled as a graduate student in the writer's program at the University of Missouri School of Journalism, Thorne Anderson eventually discovered a love for photography and became a photojournalism student at Missouri. After receiving his master's degree Anderson began teaching journalism at the American University in Bulgaria and continued working as a freelance photographer, photographing events such as the anti-Milosevic demonstrations in Serbia, the Bulgarian national strike in 1996, and the growing Kosovar refugee crises in Albania and Macedonia. Anderson says, "I wasn't photographing these events because they were exotic or adventurous. I photographed them because they were taking place in my backyard and affecting the lives of my friends, my students, and their families. It was only later that I began to appreciate how following dramatic stories like these can reveal a lot about human nature, international relations, and American foreign policy." Anderson left teaching to become a full-time freelance photographer when the Kosovo war escalated in 1999 and continued to cover the aftermath of the Kosovo war, the ensuing refugee problems, the rebuilding of Kosovo, the fall of Slobodan Milosevic and the spin off wars in Macedonia and Southern Serbia.

Following the September 11, 2001 attacks on the World Trade Center and the Pentagon, Anderson worked almost exclusively in Afghanistan and Iraq for the next five years. Anderson says, "I've always felt a bit like an outsider to this profession because I sort of slipped into it sideways and have never been tied to a full-time job in this field. In the end, I think that attitude has helped me to cultivate a healthy, sometimes alternative, perspective, and to follow roads less traveled to seek out novel angles of coverage" (Anderson, 2007).

7 Peter Howe, a leading advocate of photojournalism, worked as picture editor for the *New York Times Magazine*, director of photography for *Life* magazine and vice president of photography and creative services for Corbis.

8 "Historically, photographers have offered mostly positive images of the warrior's trade, and of the satisfactions of starting a war or continuing to fight one. If governments had their way, war photography, like most war poetry, would drum up support for soldiers' sacrifice.

"Indeed war photography begins with such a mission, such a disgrace. The war was the Crimean War, and the photographer, Roger Fenton, invariably called the first war photographer, was no less than that war's 'official' photographer, having been sent to the Crimea in early 1855 by the British government at the instigation of Prince Albert. Acknowledging the need to counteract the alarming printed accounts of the unanticipated risks and privations endured by the British soldiers dispatched there the previous year, the government had invited a well-known professional photographer to give another, more positive impression of the increasingly unpopular war" (Sontag, 2003, pp. 47, 48).

9 Howard Friel and Richard Falk in *The record of the paper* document the *New York Times'* acceptance of the Bush administration's Iraq threat argument. Instead of challenging the notion that Iraq was capable of delivering weapons of mass destruction to American soil, *N. Y. Times* writers accepted this assertion in their stories and editorials. In addition *N. Y. Times* writer Judith Miller pressed the idea of Weapons of Mass Destruction in her stories (Friel & Falk, 2004).

10 "*Los Angeles Times* columnist Robert Scheer was fired on November 11 after nearly 30 years at the paper, the last 13 as one of its most progressive political columnists . . .

Scheer's forceful and independent commentary has often placed him in the middle of national debates. He has been one of the strongest critics of the White House over the Iraq War. For instance, in a pre-war column (8/6/02) that undercuts the current notion that everyone got the WMD story wrong, Scheer wrote that 'a consensus of experts' told the Senate that Iraq's chemical and biological arsenals were 'almost totally destroyed during eight years of inspections.' Shortly after George W. Bush's 'Mission Accomplished' speech, and well ahead of the pack, Scheer (6/3/03) called White House pretexts for war a 'big lie' . . .

The *Times* has suggested that Scheer's firing was simply part of a larger revamping of its opinion pages, but Scheer says he was fired for ideological reasons and because the *Times*' corporate parent, Tribune Company of Chicago, was caving in to outside pressure from conservatives" (Fair, 2005).

References

Anderson, T. (2007). *Interview by author* [email] July, Quito, Ecuador.

Carter, B. & Steinberg, J. (2004). The struggle for Iraq: Issues of taste; to portray the horror, news media agonize. April 1, *nytimes.com*

Colombo, S. (2005). Frontline access: Online gallery boasts soldiers' wartime photos. February 11, *ojr.org*

Committee to Protect Journalists (2007). Journalists killed: Statistics and archives. July 14, *cpj.org*

Crawford, C. (2004). *Interview by author* [cassette recording] June, Los Angeles.

Dotinga, R. (2004). Press wrestles with grim clips. May 26, *csmonitor.com*

Fair (2005). *LA Times* dumps liberal columnist: Scheer out as Bush attacks Iraq War critics. November 17, *fair.org*

Fox, T. (2006). *Telephone interview by author* [digital recording] May, Miami.

Friel, H. & Falk, R. (2004). *The record of the paper: How the* New York Times *misreports US foreign policy*. New York: Verso.

Fulton, M. (1988). *Eyes of time: Photojournalism in America*. New York: Little, Brown and Company.

Gannett Foundation (1991). *The media at war: The press and the Persian Gulf conflict*. New York: Author.

Howe, P. (2004). The reality of war, sort of. March, *digitaljournalist.org*

Irby, K. (2004). War images as eyewitness. May 10, *poynter.org*

Kifner, J. (2003). A thousand words; good as a gun: When cameras define a war. November 30, *nytimes.com*

Lang, D. (2006a). Photo books show two different Iraqs. March 20, *pdnonline.com*

Lang, D. (2006b). Q & A with Toby Morris, photographer shot in Iraq. March 21, *pdnonline.com*

Lang, D. (2006c). War photographer Catherine Leroy dies in California. July 10, *pdnonline.com*

Lester, P. M. (1994). Military censorship of photographs. *commfaculty.fullerton.edu*

Lewis, J. (2004, April 5). Front page horror. *slate.com*

Loomis, R. (2007). Web stories: Rick Loomis. *kcet.org*

McBride, K. (2003). Did powerful image present an unbalanced view? April 14, *poynter.org*

Reporters Without Borders (2006). Violence still increasing, 63 journalists killed, more than 1,300 physically attacked or threatened. January 4, *rsf.org*

Reynolds, P. (2006). The return to Abu Ghraib. February 15, *news.bbc.co.uk*

Rosenblum, M. (1993). *Who stole the news*. New York: John Wiley & Sons.

Rosenblum, N. (1984). *A world history of photography*. New York: Abbeville.

Sector, C. (2006). More Abu Ghraib prison abuse photos leaked. February 15, *abcnews.go.com*

Shapiro, A. (2004). Vivid photos remain etched in memory. May 10, *npr.org*

Shook, P. H. (2004). Readers respond to Fallujah photos. April 13, *poynter.org*

Sontag, S. (2003). *Regarding the pain of others*. New York: Farrar, Straus & Giroux.

Theo, M. (2004). *Interview by author* [cassette recording] June, Chicago.
Thompson, M. (2004). Discussion is the policy. April 2, *poynter.org*
Tomkins, A. (2003). Tough call on Hussein corpse photos. July 24, *poynter.org*
Winn, S. (2004). Photos that will haunt us more than words ever could. May 19, *sfgate*
Zucchino, D. (2007). Web stories: Rick Loomis. *kcet.org*

9

Webs and Blogs

One of the things that attracted me to come to the web is that at a certain point I was seeing a declining arch in the commitment of print media and the use of photojournalism in explaining the world. I was really distressed about that state of affairs, and I thought there might be an opportunity to use the web in a certain way to bring that back and effectively create in a different environment a lot of the same sensibility that drove the great picture magazines of the 40s, 50s and the last century. (Kennedy, 2004)

Technology has always played a key role in the advancement of photojournalism. Improvements in lenses as well as in negative and print quality and the introduction of the 35 mm camera, roll film, and artificial light allowed photographers to freeze motion, photograph in low light, and move about unencumbered by heavy equipment. The invention of the halftone process enabled publications to mass produce images and include them with text. All of these advances affected the content, distribution, and social function of photojournalism.

Photojournalists have often taken the lead in using new technology, yet they have often been loath to let go of their familiar equipment and routines. I recall as a graduate student participating in debates over whether the Nikon F/3 was as good as the previous F/2 model. Later, as a photographer I commiserated with other photographers at how inferior the quality of electronic darkroom images were compared to traditional darkroom prints.

And, as a director of photography I had to convince staff photographers that they needed to exchange their film cameras for digital models. Each change brought improvements and challenges.

Today the proliferation of online news and web logs (blogs) creates opportunities as well as potential problems.[1] Many see the ability of virtually anyone to post information on the web as democratization of communication and an opportunity for a more diverse presentation of the news. Others view the web as an invitation for misinformation, banality, and unethical practices.

No one debates the fact that the Internet will continue to become more influential in the distribution of information and the exchange of ideas. And, newspapers now accept the Internet as both competition and potential salvation. Those within the newspaper industry, however, have various ideas on how best to embrace and utilize the Internet (Kirtz, 2006).

Although some newspapers like the *Washington Post* hired highly innovative people such as Tom Kennedy to lead their online publications, many newspapers initially used the Internet as an "extension" of the print newsroom. They posted the same stories that were published in print and/or hired inexperienced staff to write about the same topics that appeared in the newspaper (*The Economist*, 2006). Most newspaper publishers now realize that the Internet works differently than the traditional newspaper. They keep the print and Internet newsrooms separate or create a newsroom based on a new model so that when material is shared, it's treated appropriate to its medium. *Los Angeles Times* photo editor for projects and multimedia Gail Fisher says:

> While I'm editing for the newspaper, I'm also editing for the web. I'll do a tighter edit for the newspaper than I'll do for the website. Francine [Ore working on a six-part story on how people live in Africa on a dollar a day] will be in here and we'll lay everything [the photographs] down and I'll say, "Okay now I want you to write the script for the [website] narration. Once you arrange for the narration things will move a little bit, but I want you to think in terms of telling the story in this photo gallery, and you might need

> a few transitional images that maybe will only stay on the screen two or three seconds to get you to this one, which will stay maybe four to five seconds, or six seconds." If they [the photographers] haven't recorded narration in the field or shot video, then we come back and they'll talk about the photography [for the website]. (Fisher, 2004)

Newspaper photographers and writers are being forced to adjust to new technology and new ways of telling stories with varying degrees of success and acceptance.[2] Washington Post/Newsweek Interactive senior video journalist Travis Fox says of his early experience, "I joke that when I first started doing videos here in the fall of 1999, I was afraid that our executive editor would try to watch the videos because we knew that it would ultimately crash his computer" (Fox, 2006). At the same time Fox thinks that the online journalists at washingtonpost.com have been able to create routines and a style of reporting different from the print newspaper.

> Now what I try to achieve with all of my projects are kind of "evergreen" thematic stories because the website is unlike television or the newspaper. It doesn't come out one day and then it's gone. It's an ongoing medium so the stories will be there tomorrow and the next day if it's promoted. For example, Hamas is in the news and obviously will be reported on over and over again in the coming months. So, what I'm trying to do with this project is to explain Hamas from the Palestinian perspective, from the point of view of a 17-year-old Gaza kid who is just getting out of high school figuring out what he wants to do.
>
> It's not so much the day-to-day, what's happening in this conflict between Fatah and Hamas kind of thing. It's not the story of the day. It's the thematic story that will be paired with the story of the day. For example, when Scott Wilson, our correspondent in Jerusalem, writes the latest story about the referendum on whether they're going to accept the plan for peace with Israel, this package will be paired with it on the website, and it will give the reader more depth and more context and give a sense of place and people. (Fox, 2006)

Los Angeles Times staff writer Ken Weiss describes his first experience working with a multimedia project:

> I've done three interesting projects with the same photographer, Al Seib, that have sort of been showcased. They all ended up being multimedia projects. The first was about two and a half years ago. I went to British Colombia and did a story on farm salmon – extremely photogenic – and the director of photography, Colin Crawford, said, "Oh, we need to videotape this because the [Chicago based] Tribune Company [owner of the *Los Angeles Times* at the time] is pushing this [multimedia] concept." They're trying to turn us from scribes and photographers to "media content providers." That's a term they love. So, Al Seib and I went to British Colombia, and we took float planes to get to the fish farms and saw a fish processing house – all extremely photogenic and good material for myself as sort of a way to illustrate a story of how fish farming works and how it's gone very wrong for the local environment and causing other problems.
>
> Out of that came a front-page story that I wrote, lots of photos and a short video that we did. It was about eleven minutes long. Al had the tricky task – and this was the first time he did it – of both taking pictures and doing video and sound. You know very often TV crews will have two or three people to do that. And, I was both on-air talent as well as a scribe, but I was also being sort of the producer in a way.
>
> I was slow to warm to this I have to say because being steeped in the written word – seeing that as a high calling and photos as sort of adornment – that's sort of the other tension [for me]. This was – especially during the video – very different, but I've become a believer because there is just tremendous power, as we know, in images, and moving pictures are even more powerful. This thing ended up airing on a local PBS station, and it really had a huge splash. (Weiss, 2004)

Three years later Weiss won the 2007 Pulitzer Prize for a five-part, multi-media series, "Altered Oceans." *Times* photographer Rick Loomis worked with Weiss on the series that employed video, print journalism, still photography, graphics, and an online message board. "In a nod to the evolving nature of the newsroom, the Pulitzer committee allowed online elements to be submitted as part of the Pulitzer consideration" (Weiss, 2007).

"Media content providers," working with digital photographs, sound, and video, share images and stories with television news and documentary. Employing digital sound, photography, and video keeps production costs down allowing virtually anyone to generate multimedia content. Although this creates opportunities for innovation, it also opens the door to potential trouble. Many web "journalists" and bloggers have no journalism experience and/or are not guided by the same sets of journalism ethics that more traditional journalists follow. Even managers and editors working with their own newspaper websites are searching for balance between the medium's technical needs and journalistic standards. Tim Rasmussen, former director of photography for the *South Florida Sun Sentinel*, struggled with the integration of the *Sun Sentinel*'s website into the newsroom. He says:

> The other day one of the general managers from our dotcom and I were negotiating what the title of the video position that I had been given from their budget would be. I had written, "Video Journalist" which mirrors the photojournalist title in photography. The only difference that I saw was in the equipment that is being used. That came back to me as "Web-Specialist Videographer."
>
> I called him back and said, "Okay, let's compromise because I think that it's critical that if he's going to work for me, he's going to be a journalist and not a videographer or a web specialist," and he said, "One of the problems is that a lot of my folks have a problem with the 'J-word.'" I laughed and said, "Well, they're going to have to get over it because one way or another we are going to integrate [journalism and the web], and the web is going to have to accept journalism ethics, and we're going to have to accept how you guys put the web together." So, we compromised with, "Web-Video Journalist."
>
> It was very interesting because I think that's one of the problems. When they built the websites, they built them outside the journalism departments at most newspapers although not all. Some places were stunningly smart and hired Tom Kennedys to develop what the web would become while at other places like here, the web is a total non-editorial division operation. Two or

> three of the people [working for the website] were former journalists, but a majority are young kids who are web producers and who don't have any idea what the rules are. As with the web itself, we're making it up as we go along. (Rasmussen, 2006)

Lines become even more blurred when those outside mainstream journalism claim journalist status.[3] In California, activist Josh Wolf went to prison rather than turn over a video that he produced of a 2005 protest in San Francisco.[4] He insisted that he was a journalist and as such had the right to protect his sources. "'Journalists absolutely have to remain independent of law enforcement,' Wolf told reporters outside the gates of the prison. 'Otherwise, people will never trust journalists'" (Sites, 2007).

Yet, Wolf also claimed that he was an activist and a participant in the protest against the World Trade Organization that he videotaped.

Wolf was eventually released from prison in exchange for giving prosecutors a copy of the video. "[Family members said that] in exchange, prosecutors acceded to Wolf's key contention: that he not be made to appear before a grand jury and identify those on his videotape" (Sites, 2007).

Even journalists don't agree as to whether or not Wolf is a journalist:

> Debra Saunders, a conservative columnist for the *San Francisco Chronicle*, applauds Wolf's dedication, but doesn't believe he should be called a journalist. "I think that you can be a blogger and be a journalist. . . . There are people who fit that [description], but when you're an activist cavorting with the people you're chronicling, then you are not a journalist."
>
> Her own newspaper disagrees with that assessment and has supported Wolf on the *Chronicle*'s opinion pages. "The fact that Josh Wolf has strong political views does not disqualify him from being a journalist any more than the fact that I am an editorial page editor and have opinions disqualifies me from being a journalist," says John Diaz of the *Chronicle*. "The fact is, he was out at that rally, collecting information to disseminate to the public. I think that makes him a journalist."

> Ultimately, Saunders says, it won't be journalists and bloggers who decide the issue, but the government. "The courts are going to end up deciding who journalists are, because, unfortunately, this administration is really pushing the envelope in jailing journalists, and it won't end with the Bush administration," Saunders says. "It will get bigger as people point fingers in many ways, and that means the courts are going to decide who journalists are. You may not like it, but that's the way it is." (Sites, 2007)

Despite questions about the definition of "journalist," bloggers like Wolf represent what many see as part of the new democratization of news through the Internet. People are posting material from the profound to the mundane (Gahran, 2006) as well as from the personal to the international. A 2006 Pew Internet survey found that 57 million US adults visit blogs. Not surprisingly 54 percent of bloggers are under the age of 30, and by far the largest percentage of bloggers (37 percent) said that the "primary topic" of their blog was "My Life and Experiences," far ahead of the second most mentioned primary topic, "Politics and Government" (11 percent).[5] Only 5 percent said that their primary topic is "General News and Current Events" (Visual Editors, 2006).

Regardless of the low percentage of blogs concentrating on general news and current events, newspapers are engaging Internet users in the news-gathering business. Rebecca MacKinnon, research fellow at Harvard Law School's Berkman Center for Internet and Society says, "Any one journalist simply cannot cover the myriad of happenings he or she encounters in a given day. Devices like camera phones let people distribute their own messages, images and stories to the world" (Kirtz, 2006). Cell phone cameras now provide both television and "Moblog" (a combination of the words mobile and weblog) journalism with still and moving images.

The primary motivation for newspapers to create blogs and to include "citizen journalists" in reporting the day's news seems clear – newspaper circulations are falling rapidly, "publishers increasingly are looking online for readers, especially the younger readers who appear to be skipping their print editions entirely"

(Melamed, 2006). In an effort to attract new readers, virtually all newspapers present themselves in some fashion on the Internet. Some are radically changing the way in which they gather, organize, and present the news.

Gannett Company, for example, is reorganizing its newsroom to reflect the increasing influence of the Internet and community dialogue. "Gannett's plan renames the newsroom an 'Information Center' and divides it into seven areas: public service, digital, data, community conversation, local, custom content, and multimedia" (Ahrens, 2006).[6]

Other mainstream media are exploring myriad ways of taking advantage of multi-media production, the Internet, and its international audience.[7]

> The [*Washington*] *Post* recently added PostGlobal, an online panel discussion by international journalists, and it has created comment sections on stories, added dozens of blogs and hosted hundreds of hours of live discussions. The site handed out 50 video cameras to reporters to capture content for the web. It's also creating its own MySpace-like social networking site that will enable users to create pages and communities. (Melamed, 2006)

Washingtonpost.com has also sold edited video programming to television stations such as PBS. This benefits Washingtonpost.com in at least two ways. The station pays for the video piece and Washingtonpost.com receives on-air recognition for having produced the work. Jim Brady, executive editor of Washingtonpost.com, explains his approach to the Internet and multimedia production, "Our philosophy is that when a new thing comes out, and there's a lot of buzz about it, let's try it" (Melamed, 2006).

Los Angeles Times writer Ken Weiss extols the *Times* ability to reach an expanded audience through the Internet. "I find this very exciting because in my estimation we have a great newspaper, but people on the East Coast don't know that because they don't subscribe to West Coast papers. But, the Internet allows us to reach a worldwide audience" (Weiss, 2007).

Despite the excitement about new ways of telling stories, reaching an international audience and generating income, some believe that the newspaper industry has been slow to embrace Internet technology and that newspaper owners now face the challenge of catching up before newspaper revenues totally collapse. Michael Riley, editor of the *Roanoke Times* says:

> Looking at this as an economist, I would draw a chart with two trend lines to explain our future. On this chart, I'd look to see where the tipping point – when the weight of our news dissemination effort moves from print to online – might occur. The first line, declining steadily over time, captures the commitment of readers to print newspapers. The second one, increasing steadily, shows users going online to get news. At some point in the not-too-distant future, those lines will cross.
>
> As we head towards that tipping point, these trend lines let us know that a concomitant shift already needs to be taking place at our news operations. Gradually, we need to either add or move resources – people and money – from print to online. This redeployment of resources is one of the more critical questions ahead. Our experience tells us that efforts should already be underway to make time for journalists in the newsroom to experiment with and learn more about digital storytelling. With good planning, the tradeoffs in this transformation need not be too harsh or debilitating." (Riley, 2006)

Travis Fox adds, "The dot com is profitable. The long term answer is whether we're profitable enough to support the decline in circulation and advertising in the newspaper" (Fox, 2006).

The equation is further complicated by the inequality between advertising revenues generated by print audiences versus online audiences. "Gavin O'Reilly, president of the World Association of Newspapers in Paris, says that print readers are much more valuable than online readers, who use newspaper websites in a 'haphazard and fragmented way'" (*The Economist*, 2006). Although the numbers are not very precise – anywhere from 10 to 100 new online readers are needed to make up the revenue for every print reader lost – publishers agree that newspapers face strong challenges when trying to replace print revenue with online revenue (*The Economist*, 2006).

Internet sites face other questions as well:

> Nik Gowling, main presenter on the British Broadcasting Corporation's "World" . . . [is] concerned about something he called the "tyranny of real time." He said he wonders how journalists can measure truth and accuracy in a constant deadline situation. Viewers and readers, he said, demand that news be published quickly, and these days, many of them are helping to make that happen. "The audience wants us to share and source every bit of information," he said.
>
> But those responses, he said, don't always deliver usable information. That's what happened during the BBC's coverage of the train and bus bombings in London last July. After a chase, police killed a man who turned out to have had nothing to do with the bombings. The incident prompted a flood of instant messages and cell phone pictures. "We had credible eyewitnesses in the first three hours," Gowling said. "They were all credible and they were all wrong." (Kirtz, 2006)

The war in Iraq has produced a number of examples that magnify the Internet's potential for benefit and challenge. Perhaps the best examples are the gruesome images from Abu Ghraib – images taken by soldiers in the field and sent to friends and family via the Internet.[8] The photographs eventually reached a shocked US public and led to investigations into how prisoners are treated. Whereas the ability of soldiers to record and distribute information and images challenges government control, it also enlightens US citizens (and apparently government leaders).

> In his testimony to congressional committees, Defense Secretary Donald Rumsfeld indicated that the flood of pictures was now beyond the US authorities' control. . . . Mr. Rumsfeld was indignant at the publication of such images: "We're functioning with peacetime constraints, with legal requirements, in a wartime situation in the Information Age, where people are running around with digital cameras and taking these unbelievable photographs and then passing them off, against the law, to the media, to our surprise." However, he admitted that he had not realized the

> seriousness of the allegations until the pictures were leaked to the media. (Maceda, 2004)

The Internet provides the opportunity to post and view news from a variety of perspectives beyond those of soldiers in the field.[9] It offers the potential (not always realized) to be a real marketplace of ideas. It allows news consumers to receive stories and images that contradict the "official line" in the Iraq war (Zelizer, 2004). Because anyone with a digital camera, a computer, and Internet access can post images (Simon, 2004), the war gets told through the eyes of any number of cultures, political proponents, and activists.

One might argue that this kind of information free-for-all is laden with potential propaganda and outright falsification, yet it is exactly this kind of partisan competition that was encountered and given special privileges by the founders of the United States.

Some avoid information about the Iraq war online because the Internet hosts images that much of the print media consider too graphic to publish (Carter & Steinberg, 2004). But, others argue that the terrible consequences of war should be seen rather than hidden or sanitized. Peter Howe says:

> [W]ar is distressing and often obscene, and every time we try and put a good face on it we commit a moral crime. When we hide behind the safety of our own propaganda where no lives are lost, no injuries are too disfiguring, the people we liberate flock joyously towards our troops, and the phrases like "collateral damage" and "friendly fire" are fuzzy substitutes for "innocent victims" and "tragic incompetence" then we commit the ultimate obscenity. We convince ourselves, and, even worse, our children that war is OK. If we can produce men and women with the courage to photograph the reality of war, then we as a society should have the courage to look at what they see. (Howe, 2004)

Ultimately, no one can force the public to view disturbing images or read stories that are critical of US policy. Surveys find deep divisions over the display of graphic images. According to a 2004 survey, only a small percentage of Internet users actually search online for photographs from Iraq deemed by newspapers and television as too graphically strong to show. Additionally, more Americans think that such images should not be posted on the Internet than those who believe they should (Fallows & Rainie, 2004).

Further, media are hesitant to publish, broadcast, cablecast, or post anything that runs counter to public opinion. Unlike websites that cater to niche audiences,[10] mainstream news media try to appeal to broader audiences in hopes of generating the greatest financial returns.

"MacKinnon, formerly a foreign correspondent and producer for CNN, warned against expectations of a 'cyber Utopia.' 'New technology doesn't make us more democratic,' she said. 'It'll be what we make of it'" (Kirtz, 2006). As the Internet increasingly becomes the dominant information purveyor, it will be interesting to see how things play out. Will the Internet provide a broad and deep array of information presented in an accurate and ethical way that helps to reenergize the political electorate and inform citizens of the world around them? Or, will newspaper ownership look to the Internet as an economic panacea to declining readership at the expense of meaningful content?

Will aggregators such as Google dominate the flow of information much like mainstream newspapers did during the last century? And, will style take precedence over substance in a medium that features clever visuals and interactive capabilities?

These are important questions as the "dumbing down" of America – as some have called it – comes at a time when international and environmental issues challenge the future of the country and the planet.

Notes

1 Visual journalists extol the ability of newspapers to post more visual information on their websites than they are able to print. *New York Times* senior editor Mike Smith says, "One of the things that

happened during 9/11 was that our website went crazy with pictures. If we ran 20 pictures in the paper we would have 50 on the web, and people reacted all over the world to these pictures. It was clear from the reaction of readers that they got it and that they appreciated it" (Smith, 2004).

2 Newspaper journalists also must learn to communicate directly with the readership through the newspaper blogs. Some embrace the task; others are less enthusiastic. *Washington Post* ombudsman Deborah Howell "notes that 'Reporters today get more daily feedback from readers than any journalists in history,' and surveys several editors and reporters at the *Post* about how they manage the email they receive from the public. The response was mixed, with some reporters loving it, and others hating the 'rude, crude, sexist, racist, anti-Semitic email' that seems to come as knee-jerk reactions to stories" (Grier, 2006).

3 "A third (34%) of all bloggers considers their blog a form of journalism, according to a study from the Pew Internet & American Life Project" (Vaina, 2007).

4 Life for bloggers (as with traditional journalists) can be considerably more dangerous in countries ruled by repressive regimes. "Reporters Without Borders has drawn up a list of 15 'enemies of the Internet' (Belarus, Burma, China, Cuba, Iran, Libya, the Maldives, Nepal, North Korea, Saudi Arabia, Syria, Tunisia, Turkmenistan, Uzbekistan, Vietnam) . . .

The information ministry in Iran boasts that it blocks access to hundreds of thousands of websites. The ruling ayatollahs target any kind of sexual content and also independent news sites. Iran has the grim distinction of having arrested and jailed the most bloggers – a score of them were thrown in prison between autumn 2004 and summer 2005" (Reporters Without Borders, 2006).

5 On July 23, 2007 YouTube, Google, and CNN sponsored a two-hour presidential debate in Charleston, South Carolina. CNN editors chose questions from among videos submitted to YouTube. " 'The greatest innovation of this debate is that we're seeing candidates respond to real voters instead of polished TV personalities,' said Michael Silberman of the online consulting firm EchoDitto. 'It's a win for the candidates who are at their best when addressing voters. It's a win for democracy, since average Americans outside of the early primary states now have the opportunity to ask direct questions of candidates' " (Pickler, 2007).

Not all viewers were impressed however. "[W]hile there was a new format for the debate . . . the change went only so far: Candidates frequently lapsed into their talking points, and there was little actual debate among them" (Healy & Zeleny, 2007).

The political movement, "unity08," (unity08.com) is built completely around the Internet. The party is soliciting nominations for president online through the "first ever online virtual convention" and hosting an online conversation through its blog.

6 "[T]he company's news will be 'platform agnostic,' meaning it will be delivered however the reader desires – on paper, on the Web, on a mobile device and so on" (Ahrens, 2006). Keeping the content separate from the design so that the same content can be repurposed for several mediums facilitates this process.

7 Norwegian newspaper firm, Schibsted, has its own home page. This makes a significant difference in the amount of money it can collect from advertisers. " 'If visitors come from Google to stories deep in the paper and then leave,' explains Mr. Munck, [executive vice-president for Schibsted] 'Google gets the dollars and we get only cents, but if we can bring them in through the front page we can charge 19,000 Euros ($25,000) for a 24-hour banner ad.' In spite of this, most newspapers still depend on news aggregators" (*The Economist*, 2006).

8 Photojournalist Kim Newton has created an online collection of photographs produced by soldiers serving in Iraq. The site called "Digital Warriors," "aims to present the culmination of the work produced by these soldiers" (Colombo, 2005).

9 A 2007 content analysis of one-week's Iraq stories designed to investigate differences between newspaper and blog sourcing found "Blogs were slightly more diverse in their sourcing. . . . [And] compared to newspapers, blogs were considerably less likely than newspapers to include official Iraqi sources" (Vaina, 2007).

10 One site called NowThatsFuckedUp.com (NTFU) "started out as a place for people to trade amateur pornography of wives and girlfriends. According to the site's owner, Chris Wilson . . . the site was launched in August 2004 and soon became popular with soldiers in Iraq and Afghanistan" (Glaser, 2005). When the US military subsequently banned access to NTFU from its computers in response to women soldiers appearing nude on the site, Wilson offered free access if soldiers could prove their military status.

Although many posted innocuous photographs showing the everyday activities of soldiering, some posted more graphic images. "Now there's an entire forum on the site . . . where these bloody photos show body parts, exploded heads and guts falling out of people. Along with the photos is a running commentary of people celebrating the kills, cracking jokes and arguing over what kind of weaponry was used to kill them. But the moderators will also step in when the talk gets too heated, and sometimes a more serious discussion about the Iraq war and its aims will break out . . .

Capt. Chris Karns, a Centcom spokesman [said] there are Department of Defense regulations and Geneva Conventions against mutilating and degrading dead bodies, but that he wasn't sure about regulations concerning photos of dead bodies. He noted that the Bush administration did release graphic photos of the dead bodies of Uday and Qusay Hussein to the media" (Glaser, 2005).

References

Ahrens, F. (2006). Gannett to change its papers' approach. November 7, *washingtonpost.com*

Carter, B. & Steinberg, J. (2004). The struggle for Iraq: Issues of taste; to portray the horror, news media agonize. April 1, *nytimes.com*

Colombo, S. (2005). Frontline access: Online gallery boasts soldiers' wartime photos. February 11, *ojr.org*

The Economist (2006). Special report: The newspaper industry, more media, less news. *The Economist*, August 26, pp. 52–54.

Fallows, D. & Rainie, L. (2004). Reports: Major news events. July 8, *pewinternet.org*

Fisher, G. (2004). *Interview by author* [cassette recording] June, Los Angeles.

Fox, T. (2006). *Telephone interview by author* [digital recording] May, Miami.

Gahran, A. (2006). New Pew blogger study. July 20, *poynter.org*

Glaser, M. (2005). Porn site offers soldiers free access in exchange for photos of dead Iraqis. September 20, *ojr.org*

Grier, T. (2006). Can we all just learn to interact? June 13, *ojr.org*

Healy, P. & Zeleny, J. (2007). Novel debate format, but same old candidates. July 24, *nytimes.com*

Howe, P. (2004). The reality of war, sort of. March, *digitaljournalist.org*

Kennedy, T. (2004). *Interview by author* [cassette recording] June, Washington, DC.

Kirtz, B. (2006). Fear not the new media. October 19, *poynter.org*

Maceda, J. (2004). Terrorists and the Internet. June 24, *msnbc.msn.com*

Melamed, S. (2006). A sea of change for paper's web sites. July 14, *medialifemagazine.com*

Pickler, N. (2007). YouTube questions take a different tack. July 23, *Associated Press.*

Rasmussen, T. (2006). *Telephone interview by author* [digital recording] May, Miami.

Reporters Without Borders (2006). Violence still increasing: 63 journalists killed, more than 1,300 physically attacked or threatened. January 4, *rsf.org*

Riley. M. (2006). Lessons from a newsroom's digital frontline. Spring, *nieman.harvard.edu*

Simon, E. (2004). Digital cameras change perception of war. May 7, *msnbc.msn.com*

Sites, K. (2007). Journalist or activist? April 3, *hotzone.yahoo.com*

Smith, M. (2004). *Interview by author* [cassette recording] June, New York.

Vaina, D. (2007). Newspapers and blogs: Closer than we think? April 23, *ojr.org*

Visual Editors (2006). The facts of life . . . blogging, newspapers and convergence. July, *visualeditors.com*

Weiss, K. R. (2004). *Interview by author* [cassette recording] June, Los Angeles.

Weiss, K. R. (2007). *Telephone interview by author.* August, Miami.

Zelizer, B. (2004). Which words is a war photo worth? Journalists must set the standard. April 28, *ojr.org*

10

Conclusion

I recently returned to Ecuador to spend two weeks working with *El Universo*. A month before my arrival an outside group redesigned the newspaper increasing the size of the banner, emphasizing ads, and limiting the size of photographs on the front page. Colorful design elements and very large headlines vie for the reader's attention.

The design group left a binder with a number of models for designing the front pages. The lack of flexibility bothered me, and I talked about it with the publisher. At first my objections were directed at the limitations in the use of photographs. Later, I realized that I was more concerned with the preeminence of packaging over substance.[1]

I don't want to single out *El Universo*, a newspaper that I respect. Most newspapers in the United States have gone through redesigns during the past decade attempting to increase readership – newspapers worry about marketability (Meyer, 2004).

But US newspapers – and news media in general – are given special privileges in exchange for performing a public service. In 1947 the Commission on Freedom of the Press defined that service as:

> [F]irst, a truthful, comprehensive, and intelligent account of the day's events in a context which gives them meaning; second, a forum for the exchange of comment and criticism; third a means of projecting the opinions and attitudes of the groups in the society to one another; fourth, a method of presenting and clarifying the

> goals and values of the society; and fifth, a way of reaching every member of the society by the currents of information, thought, and feeling which the press supplies." (Commission on Freedom of the Press, 1947, pp. 20, 21)

Those who created the US Constitution clearly thought that a free press was instrumental to the democratic process. Thomas Jefferson wrote:

> "The basis of our governments being the opinion of the people, the very first object should be to keep that right; and were it left to me to decide whether we should have a government without newspapers or newspapers without a government, I should not hesitate a moment to prefer the latter." (Commission on Freedom of the Press, 1947, p. 13)

In the early years of the nation, however, the press differed greatly from today's news media. I'm not referring to the technological advances but rather to the small amount of money that was once necessary to begin a newspaper and to their partisan nature. Newspapers of all political persuasions existed during the first century after the founding of the nation. Newspapers as big business began just over a century ago, not coincidentally about the same time that "objectivity" became a journalism mantra.

These two factors – news media as big business and the concept of "objectivity" – play a key role in the state of today's news industry. The financial success of newspapers throughout the twentieth century (first privately owned and later as corporate owned entities) led to an oligarchy of powerful ownership, fewer voices, and a greater demand to increase profits. "[For generations] monopoly newspapers were [like] tollgates through which information passed between the local retailers and their customers. . . . Owning the newspaper was like having the power to levy a sales tax." (Meyer, 2004, pp. 34)

Economic strategies urge news organizations to avoid controversy and to steer clear of anything that might alienate news consumers. From the beginnings of the United States, however, the primary social function of the free press was to serve as a foundation for the exchange of disparate ideas and as a protection against elite rule.

Current news media concentration endangers the role of the press as a marketplace of ideas. Furthermore, the economic interests of corporate media ownership conflict with the press function as a watchdog against governance by the elite. Bill Moyers observes:

> What would happen . . . if the contending giants of big government and big publishing and broadcasting ever joined hands? Ever saw eye to eye in putting the public's need for news second to free-market economics? That's exactly what's happening now under the ideological banner of "deregulation." Giant megamedia conglomerates that our founders could not possibly have envisioned are finding common cause with an imperial state in a betrothal certain to produce not the sons and daughters of liberty but the very kind of bastards that issued from the old arranged marriage of church and state . . .
>
> Never has there been an administration so disciplined in secrecy, so precisely in lockstep in keeping information from the people at large and – in defiance of the Constitution – from their representatives in Congress. Never has so powerful a media oligopoly – the word is Barry Diller's, not mine – been so unabashed in reaching like Caesar for still more wealth and power. Never have hand and glove fitted together so comfortably to manipulate free political debate, sow contempt for the idea of government itself, and trivialize the people's need to know. (Moyers, 2003)

Today's news media offer "objective" reporting as a substitute for diverse and competitive partisan reportage – if journalists report the news "objectively," there is little need for alternative perspectives (Tuchman, 1972). Journalism schools and newsroom culture preach "objectivity" as a realizable and desirable goal for all journalists. Chomsky suggests, however, "objectivity" subjectively presents "the ideology of dominant economic interests" as a politically neutral perspective (Chomsky, 1979).

The concept of "objectivity" is used by the mainstream news media, in part, as justification for limited newsroom diversity.

Newsrooms have traditionally employed relatively low numbers of minorities, particularly minority women. And, the percentage of minorities working in newsrooms is increasing at a much slower pace than the percentage of minority members in the general population (Weaver & Wilhoit, 1996; Weaver et al., 2007).

Limited newsroom diversity makes the Commission on Freedom of the Press mandates more difficult to achieve. Stories that may be important to particular groups fail to make it onto the list of story ideas compiled by editors and writers who for the most part are white.[2] Other factors further prevent a "comprehensive account of the day's events." Newsroom culture and routines create a kind of autopilot mentality when reporters and editors are forced to make rapid decisions about stories and photographs under deadline pressure. In addition, journalism school training guides journalists in their judgment of "newsworthiness."[3] Finally, "The skew in news today reflects not just who sits in the newsroom, but whom we consult and whom we cover. . . . 'Journalists default to male and white as authority figures, as experts'" (Lehrman, 2006).

Sources and experts are also chosen based on socio-economic and power status. In his 1993 book *Who stole the news*, Mort Rosenblum says, "Head-of-state interviews are treasured by editors, most of whom refuse to let correspondents quote taxi drivers because they sound too easy. In fact, cabbies usually reveal more" (Rosenblum, 1993).[4]

Journalists must seek the ideas, dreams, frustrations, etc. of people from all walks of life. I once recommended to *El Universo*'s publisher that the photographer's workweek be reduced from six days to five. I reasoned that photographers would spend that extra free day exploring the city with their families. Photographers would not only feel more refreshed and alert but would also interact with various members of society – potential news sources.

The failure of US mainstream newspapers (and news media in general) to present minority perspectives has not only earned it the moniker, "The White Press" in some quarters but has also been blamed for contributing to political unrest[5] and may explain in part why newspapers are facing uncertain economic futures. "Journalism involves telling stories that the audience finds relevant. We ignore great numbers of news consumers at our own peril. If we want to stay in business, we must seek news that is important or interesting to our readers, listeners and viewers" (Lehrman, 2006).

For generations mainstream newspapers dominated the flow of information without regard for many sectors of society. As the number of newspapers declined and ownership became more centralized in the late 1900s profits soared. Now, information flows from a variety of sources. The days when newspapers could expect 20 to 40 percent profit have passed with the coming of the Internet and cable television. "The glory of the newspaper business in the United States used to be its ability to match its success as a business with self-conscious attention to its social service mission. Both functions are threatened today" (Meyer, 2004, p. 4).

The Internet offers the potential for broader and deeper reportage – an alternative to mainstream print media. But, the Internet presents both opportunities and challenges for photojournalism and photojournalists (Fox, 2006; Kennedy, 2004). The online medium is seemingly a perfect fit for visual journalism. Website producers understand that potential viewers are attracted to individual websites because of the visuals. The technology facilitates the mixing of still images with video and graphics and sound as well as words. And, there are no space limitations, a constant concern for print media.

At the same time, the web has a voracious appetite. The public clamors for instantaneous news about celebrities, wars, athletic events, political scandals, and the like.[6] The Internet supplies a non-stop flow of information, sometimes accurate, other times not much more than rumor and gossip. *Los Angeles Times* editor Kirk McKoy says:

> It used to be if you needed news, you went to the newspaper. Now you go to the TV or the Internet and you get it ASAP. But, the

> problem with that is that it breeds sensationalist news. I remember listening to a lot of radio and TV stations and their tag line is, "Remember who brought it to you first." You know, who cares if we brought it to you first, we gave it to you right. If it's wrong, what good is it? (McKoy, 2004)

In an attempt to compete in the non-stop world of information dissemination, news media are under pressure to gather and report news as it happens in an interesting and entertaining way. Many now solicit "user-generated content," (UGC) from the general public. The 9/11 attacks, the 2004 tsunami and most recently the killings at Virginia Tech generated significant amounts of amateur video and still photography that were disseminated by mainstream media and Internet sites.

The coming of the Internet, blogging, and UGC may be a mixed blessing. Because sites like YouTube dramatically widen the pool of news sources and news producers, viewers are exposed to a much more diverse worldview and receive news from a variety of perspectives. In some ways it mirrors the diversity of newspapers in the early days of the Republic. At the same time, the most common blog topic by far is "My Life and Experiences." Politics and government as well as general news lag far behind in what bloggers write about (Gahran, 2006). Blogs may be more akin to eighteenth-century diaries (or twenty-first-century reality TV) than eighteenth-century newspapers.

In addition, the Internet's need to always be up to the minute increases the pressure on mainstream journalists. Photographers, for example, are expected to create images that are immediate, compelling, and aesthetically strong. And, although digital cameras and darkrooms expedite the process of photographic reportage, they also raise the expectations of productivity and the possibilities of deceit.

Photojournalists who don't have sufficient time to complete their assignments well are tempted to take shortcuts. Sometimes – although rarely – they digitally alter images.[7] More routinely photojournalists, lacking the time necessary to produce a visual story with context and meaningful content, settle for stereotypical images that symbolize the concepts that their editors have called for. These images, intended as visual symbols, become a reality for viewers and often reinforce stereotypes already held.

Perhaps most disturbing, media conglomerates now realize the moneymaking potential of the Internet and are taking action.

> We have to fight to keep the gates to the Internet open to all. The web has enabled many new voices in our democracy – and globally – to be heard: advocacy groups, artists, individuals, non-profit organizations. Just about anyone can speak online, and often with an impact greater than in the days when orators had to climb on a soap box in a park. The media industry lobbyists point to the Internet and say it's why concerns about media concentration are ill founded in an environment where anyone can speak and where there are literally hundreds of competing channels.
>
> What those lobbyists for big media don't tell you is that the traffic patterns of the online world are beginning to resemble those of television and radio. In one study, for example, AOL Time Warner (as it was then known) accounted for nearly a third of all user time spent online. And two others companies – Yahoo and Microsoft – bring that figure to fully 50%. As for the growing number of channels available on today's cable systems, most are owned by a small handful of companies. Of the 91 major networks that appear on most cable systems, 79 are part of such multiple network groups such as Time Warner, Viacom, Liberty Media, NBC, and Disney. In order to program a channel on cable today, you must either be owned by or affiliated with one of the giants.
>
> If we're not vigilant the wide-open spaces of the Internet could be transformed into a system in which a handful of companies use their control over high-speed access to ensure they remain at the top of the digital heap in the broadband era at the expense of the democratic potential of this amazing technology. So we must fight to make sure the Internet remains open to all as the present-day analogue of that many-tongued world of small newspapers so admired by de Tocqueville. (Moyers, 2003)

How do all of these factors affect the practice and profession of photojournalism? I recall a conversation that I had with award-winning photographer Randy Olson several years ago. He and

Melissa Farlow (Randy's wife and fellow photographer) examined decades of winning news photographs from the *Pictures of the Year* competition. I asked Randy if he had noticed any tendencies over time. He replied the most obvious trend was the movement from documentary work to illustration photography.

This phenomenon strikes at the heart of my complaint registered at the beginning of this chapter – packaging over substance. Photo illustrations are at the base level of photojournalism. Writers and editors frequently like them because they are literal visual illustrations of concepts chosen by word journalists. Some photographers enjoy shooting them because they control the light, composition, and subject. And, some photo editors prefer illustrations because the unpredictability of working with "real" subjects has been eliminated so they know the photographer will get a useable photograph. Designers working at newspapers that are tightly formatted frequently embrace photo illustrations because the photographs can be fitted to space. And, photo technicians – those responsible for adjusting the tonal quality of the images – prefer photographs in which the light has been carefully controlled.

Photojournalism at its best, however, has always been intentionally subjective, emotional, and intimate. We remember Joe Rosenthal's photograph of the marines raising the flag at Iwo Jima and Robert Capa's photograph of allied soldiers coming ashore under fire during D-Day more than we do the written reports from World War II. Nick Ut's photograph of Kim Phuc – burned and naked from a napalm strike – as well as Eddie Adams' photograph of Nguyen Ngoc Loan executing a Viet Cong prisoner symbolizes the tragic consequences of the Viet Nam War. Howard Chapnick explains:

> Photojournalism is rooted in the consciousness and consciences of its practitioners. The torch of concern, a heritage of humanistic photography, has passed from generation to generation, lighting the corners of darkness, exposing ignorance, and helping us to understand human behavior. It bares the naked truth and sometimes lies. It informs, educates and enlightens us about the present.

> It illuminates the past. It records beauty and ugliness, poverty and grandeur. (Chapnick, 1988, Foreword)

The best visual newspapers "play all the notes." Newspapers like the *Los Angeles Times*, the *Hartford Courant*, the *Portland Oregonian*, the *New York Times* and the *Rocky Mountain News* publish a variety of photographs – from photo illustrations to in-depth documentary photo reportage. But, a great many newspapers rely on photo illustration and shun powerful photographs that document the more discomforting aspects of life.

James Nachtwey, arguably the most honored war photographer in history, suggests, "Photography can be a powerful anecdote to war." Governments and militaries know the persuasive power of the photograph and have historically tried to control the visual image of war. When newspapers keep photographs of civilian war casualties off the front page (or out of the newspaper altogether) to avoid the potential financial consequences of angry readers and/or advertisers, they are abandoning their obligation to provide "a truthful, comprehensive, and intelligent account of the day's events in a context which gives them meaning." And they are doing their country a disservice by not allowing its citizenry to see the consequences of war.

Some have said that photojournalism is in trouble because of the highly publicized (yet infrequent) lapses in ethics and the competition from "user generated content." I believe, on the contrary, that photojournalism is perfectly positioned to take the lead in a new kind of journalism that does a better job of representing those portions of society that have been traditionally underrepresented by the mainstream media and of giving a more "truthful, comprehensive, and intelligent account of the day's events in a context which gives them meaning."

Photojournalists spend more time "in the streets" than word journalists. They are more accustomed to creating relationships with people of all socioeconomic levels because they cannot do their reporting by phone or over the Internet. The stories that many photojournalists pursue have to do with the joys and difficulties of living, working, loving, dying, practicing faith, raising families, etc. across all strata of society. Photojournalists, I believe, also relate to minorities more easily because of their own minority (and in some cases "second-class") status within newsrooms.

Finally, photojournalists know that their photographs subjectively tell stories, and I think that most of them embrace the idea of "committed journalism" – using photography to tell a story from a particular perspective. This does away with the pretense of objectivity and instead suggests a "forum of ideas" approach.

Bill Moyers asserts, "journalism and democracy are deeply linked in whatever chance we human beings have to redress our grievances, renew our politics, and reclaim our revolutionary ideals" (Moyers, 2003). Strong visual images used effectively can engage readers, rouse their emotions, and inform them about all aspects of life. Photographers have always pursued a wide gamut of subject matter, but editors often decide against using a photograph because it is "too difficult to read" or "too difficult to view," or it's "not newsworthy." In many cases editors declare, "It's not what our readers want." As Peter Howe, in referring to the Iraq war, says, "I do not believe that more graphic photographs haven't been taken. . . . What I think we are seeing here is a selection process that is the result of internal media company censorship" (Howe, 2004).

The nation's founders gave the news media special rights and protections, believing that an informed citizenry is essential to good governance. Some believe that a new media ownership model is coming, one in which owners accept lower financial returns on their investments and put more emphasis on their public service responsibilities (Knight Foundation, 2006).

I believe that such a transition would bode well for visual journalism. Newspapers have often underappreciated the storytelling power of the image and/or been loathe to employ photographers fully as journalists. News media, attempting to reach a broader audience and cover more diverse and globally important topics, and searching for new ways to tell stories, will embrace visual journalism. Photojournalists have throughout history shown a readiness to "bear witness," "[to] make visible the unseen, the unknown, and the forgotten" (Fulton, 1988, p. 107). Visual images inform people about the world and about life in ways that words cannot. And, the best images can motivate people to work toward a better world.

Notes

1 Fox television provides perhaps the ultimate example of packaging over substance. In yet another "reality" series ("Anchorwoman") Lauren Jones, a "swimsuit model and actress [with] no journalism experience," will co-anchor a 5 p.m. newscast in Tyler, Texas. Some journalists and journalism organizations like the Poynter Institute have criticized the station (KYTX) for hosting the show: "KYTX station president and GM Phil Hurley [however] shrugs off the criti cism. . . . 'Journalism credibility? I think that's somewhat amusing when all I see today on the cable news is Paris Hilton, nonstop,' he said. 'This is a TV show. It's going to be a comedy. They just chose to shoot it at our station.'" (Gough, 2007).

2 "Today, even though media executives have pledged their commitment to diversity for more than two decades, at least 86 percent of newspaper editorial employees . . . are white. . . . [And] even as recently as 2005, at least 346 U.S. newspaper newsrooms, or about one of four, were 100 percent white" (Lehrman, 2006).

3 In an op-ed piece John Tierney says that university journalism faculties are predominantly liberal and Democratic and that they are training journalists of the same ilk (Tierney, 2005). One could also make the point that journalism faculties are overwhelmingly white and so journalists trained at these institutions see the world from a predominantly white perspective.

4 During my many visits to Ecuador in the 1990s and 2000s, I listened as cabbies consistently complained about corruption in the government. They couldn't understand, for example, how gasoline prices could be so high in an oil-exporting nation. It was easy to predict the political instability that has plagued Ecuador in recent years and the voters' constant search for a populist president whom they deem honest.

Ecuador has had eight presidents in the past ten years. Current president, Rafael Correa, is a populist president who enjoys strong popular support.

5 "In analyzing why riots had seethed in U.S. city streets for four summers in a row, the [1968 Kerner Commission report] pinpointed the isolation and neglect of black Americans by white society. They chastised the news media for its part – both before and during the uprisings . . . [saying], 'by and large, news organizations have failed to communicate to both their black and white audiences a sense of the problems America faces and the sources of potential solutions,' the commission concluded bluntly. 'The media report and write from the standpoint of a white man's world' " (Lehrman, 2006).

6 This is certainly true of the print media as well. "Many newspapers and magazines flee from reality and see themselves as part of the entertainment media, seeking out escapist subject matter divorced from the reality of our times" (Chapnick, 1988, Foreword).

7 Photojournalists rarely alter their images digitally beyond the accepted standards of cropping, minimally dodging, burning and toning. Virtually all photojournalists know the ethical implications of digital manipulation and shun the practice. In addition, photographers who do alter their photographs beyond the accepted norms almost always lose their jobs.

As the twentieth century began the general public became more interested in photojournalism and understood the mechanics of photography better because roll film made photography accessible to amateurs (Carlebach, 1997). Likewise, today news consumers are more interested in and avidly aware of darkroom techniques because Photoshop and other digital imaging software are available to anyone with a computer. News consumers know that photographs can be altered, and they keep an eye out for transgressions.

References

Carlebach, M. L. (1997). *American photojournalism comes of age.* Washington DC: Smithsonian Institution Press.

Chapnick, H. (1988). Forward. In M. Fulton (Ed.), *Eyes of time: Photojournalism in America.* New York: Little, Brown and Company.

Chomsky, N. (1979). Ideological conformity in America. *Nation*, January 27.

Commission on Freedom of the Press (1947). *A free and responsible press.* Chicago: University of Chicago Press.

Fox, T. (2006). *Telephone interview by author* [digital recording] May, Miami.

Fulton, M. (1988). *Eyes of time: Photojournalism in America.* New York: Little, Brown and Company.

Gahran, A. (2006). New Pew blogger study. July 20, *poynter.org*

Gough, P. (2007). Fox reality show roils Texas town. June 11, *yahoonews.com*

Howe, P. (2004). The reality of war, sort of. March, *digitaljournalist.org*

Kennedy, T. (2004). *Interview by author* [cassette recording] June, Washington DC.

Knight Foundation. (2006). Newspaper industry needs new owners, says former *LA Times* editor. April 26, *Knight Foundation News Release.*

Lehrman, S. (2006). News in a new America. July 24, *knightfdn.org*

McKoy, K. (2004). *Interview by author* [cassette recording] June, Los Angeles.

Meyer, P. (2004). *The vanishing newspaper: Saving journalism in the information age.* Columbia, MO: University of Missouri.

Moyers, B. (2003). Keynote address to the National Conference on Media Reform. November 8, *commondreams.org*

Rosenblum, M. (1993). *Who stole the news.* New York: John Wiley & Sons.

Tierney, J. (2005). Where cronies dwell. *The New York Times*, October 11, p. A27.

Tuchman, G. (1972). Objectivity as strategic ritual: An examination of newsmen's notions of objectivity. *American Journal of Sociology, 77*, 660–679.

Weaver, D. H. & Wilhoit, G. C. (1996). *The American journalist in the 1990s: U.S. news people at the end of an era.* Mahwah, NJ: Lawrence Erlbaum Associates.

Weaver, D. H., Beam, R. A., Brownlee, B. J., Voakes, P. S., Wilhoit, G. C. (2007). *The American journalist in the 21st century: U.S. news people at the dawn of a new millennium.* Mahwah, NJ: Lawrence Erlbaum Associates.

Index